SCRIPTURAL TRACES:
CRITICAL PERSPECTIVES ON THE RECEPTION AND INFLUENCE OF THE BIBLE

34

Editors
Matthew A. Collins, University of Chester
Michelle Fletcher, King's College London, UK
Andrew Mein, Queen's Foundation for Ecumenical Theological Education, UK

Editorial board
Michael J. Gilmour, David Gunn, James Harding, Jorunn Økland

Published under

LIBRARY OF NEW TESTAMENT STUDIES
674

Formerly the Journal for the Study of the New Testament Supplement series

Editor
Chris Keith

Editorial Board
Dale C. Allison, Lynn H. Cohick, Kylie Crabbe, R. Alan Culpepper,
Craig A. Evans, Jennifer Eyl, Robert Fowler, Juan Hernández Jr.,
John S. Kloppenborg, Michael Labahn, Matthew V. Novenson,
Love L. Sechrest, Robert Wall, Catrin H. Williams, Brittany E. Wilson

KEIR HARDIE, THE BIBLE, AND CHRISTIAN SOCIALISM

The Miner's Prophet

By Daniel L. Smith-Christopher

t&tclark
LONDON • NEW YORK • OXFORD • NEW DELHI • SYDNEY

T&T CLARK
Bloomsbury Publishing Plc, 50 Bedford Square, London, WC1B 3DP, UK
Bloomsbury Publishing Inc, 1359 Broadway, New York, NY 10018, USA
Bloomsbury Publishing Ireland, 29 Earlsfort Terrace, Dublin 2, D02 AY28, Ireland

BLOOMSBURY, T&T CLARK and the T&T Clark logo are trademarks
of Bloomsbury Publishing Plc

First published in Great Britain 2024
Paperback edition published 2026

Copyright © Daniel L. Smith-Christopher, 2024

Daniel L. Smith-Christopher has asserted his right under the Copyright,
Designs and Patents Act, 1988, to be identified as Author of this work.

For legal purposes the Acknowledgments on p. xv constitute an
extension of this copyright page.

Cover image: James Keir Hardie by John Furley Lewis,
1902 © Historic Images / Alamy Stock Photo

All rights reserved. No part of this publication may be: i) reproduced or transmitted in any form, electronic or mechanical, including photocopying, recording or by means of any information storage or retrieval system without prior permission in writing from the publishers; or ii) used or reproduced in any way for the training, development or operation of artificial intelligence (AI) technologies, including generative AI technologies. The rights holders expressly reserve this publication from the text and data mining exception as per Article 4(3) of the Digital Single Market Directive (EU) 2019/790.

Bloomsbury Publishing Plc does not have any control over, or responsibility for, any third-party websites referred to or in this book. All internet addresses given in this book were correct at the time of going to press. The author and publisher regret any inconvenience caused if addresses have changed or sites have ceased to exist, but can accept no responsibility for any such changes.

A catalogue record for this book is available from the British Library.

Library of Congress Cataloging-in-Publication Data

Names: Smith-Christopher, Daniel L., author.
Title: Keir Hardie, the Bible, and Christian socialism : the miner's prophet / by Daniel L. Smith-Christopher.
Description: London ; New York : T&T Clark, 2024. | Series: Scriptural traces ; critical perspectives on the reception and influence of the bible ; 34 | Includes bibliographical references.
Identifiers: LCCN 2023051368 (print) | LCCN 2023051369 (ebook) |
ISBN 9780567707604 (hardback) | ISBN 9780567707642 (paperback) |
ISBN 9780567707611 (pdf) | ISBN 9780567707635 (ebook)
Subjects: LCSH: Hardie, James Keir, 1856-1915. | Bible–Criticism,
interpretation, etc. | Christian socialism–Great Britain–History. |
Labor movement–Religious aspects–Christianity.
Classification: LCC HD8393.H3 S66 2024 (print) | LCC HD8393.H3 (ebook) |
DDC 328.41/092 [B]–dc23
LC record available at https://lccn.loc.gov/2023051368
LC ebook record available at https://lccn.loc.gov/2023051369

ISBN: HB: 978-0-5677-0760-4
PB: 978-0-5677-0764-2
ePDF: 978-0-5677-0761-1
eBook: 978-0-5677-0763-5

Series: Library of New Testament Studies, volume 674
ISSN 2513-8790
Scriptural Traces volume 34

Typeset by Integra Software Services Pvt. Ltd.

For product safety related questions contact productsafety@bloomsbury.com.

To find out more about our authors and books visit www.bloomsbury.com
and sign up for our newsletters.

By and large, the world of biblical interpretation is detached from the problems of the contemporary world and has become ineffectual because it has failed to challenge the status quo or work for any sort of social change ...

R. S. Sugirtharajah, 2002

The first duty of the Church to the social question is to understand it. This done, then to denounce fearlessly and in unmistakable language whatever causes are producing suffering, and next to aid in building up a system founded on righteousness, the operation of which would predispose men to true living and faith in the goodness of God.

Keir Hardie, 1893

CONTENTS

Foreword — ix
Acknowledgments — xv

Chapter 1
WADING IN THE "STREAMS" OF A METHODOLOGICAL RIVER DELTA — 1

Chapter 2
KEIR HARDIE: A LIFE AND CONTEXT — 27

Chapter 3
HARDIE (AND HIS BIOGRAPHERS) ON HARDIE'S RELIGION — 59

Chapter 4
THE "FAMILY OF FAITH": HARDIE'S CLOSE ALLIES IN "BIBLICAL" CHRISTIAN SOCIALISM — 91

Chapter 5
HARDIE AND HIS BIBLE — 129

Chapter 6
THE MINER'S BIBLE: HARDIE IN DIALOGUE WITH NEW TESTAMENT DEBATE — 183

Bibliography — 223
Index — 232
Selected Scripture Index — 236

FOREWORD

Why should anyone be interested in how a Scottish miner from the late nineteenth and early twentieth centuries read his Bible? Didn't thousands of Scots read the Bible? Even if I clarify that this particular Scottish miner was blacklisted for union organizing, and later became a critically important socialist organizer in the UK, and was among the central founders of the British Labour Party, perhaps this still doesn't answer the question?

What if, however, it could be argued that this particular miner was INSPIRED in his socialist activism precisely through his Christian faith and his reading of the Bible? What if I further propose that the ways he read his Bible, and wrote about the Bible, may well have significance far beyond his own biography? *What if this particular miner has something to teach us about the Bible?* Are we intrigued now?

It is the promise of a form of study known as "Reception History of the Bible" that these kinds of questions can be important. The ways that people have read the Bible in unusual circumstances, and usually outside of academic institutions, may well hold the promise of suggesting new ideas, new possibilities, and open new areas of investigation for anyone who is invested in the importance of the Bible both historically, academically, and even personally. We are, to continue the mining theme, panning for intellectual gold here. We are looking for those moments when readers of the Bible can reflect on historical readings that suggest new directions of analysis—new ideas—new possibilities. We are looking for those moments when we say, "Now THAT is interesting ... and significant! ... *and raises questions about how I read those passages in my own study."*

This project was inspired by all these ideas—but it began when I first started reading editorials in an older Socialist newspaper called *The Labour Leader* written by the editor, Keir Hardie. I was struck by how often Hardie discussed Scripture ... and as I kept reading ... I continued to be surprised and impressed. This book unfolded like the pages of his newspaper as I gingerly turned the (sadly sometimes crumbling) pages of archived newspapers in London libraries and worked through (often incomplete) digitalized versions online. I have dabbled a bit in projects that could be classified "Reception History" of the Bible, but this is my first major project along these lines.

Because this work is somewhat unusual—and published in a series dedicated to the "unusual" work in Biblical Studies—it may be helpful to make some comments about what follows. I presume (and hope) that readers from different disciplines will find this work of interest, as I have found published work in many other disciplines to be of great interest in my work on this project. As I am normally a student of "Historical-Critical" studies of the Bible who focuses mostly on Hebrew Bible/Old Testament studies (albeit with an eye toward contemporary issues), this project represents a rather sharp turn in my previous academic interests.[1] Especially for readers whose predominant interest is in History (esp. British labour history) or perhaps Political Science (esp. nineteenth- to twentieth-century socialist thought), or Historical Theology (esp. those interested in Christian Socialism), it may be helpful for me to summarize here why I have laid out the following chapters in the manner that I have arranged them.

First of all, "Reception History" within Biblical Studies remains a somewhat controversial topic, which explains my attempt in Chapter 1 to try to carefully articulate the methodologies I am experimenting with. As I try to explain therein, I have been inspired by work in a variety of disciplines and academic areas which all seemed to "flow" together[2] into arguments in support of the possible significance of the project as a whole. What was especially interesting for me was the fact that I was able to both draw on very recent arguments (e.g., starting with work by Christopher Rowland, Ian Boxall, and Susan Gillingham on "Reception History") but then also found myself returning to much older arguments in twentieth-century "Labour History" that seemed to me to be quite important to the project, even though none of the people involved in those older arguments would likely have anticipated the serious interest of a (Quaker) Biblical scholar. Therefore, I move through a variety of materials, noting how they may contribute to thinking about "Reception History of the Bible" in different ways. For example, I became fascinated by revisiting Michael Gold's famous call from the 1930s for a "proletarian literature." Featured in his manifesto was his argument that readers (and scholars) need to pay attention to previously overlooked sources among working people—and not only published books. Gold's stirring call sustained me as I paged through Hardie's newspapers. Noting the more recent (but still mainly twentieth-century) discussions of Gold's project, I found that it was easy for me to translate Gold's ideas toward new possibilities in Biblical Studies. I also recognized, for example, how older arguments surrounding Herbert Gutman's famous 1966 essay on the role of religion in labour history reveals, on close inspection, some very interesting possibilities for a study of the role of the Bible in labour activism, irrespective of the viability of his other arguments in that famous essay. Finally, I acknowledge with profound gratitude the recent turn in even more recent Labour Studies in the

---

1. Although perhaps anticipated a bit by my recent book on the Hollywood "Blacklisted" films in relation to what I argue are radically Biblical values of social justice that are quite compatible with the values represented in ten "blacklisted" films. These films, among many others I could have included, were unfortunately thought at the time to be "un-American," or even "communist propaganda" by Congress, press, and even by clergy. That project was intended to be a kind of "workbook" for potential Adult Education series where folks may be interested in watching the ten films that I featured and discussing the Biblically based arguments that I tried to make in relation to each of them: *The Blacklisted Bible: Biblical Justice and the Hollywood Panic 1947–1955* (Eugene, OR: Cascade Books: 2022).

2. Thus the river imagery that I risk over-using, perhaps to be forgiven in a Oregonian from Portland?

UK and the USA toward re-assessing the role of religion in labour movements, which I found deeply encouraging—and even exciting. I believe that these works are pointing toward a radical rethinking, for example, of what we normally think of as "Religious History" in the UK, but in the US especially, and (I contend) with it the role of Biblical interpretation. I finish this chapter with a summary of why I believe that Keir Hardie represents the ideal "case study" for bringing these borrowed discussions from other disciplines together by proposing that Biblical Studies can and should participate in this "Second Wave" of Labour Studies and Religion. Arguably, the rest of the book tries to defend precisely that contention.

While the discussion in Chapter 1 may be of particular interest to scholars in many of the various disciplines where I am both a shameless but grateful interloper, it is also quite reasonable for readers to delay (or skip) this chapter with its heavier methodological discussions, and dive right into Chapter 2, which is a biographical summary of the life of Keir Hardie himself as preparation for the chapters that follow.

In Chapter 2, I do not attempt to improve on the excellent biographies of Hardie, but simply summarize Hardie's life with particular attention to the role of religion in his life and context. This topic is always included in the biographies—but usually dealt with quite briefly (and is occasionally somewhat dismissive). Yet some of these issues are of clear importance in providing further context for any study of Hardie's reading of the Bible.

This central significance of religion for Keir Hardie, then, is the focus of Chapter 3, where I go into more detail on four significant issues in Hardie's life that have had far too little attention in much of the biographical material on Hardie as a Labour hero in history. Here, I discuss (1) Hardie's early interest in an off-shoot Scottish Christian movement led by James Morison and his "Evangelical Union"; (2) the role of Hardie's interest and involvement in "Temperance" issues; (3) the fascination with "heterodox" religious interests that have clearly been exaggerated—or misunderstood—by biographers wanting to distance Hardie from too many religious concerns; and finally (4) a highly significant event in 1910 when Hardie attended and addressed a large convention in Lille, France, and where Hardie's story (and theology) briefly but significantly intersects with French Christian socialism. Here, in one of those wonderful historical moments, Hardie crosses paths with such highly significant figures as André Trocmé, the hero of Le Chambon sur Lignon (and justifiable hero for many Christians because of his courageous hiding of Jews during Nazi occupation). Yet, Trocmé's *socialist* convictions are rarely acknowledged by the same Christians who are so impressed with Trocmé's life.

In Chapter 4, I try to acknowledge the importance of a few of Hardie's allies in his Christian radicalism. Once again, because Hardie's religious interests have not been a significant emphasis in the available biographies (with some exceptions that I do acknowledge), the potential importance of these figures has not been (in my view) sufficiently considered. Here, I try to propose that Hardie's most significant allies in Christian Socialism especially include Caroline Martyn (1867–1896), Dennis Hird (1850–1920), and John Morrison Davidson (1843–1916), none of whom have been the subject of major historical studies that I am aware of. As a Scottish radical Christian, Davidson's influence, especially, is important to note because we have excellent published sources from his pen.

Chapter 5 gets to the heart of the matter—here I survey a large number of examples of Hardie's use of the Bible, and how extensive and interesting many of these discussions actually are. It is the nature of the case that this chapter will feature extensive quotation because part of the indisputable charm of Hardie was his rhetorical flourish—it was widely acknowledged that he was a stirring speaker. Happily, some of the sources even note moments of applause, making it easier to imagine the events.

Finally, Chapter 6 represents the attempt to answer the inevitable question I will be asked: "So what, Daniel?" Here is where I hope to make a contribution to the critical potential of "Reception History" as proposed in Chapter 1 by citing the work of Rowland, Boxall, and Gillingham. I have selected four classic Biblical passages frequently noted in Hardie's work—and I try to place them into some kind of dialogue with contemporary New Testament research on precisely these passages. Do Hardie's observations deserve a "place at the table" for these contemporary Biblical debates? I contend that they do—and try to establish this here. In fact, Hardie's work is more than passingly interesting—and I contend that in a few of these cases (especially with regard to debate on 2 Thessalonians 3:10 and Matthew 23) Hardie makes genuine and significant contributions to the debate.

Any success which these arguments may be thought to have achieved in this book, of course, is entirely up to my patient readers. I would, however, consider the most rewarding success of this project to be greater attention given to the often unsung[3] heroes of Christian Socialism in its classic period—although I might contend that the *most* heroic are the crowds of working families who cheered them on and who will remain anonymous throughout time. I consider this "classic period" of Christian Socialism to be *c.* 1870–1930 in both Europe and the United States, and I refer my readers to my footnotes for suggestions on where to begin the delightful task of rediscovering these men and women of profound faith in God—and therefore also a faith in human hope.

A Note on Socialism and Contexts for This Project

For Americans like me, raised in the Cold War hysteria surrounding the word "Socialism" (much less "Communism"), the resurrection of socialism as an acceptable political term in the USA is nothing short of astonishing. The shift is clearly visible not only in a few scattered local elections in US cities won by

---

3. More than a figure of speech since Christian Socialism from this era also featured a fascinating body of music as well! My colleague, Christophe Chalamet, and I are currently editing *The Cambridge Companion to Christian Socialism* which will feature a chapter sampling some of these wonderful Christian socialist hymns and songs.

explicitly socialist candidates (e.g., Kshama Sawant, City Councilwoman in Seattle, WA), but also in more general political trends among Americans under thirty. By the nature of the case, the literature is still largely in the popular press, but examples abound with rather striking titles such as: "'The S-word': How Young Americans Fell in Love with Socialism"; "Why Millennials Aren't Afraid of Socialism"; "Bernie Sanders and the Resurgence of Socialist Sentiment in America."[4] In the early 2020s, of course, "socialism" is still considered the "ultimate insult" hurled at the Democratic party by Republicans of all hues in the USA—but for many modern younger Americans, that supposed insult is easily brushed aside. I have come to realize that a book proposing a "Proletarian Exegesis of the Bible" is therefore perhaps more of a reflection of the times than I even originally intended.

It is important to clarify, however, that "Socialism" in this book is going to be used as a set of moral ideas rather than a *specific* economic or partisan political program. Marx will make very few appearances in this project.[5] In British history (and I am discovering, more than is often acknowledged in American history as well), the Bible was a primary source of a moral attitude that motivated many women and men to seriously consider programs and projects identified with socialism. Therefore, "Christian Socialism" was always at its best when it participated in ethical and moral debates, but its openness to various definitions or political programs (often spanning a spectrum of practical ideas from cooperative retail shops, worker-owned factories, "New Towns," as well as nationalized industry or essential services like health care) has often drawn severe criticism from doctrinaire Marxists. If we are interested precisely in the citation and debates by socialists using the Bible, however, it will be moral ideas and idealism that we will be most interested in. So, let me state matters here clearly—I am not interested in the partisan debates about Hardie's socialist "doctrine," especially the endless debates about how purely "Marxist" Hardie was or wasn't (clearly he wasn't). To the contrary, I am interested in Hardie's *reading of his Bible* as an inspiration to his passion for justice, because I believe his ideas have significance historically, but also potential significance in Biblical Studies in the twenty-first century. Clarifying this will require a few comments on Biblical "methodology," so I apologize that there is a bit more to be said about this before commencing the work on Hardie himself.

---

4. Chris McGreal, "'The S-word': How Young Americans Fell in Love with Socialism," *The Guardian*, September 2, 2017; Julia Mead, "Why Millennials Aren't Afraid of Socialism," *The Nation*, January 10, 2017; Ralph Benko, "Bernie Sanders and the Resurgence of Socialist Sentiment in America," *Forbes*, December 14, 2017.

5. Roland Boer, *Marxist Criticism of the Bible*, 2nd edn (London: Bloomsbury/T&T Clark, 2015).

ACKNOWLEDGMENTS

I want to express my appreciation to friends and colleagues who encouraged this project, especially Sarah Blake and Andrew Mein who work with the series "Scriptural Traces." I am honored to have this work published in this fascinating series, and humbled by the company I am keeping with such creative works in this series. Thanks to R. S. Sugirtharajah for his ever-present encouragement for new ideas and his treasured friendship. Thanks to my new friend Dr. Christophe Chalamet for his own excellent work that I drew upon, but also his encouragement, and a special thanks to Christopher Rowland who encouraged the project from the beginning. I want to acknowledge the appreciation I felt, and the dependence that is obvious, for the previous biographies of Hardie that have been published. I hope that I have contributed a worthy addition to that literature.

I owe an immense debt of gratitude to a few Grad Students at Loyola Marymount University who helped with editing—Shayne Yano early on, and especially Laura Boysen Aragon who helped me edit the entire manuscript. I could not have completed this work in any timely manner without their tremendous help. Remaining errors remain entirely my own oversights.

I would like to thank Kate Clissold-Jones, Ayesha Hussain and Katherine Jenkins from Bloomsbury, Anne Hunt and Vidhya Mohan from Integra, and the copyeditor, Elizabeth Nichols, for all of their hard work on the production of this book.

My wife, Zsa Zsa J. Christopher, continues to patiently endure the hours spirited away in reading, visiting libraries, and writing. This work, such as it is, is quite rightly dedicated to her. If there is to be a shared dedication, however, then it would include all the thousands of people, known only to themselves in history, who gathered to hear Keir Hardie speak, cheer him on, and vote him in! In a democracy—you are the heroes.

Figure 1.1 Keir Hardie, "Men of the Movement," *The Labour Leader*, June 30, 1894.

Chapter 1

WADING IN THE "STREAMS" OF A METHODOLOGICAL RIVER DELTA

This book, and the on-going study project it represents, is intended to be a contribution primarily to Biblical Studies. However, it is immediately obvious to most readers that such a statement cannot be so simply stated. In the twenty-first century, the discipline(s) of Biblical Studies have divided like the separate streams of a river delta, and these different "streams" (I understand that the technical term is "rivulets") represent different methodological approaches. More importantly, these different "streams" also presume and debate different sets of questions that are considered pertinent to the particular "stream" in question. Even more problematic, some of these "streams" develop their own dialect and vocabulary. A further complication results if one is willing to read more widely and beyond the disciplinary boundaries where Biblical scholars are expected to dwell. I hope to acknowledge the insights and sparks of inspiration that come from different disciplines and their conversations, with apologies that I may not be fully conversant in the niceties of those debates in other disciplines. These inspirations, however, can create yet more "streams" for Biblical analysis.

Given these separate "streams"—it is now usually considered an important point of clarification to state, at the outset of a monograph in Biblical Studies, which methodological "stream" (or "school") that the work is aspiring to be associated with (and therefore, as noted, which "set of questions" is being taken up). This would presumably assist in understanding the work and its goals, but also provide at least something of a criterion by which to assess whatever success the work may be deemed to have accomplished.

As noted, however, this present project crosses a few of those "streams," and therefore in this first chapter I will try to locate this project within certain established lines of inquiry in modern Biblical Studies. I am very pleased that this work is to appear in the series entitled *Scriptural Traces*, and the fact that other works in this series identify themselves as works in "Reception History" is a strong indication of where I also try to locate the present study. I am somewhat averse to extended methodological discussions, however, so I will try to keep the following comments to a minimum. As the reader is likely to be, I am also anxious to get to Mr. Hardie.

"Reception History" or "History of Interpretation"?

Given the number of recent works that try to define, and give examples, of "Reception History" of the Bible, I need only briefly indicate that I have few disagreements with these generally very helpful recent publications. There may, however, be some confusion between scholars who work in what they define as "History of Interpretation" as opposed to "Reception History." For example, in a clearly written essay appearing in the 2013 reference work, *The Oxford Encyclopedia of Biblical Interpretation*, Christopher Rowland and Ian Boxall explain that "Reception History" and/or "Reception Criticism" is arguably different from the somewhat generically named "History of Interpretation" because: "Reception history or reception criticism does not restrict its interests to professional interpreters, but is open to a wide range of interpreters (marginal and even maverick as well as magisterial)."[1] Echoing these concerns, the first thing to say is that the present project clearly represents an experiment that is written in hopes of contributing to Rowland and Boxall's proposed "maverick" Biblical Studies. However, others have also helped with further elaborations on the meaning and significance of "Reception History" as opposed to a narrower emphasis on "History of Interpretation" which—as we have noted—tends to focus on the history of clerical and/or scholarly interpretation. In an *Oxford Handbook* dedicated to "Reception History," for example, one of the editors (Jonathan Roberts) began his Introductory essay with the following striking observation:

> The reception of the Bible comprises every single act or word of interpretation of that book (or books) over the course of three millennia ... Reception *history*, however, is a different matter. That is usually—although not always—a scholarly enterprise, consisting of selecting and collating shards of that infinite wealth of reception material in accordance with the particular interests of the historian concerned, and giving them a narrative form. In other words, to get from the plenitude of reception to the finitude of reception history requires that historians of reception—like any others—envisage parameters: in particular when reflecting on the history of responses to the Bible, whose responses do they deem to be of importance?[2]

Taking Roberts's helpful instructions, I will define the parameters of this study below in my discussion of "Proletarian Exegesis." Furthermore, however, in a

---

1. Ian Boxall and Christopher Rowland, "Reception History," in *The Oxford Encyclopedia of Biblical Interpretation*, ed. Steven McKenzie (Oxford and New York: Oxford University Press, 2013), 206–15, here 207.

2. Jonathan Roberts, "Introduction," in *The Oxford Handbook of the Reception History of the Bible*, ed. Emma Mason, Michael Lied and Jonathan Roberts (Oxford and New York: Oxford University Press, 2011), 1–9, here 1.

third, helpful volume that appears in the same series as the present project,[3] Susan Gillingham proposes that "Reception Studies" certainly contributes a wide variety of new perspectives and potential projects within Biblical Studies, but Gillingham also rather more provocatively proposes (in line with Rowland's "maverick" comment we cited earlier) that "Reception Studies" can provide: " ... a challenge to a traditional set of priorities which has evolved in historical and literary studies of the Bible over the last two centuries."[4] Finally, Boxall also notes that some scholars argue that some projects within "Reception Studies" might even try to *contribute to historical-critical work*: " ... as a 'corrective,' in order to do historical criticism better: asking how earlier receptions might force us to rethink consensus views about original context and meaning."[5] It is my aspiration to try to similarly bridge between "Reception Studies" and Historical-Critical Studies with this project, particularly in Chapter 6 below. There is, for my patient reader, unfortunately a bit more to be said, however.

We have noted that some scholars working in "Reception History" hope to "retrieve" something of value to Biblical Studies. It is interesting, along these lines, to acknowledge a similar concern in a different disciplinary context, namely "Folkloristics" (increasingly used in place of the older term, "Folklore Studies"). There is obvious similarity to concerns among Folkloristics scholars to defend their selection of subjects for their analysis—especially resisting past dismissal of certain topics as "trivial." In their introduction to a fascinating "state of the question" volume entitled *Advancing Folkloristics* (2021), editors Fivecoate, Downs, and McGriff state their concern that:

> The act of trivialization is an act of both asserting power and removing power. We assert that countertrivialization therefore works against the forces in society that create and maintain power differentials between dominant and marginalized groups. In folkloristics, this countertrivialization ought to carry out its work oriented toward and in dialogue with intersectional, feminist, postcolonialist, queer, and anti-racist scholarship.[6]

I quite like the term "countertrivialization" in relation to "Reception Studies" because it suggests that there may be *ideological* "parameters" for one's project in "Reception Studies" of the Bible.

3. E. England and W. Lyons, eds., *Reception History and Biblical Studies Theory and Practice* (London: Bloomsbury/T&T Clark, 2015).

4. Susan Gillingham, "Biblical Studies on Holiday? A Personal View of Reception History," in *Reception History and Biblical Studies Theory and Practice*, ed. E. England and W. Lyons (London: Bloomsbury/T&T Clark, 2015), 17–30, here 17.

5. Ian Boxall, "Tracing Patmos Through the Centuries," in *Reception History and Biblical Studies Theory and Practice*, ed. E. England and W. Lyons (London: Bloomsbury/T&T Clark, 2015), 155–68, here 156.

6. Jesse A. Fivecoate, Kristina Downs, and Meredith McGriff, "The Politics of Trivialization," in *Advancing Folkloristics*, ed. Jesse A. Fivecoate, Kristina Downs and Meredith McGriff (Bloomington: Indiana University Press, 2021), 59–76, here 60.

Proletarian Exegesis of the Bible: Reviving Michael Gold's project?

In order to further signal this intention on my part, I am proposing to use a different term for this particular project, namely "Proletarian" Biblical exegesis. I am not merely trying to be fashionable and coin a term: in fact, there is a history to the use of this term, and I consider it important to acknowledge that I am intentionally drawing on (older) debates in other disciplines here as well. Specifically, I wish to use this term to intentionally relate this project to the debates that still circulate around the early twentieth-century Jewish-American leftist political commentator, Michael Gold, and his call in the 1920s for a "Proletarian Literature." I wish to also point out, however, that Rev. Dr. H. F. Ward's interesting (but unrelated) essay published soon after Gold's famous "call" should be acknowledged here. Finally, I will bring the work of both of these figures into dialogue with older debates surrounding "New Labor History" and especially the reactions to Jewish-American labour historian, Herbert Gutman (1928–1985). I propose to clarify all of these contexts in this chapter before we take up the analysis of Keir Hardie and his reading of the Bible.

Michael Gold and "Proletarian literature"

The term "Proletariat" or the adjectival form, "Proletarian," is certainly a dated term. However, as I have suggested, I am intentionally using this historically significant term because I want to acknowledge my indebtedness to a fascinating literary movement from the early twentieth century, usually attributed to the work of Michael Gold (1894–1967, born Itzok Granich), who served as the editor of the early twentieth-century American left-wing journal, *New Masses*. Gold is credited with issuing a significant call for the development of an American "Proletarian literature" in the 1920s.[7] Yancey, also discussing Gold's call, concludes that: " ... his

---

7. The literature is substantial, but I found Barbara Foley's work an excellent orientation to the entire set of questions, *Radical Representations: Politics and Form in U.S. Proletarian Fiction, 1929-1941* (Durham and London: Duke University Press, 1993), and among the most interesting essays are Eric Homberger, "Proletarian Literature and the John Reed Clubs 1929–1935," *Journal of American Studies* 13, no. 2 (1979): 221–44; Peter Yancey, "Steinbeck's Relationship to Proletarian Literature," *The Steinbeck Review* 9 (2012): 38–52; Jon-Christian Suggs, "Marching! Marching! And the Idea of the Proletarian Novel," in *The Novel and the American Left: Critical Essays on Depression Era Fiction*, ed. Janet Galligani Casey (Iowa City: University of Iowa Press, 2004), 151–71; Lawrence Hanley, "'Smashing Cantatas' and 'Looking Glass Pitchers': The Impossible Location of Proletarian Literature," in *The Novel and the American Left: Critical Essays on Depression Era Fiction*, ed. Janet Galligani Casey (Iowa City: University of Iowa Press, 2004), 132–50. Whether the entire project of a "Proletarian Novel" was successful or not does not really impact my present project, but I found the entire debate both fascinating and informative. Too much of the debate, it seems, founders on "definitions," which sounds painfully familiar to those of us in Biblical Studies,

contribution to the development of Proletarian literature in America is difficult to overstate. As editor of *New Masses*, Gold was in a unique position to act as arbiter of the new literature."[8]

Gold was already calling for a "Proletarian art" in pages of *The Liberator* in a 1921 issue,[9] but then articulated some further ideas about what this might actually look like in later writings. Of course, Gold contributed a famous novel of his own to the cause: *Jews Without Money*.[10] Homberger notes that Gold's ideas about the working class and the significance of art were inspired by Gold's own context in immigrant Jewish New York:

> Literacy and education were matters of great importance within the Jewish ghetto in the lower East Side of New York, where Gold grew up. As well as there being a tradition of religious study and scholarship in the ghetto, workers' circles and educational alliances, groups sponsored by unions, Zionists, uptown German Jews, and by innumerable *landsmannschaftn* (fraternal associations of emigrants from a particular village or province) competed to provide cultural and educational facilities … It is clear that Gold based his hope for a proletarian literary movement in America upon his experience of the Jewish proletariat in New York. But the Jewish worker was not typical of other immigrants, nor of the native American working class …[11]

unfortunately. On Michael Gold's life, we now have the excellent biography by Patrick Chura, *Michael Gold: The People's Writer* (Albany: SUNY Press, 2020). Interest in Gold, thankfully, shows little sign of abating, and one can follow continued debates in James Murphy, *The Proletarian Moment: The Controversy over Leftism in Literature* (Urbana: Univ. of Illinois Press, 1991), and two good reviews of Murphy's work, Alan Wald, "Literary 'Leftism' Reconsidered," in *Science and Society* 57 (1993): 214–22, and Philip Jenkins, "Review: James Murphy, The Proletarian Movement," in *Comparative Literature Studies* 31 (1994): 195–8. Janet Galligani Casey renews the debate again in "Reviving the Thirties: The Case for Teaching Proletarian Fiction in the Undergraduate American Literature Classroom," *College English* 70 (2008): 233–48. Finally, Alan Wald's wonderful three-volume study from University of North Carolina Press is a master class: Vol. 1, *Exiles from a Future Time: The Forging of the Mid-Twentieth-Century Literary Left* (Chapel Hill: The University of North Carolina Press, 2002), featuring Gold on the cover; Vol. 2, *Trinity of Passion: The Literary Left and the Antifascist Crusade* (Chapel Hill: The University of North Carolina Press, 2007); and Vol. 3, *American Night: The Literary Left in the Era of the Cold War* (Chapel Hill: The University of North Carolina Press, 2012). This list must now happily be supplemented, especially given our religious interests by the provocative work of Jonathan McGregor, *Communion of Radicals: The Literary Christian Left in Twentieth Century America* (Baton Rouge: Louisiana State University Press, 2021).

    8. Yancey, "Steinbeck's Relationship to Proletarian Literature," 40.

    9. Homberger, "Proletarian Literature and the John Reed Clubs," 221.

    10. Michael Gold's novel has passed through many printings, a recent edition is *Jews Without Money* (New York: Public Affairs, 2009).

    11. Homberger, "Proletarian Literature and the John Reed Clubs 1929–1935," 226–7.

What I found particularly interesting, however, is how Gold attempted to fill in the details for his call for a "Proletarian literature" in *New Masses* in 1928. Where, Gold asked, would these "proletarian" expressions and thoughts be found? Gold had some ideas—and asked people to send in:

> Confessions—diaries—documents
> Letters from hoboes, peddlers, small town atheists, unfrocked clergymen and schoolteachers—
> Revelations by rebel chambermaids and night club waiters—
> The sobs of driven stenographers—
> The poetry of steelworkers—
> The wrath of miners—the laughter of sailors—
> Strike stories, prison stories, work stories—
> Stories by Communist, I.W.W. and other revolutionary workers …[12]

In my judgment, it would be hard to articulate a more provocative agenda for seeking out interesting perspectives on the Bible! In the "Preface" to her marvelous 1993 work that calls for a reconsideration of the early twentieth-century movements toward a "Proletarian literature" and especially the "Proletarian novels," Barbara Foley also notes that the term "Proletarian," as much as "Proletarian Novel," undoubtedly sounds to the contemporary ear to be a term that is, at best, an "antiquarian curiosity."[13] Nonetheless, in defending her call to pay renewed attention to these early twentieth-century American attempts at "Proletarian literature," and specifically the writing of novels, Foley makes very interesting observations. It is true, she writes, that the: "routine depiction of proletarians as workers in heavy industry may seem out of joint with a U.S. economy moving increasingly away from the productive and toward the service sector," and Foley agrees that these are antiquated references, and thus continues: "I do not deny that proletarian novels are irrevocably dated in some ways. Reading them puts us in a time warp … the frequent mention of machines echoes emptily over steel and auto plants with silenced furnaces and assembly lines."[14] However, she then mounts a spirited defense of her concern for workers and the poor that reads, if anything, even more profoundly stirring in the first quarter of the twenty-first century as it did when she wrote it in the early 1990s:

> Even if the configuration of the working class has changed since the 1930s, the United States still has a massive proletariat, native as well as foreign-born. Situated in both manufacturing and service industries, these workers fit Marx's definition of proletarians as those who, owning no means of production, have to sell their labor power in order to live. There is every indication that these workers'

---

12. Cited in Homberger, "Proletarian Literature and the John Reed Clubs," 229.
13. Foley, *Radical Representations*, vii.
14. Foley, *Radical Representations*, vii–viii.

situations will continue to deteriorate in the foreseeable future. If we look beyond national boundaries, moreover, we witness the steady proletarianization—and impoverishment—of the globe.[15]

In my view, I could not have argued the case for revisiting early Christian Socialist readings of the Bible in order to identify and reconsider a "Proletarian Exegesis of the Bible" any better than Foley's defense of revived interest in early twentieth-century American Proletarian novels.

As I grew increasingly interested in following Gold's lead on reading "maverick" Biblical reflections featured in old Socialist newspapers in the USA and the UK, I also read through archives of Migrant Camp Newsletters in Dust Bowl era California (1925–1945);[16] studied the lyrics of Labor poems and songs;[17] studied the iconography of union banners;[18] and I have come to believe that Gold's notable hopes for his proposed project have turned out to have more than a "passing resemblance" to some of the goals for the present project. Here, too, I have had to deal with finding the sources for a proposed "Proletarian Exegesis," and the answer provided here—at least initially—is particularly settled on examining the newspapers, newsletters, and pamphlets—in sum the late nineteenth- and early twentieth-century journalistic productions of individual Christian Socialists and Christian Socialist organizations. Here we find not only the sermons and

---

15. Foley, *Radical Representations*, vii–viii.

16. Special thanks to the Librarians at California State University, Bakersfield (The Dust Bowl Oral History Project) and California State, Northridge, who both have good collections of Dust Bowl camp newsletters and oral interview transcripts.

17. Start with Clark D. Halker, *For Democracy, Workers, and God: Labor Song-Poems and Labor Protest, 1865–95* (Urbana and Chicago: University of Illinois, 1991), and then survey early collections like Bouck White's edited collection, *Songs Of The Fellowship, For Use In Socialist Gatherings, Propaganda, Labor Mass Meetings, The Home, And Churches Of The Social Faith* (1912), but now public domain, and Mabel H. B. Mussey, *Social Hymns of Brotherhood and Aspiration* (Boston: Universalist Publishing House, 1914), but also now in public domain.

18. Start with John Gorman's beautiful book: *Banner Bright: An Illustrated History of the Banners of the British Trade Union Movement* (London: Allen Lane, 1973), and notice the frequent use of Solomon's Temple motifs in trades banners for builders. See Annie Ravenhill-Johnson, *The Art and Ideology of the Trade Union Emblem, 1850–1925* (London and New York: Anthem Press, 2013), where you will see Solomon's Temple featured on the banner of the Stone Masons Friendly Society of 1868 (plate PS10); somewhat humorously, Adam and Eve leaving Eden (and thus needing to make clothes) are pictured on the 1898 banner of the Amalgamated Society of Taylors (plate 48); The Tower of Babel in Genesis appears on various versions of the Operative Bricklayers Society (plates 37, 38, and 46); and David's defeat of Goliath is center stage on the banner of the Worker's Union of 1920—implying that their Union struggles are a direct comparison (!).

editorials, but also the poems, songs, and artwork of Christian Socialism.[19] At this point I will play the ventriloquist for my readers and ask: "This is all very interesting, but are we still doing 'Biblical Studies'?" I believe the answer is yes—and so I ask for a bit more patience with this methodological discussion of context.

Rev. Dr. Harry Ward and Rev. George Washington Woodbey: Foundations for a "Proletarian" reading of the Bible

Despite my admiration for Gold's program, it is also to be acknowledged that before, and during, Gold's interesting work toward encouraging a "Proletarian literature," there were already Christians on the left in the USA and the UK who were consciously thinking about this need for a progressive, "working-class" reading of the Bible. Already in the *same year* as Gold's call for a "Proletarian literature," the British-born, but later naturalized American Methodist theologian, Harry F. Ward, called for consideration of "The Bible and the Proletarian Movement."[20] Ward observed that the "proletarian movement" represented a social phenomenon "whose like the world has not yet seen," and noted how powerful the working class organizing efforts had become in both the USA and in Europe. He then wrote:

> If this be the situation … then those who are studying, teaching, and preaching the Bible because they believe it contains the truths by which alone the feet of humanity can be guided into the way of life will need to inquire what relation, if any, there is between the principles taught in the Bible and those around which the proletarian movement is forming, and also what likelihood there is that the teaching of the Bible will influence a movement which has already become so powerful.[21]

Against what he perceived as a lack of interest in religion generally among "proletarian movements" (and he already noted some exceptions to this in the UK), Ward continued his essay by noting that the Bible contains themes of direct

---

19. Walter Crane's artwork, for example, is widely noted, but more rarely an appreciation of his socialist drawings. See Morna O'Neill, "Pandora's Box: Walter Crane, 'Our Sphinx-Riddle,' and the Politics of Decoration," *Victorian Literature and Culture* 35 (2007): 309–26. Occasionally he drew on Biblical motifs, see appendix for a Crane illustration he sent to Hardie's newspaper for Christmas, and Crane's *Cartoons for the Cause* (1896) is now a public domain pamphlet.

20. Harry F. Ward, "The Bible and the Proletarian Movement," *The Journal of Religion* 1 (1921): 271–81. Ward bickered frequently with his more well-known colleague, Reinhold Niebuhr at Union. Unfortunately, Ward was late in condemning Stalinism, and it tarnished his legacy. See the excellent biography by David N. Duke, *In the Trenches with Jesus and Marx: Harry F. Ward and the Struggle for Social Justice* (Tuscaloosa and London: University of Alabama, 2003).

21. Ward, "The Bible and the Proletarian Movement," 273.

relevance to the rise of working-class politics, e.g.: "The Hebrew law stands for the producer as against the possessor, because its ideal of life is production as against possession ...."[22] Ward did not develop this further as an explicit agenda for Biblical Studies, but I acknowledge his voice here.

The Reverend George Washington Woodbey (1854–1937), on the other hand, is a crucial voice from the other US coast—he settled in California. One of his most interesting documents for our purposes is his lengthy pamphlet, *The Bible and Socialism* (1904), included in Foner's edited collection on Woodbey.[23] Woodbey has yet to find his champion as an important African-American Christian Socialist (and I consider this to be a task for a modern African-American Biblical scholar) but the little existing literature on Woodbey illustrates an important point. For example, in the Introduction, when this extensive pamphlet is discussed (briefly) by Foner, the editor is more impressed with references therein to Marxist thought than any serious discussion of Woodbey's impressive reading of Biblical texts. Yet here is another important voice suggesting that "Biblical" Christian Socialism is a neglected area of investigation in the history of Christian Socialism. Woodbey, and Ward, both provide encouragement toward the importance of tasks such as the present project.

Finally, along these lines, I also acknowledge a tremendous methodological debt to my colleague and friend R. S. Sugirtharajah, who has often struck intellectual, textual, and historical "gold" in precisely the reading of non-Western reflections on Scripture. While not necessarily and explicitly based in "class-based" reading more directly related to the present project, Sugirtharajah's methodology of taking seriously the readings of Scripture from outside the (allegedly) normal parameters of European/American historical-critical studies is a helpful guide that "recovery" and "retrieval" of "marginalized" readings of the Bible can have powerful contributions to make to both exegesis, and Biblical theology.[24] Finally, in terms of

22. Ward, "The Bible and the Proletarian Movement," 280.

23. Philip S. Foner, ed., *The Bible and Socialism* is reprinted in *The Black Socialist Preacher: The Teachings of Reverend George Washington Woodbey and His Disciple, Reverend G. W. Slater, Jr.* (San Francisco: Synthesis Press, 1983), 87–201.

24. The reading list is substantial and crucial, including: *Vernacular Hermeneutics* (Sheffield: Sheffield Academic Press, 1999); *Asian Biblical Hermeneutics and Postcolonialism: Contesting the Interpretations*, Biblical Seminar (Sheffield: Sheffield Academic Press, 1999); *The Bible and the Third World: Precolonial, Colonial and Postcolonial Encounters* (Cambridge: Cambridge University Press, 2001); *Postcolonial Criticism and Biblical Interpretation* (Oxford: Oxford University Press, 2002); *Postcolonial Reconfigurations: An Alternative Way of Reading the Bible and Doing Theology* (Des Peres: Chalice Press, 2003); *The Bible and Empire: Postcolonial Explorations* (Cambridge: Cambridge University Press, 2005); *Exploring Postcolonial Biblical Criticism: History, Method, Practice* (London: Wiley-Blackwell, 2011); *The Bible and Asia: From the Pre-Christian Era to the Postcolonial Age* (Cambridge: Harvard University Press, 2013); *Jesus in Asia* (Cambridge: Harvard University Press, 2018); and the classic edited volume, R. S. Sugirtharajah, ed., *Voices from the Margin: Interpreting the Bible in the Third World*, 25th Anniversary edn (Maryknoll: Orbis Books, 2016).

acknowledging related work, the questions being raised here, I suspect, also raise for many readers a comparison with certain aspects of Liberation Theology and most particularly its call for "peasant readings" of the Bible, which was heralded especially by Ernesto Cardenal in his series: *The Gospel in Solantiname* (vol. 1 of 4 began in 1982) and his descriptions of Nicaraguan peasant engagements with Bible Study, and a method summarized well in Carlos Mester's classic: *Defenseless Flower* (1989). While these particular conversations must be closely related to their South American contexts, they raise similar methodological questions to seeking readings "outside the normal" venues for academic Biblical Studies.

"Proletarian Exegesis" of the Bible in relation to work of Herbert Gutman, "New Labor Studies," and the Bible

Some historians have identified the recent interest in left-wing *American* Christian history as a kind of American historian's "second wave"—in recognition of a "first wave" that was launched by the debates over the seminal essay written by the Jewish-American "New Labor" historian Herbert Gutman (1928–1985). We will briefly summarize that "second wave" below, but there is significance to pointing to one particular debate that ensued upon the publication in 1966 of an influential essay by "New Labor" historian Herbert Gutman. Gutman's essay, appearing in *The American Historical Review*, was entitled "Protestantism and the American Labor Movement: The Christian Spirit in the Gilded Age." This essay is invariably cited in the recent work on Christian labour activism in the USA, because it is typically considered an important early "call" to American labour historians to pay attention to *religious-based* working-class activism in the face of a stubborn doctrinaire Marxist ideological line that tended to dismiss the significance of religious leaders (but especially Protestant Christian leaders) as invariably anti-union, anti-labour, and certainly anti-socialist. Gutman, in turn, was largely inspired by the ground-breaking, and controversial, work of British labour historians E. P. Thompson and Eric Hobsbawn, so there is clear evidence for drawing attention to the "trans-Atlantic" nature of these scholarly debates.[25] Arguably, then, American "Labor History" has roots in an exchange of ideas between British and American historians, but we shall soon note that there is reason to expand this to take note of important studies in European *Christian* radical history as well. In Gutman's important essay, he had written:

> Unless one first studies the varieties of working-class community life, the social and economic structure that gave them shape, their voluntary associations (including churches, benevolent and fraternal societies, and trade-unions) their

---

25. This is helpfully outlined by Shelton Stromquist, "Labor Historians and Traditions of Engaged Scholarship: Progressives, Insurgents, and the Making of a New Labor History," in *Civic Labors: Scholar Activism and Working-Class Studies*, ed. Dennis Deslippe, Eric Fure-Slocum, John McKerley, Kristen Anderson, Matthew Mettler, and John Williams-Searle (Chicago: University of Illinois Press, 2016), 11–34.

connections to the larger community, and their particular and shared values, one is likely to be confused about the relationship between the worker, institutional religion, and religious beliefs and sentiments.[26]

"New Labor Studies" was also, however, a movement among historians with an explicit ideological interest and commitment (like Thompson himself), and thus resembles the post-modern turn in Biblical Studies—a turn toward what is often called "Interested Perspectives" in Biblical textual analysis.[27] As such, very similar debates ensued among historians (even among those who shared certain political interests in their personal as well as professional life) about the role of activism and historical studies, the problems of "bias," "objectivity," etc. It would be a separate work entirely to do justice to the wide variety of contributions to the ongoing assessment of Gutman's work (and I am not the one to write such an assessment), but I am interested in one specific aspect of it—namely the nature of Gutman's *evidence* used in his argument, and Cornell historian Nick Salvatore's severely critical review of that essay over thirty years after it was published (and some thirteen years after Gutman's own premature death).[28] In his review of Gutman's famous essay (it was not the only one of Gutman's writings that he considered), Salvatore writes:

> Gutman's 'Protestantism and the American Labor Movement: The Christian Spirit in the Gilded Age' begins with a bracing (if, by now, a repetitive) call for historians to transcend the 'simple 'economic' terms' of the traditional institutional historians. Calling instead for a study of 'the 'mind' of the worker the modes of thought and perception through which he confronted the industrialization process, and which helped shape his behavior,' Gutman proposed to examine 'the disaffected worker's thought: the way certain strands of pre-Gilded Age Protestantism affected him in a time of rapid industrialization and radical social change.'[29]

Salvatore continued his brief review stating, positively, that Gutman was surely right that we cannot understand the "hearts and minds" of working-class people

---

26. Herbert G. Gutman, "Protestantism and the American Labor Movement," *The American Historical Review* 72, no. 1 (1966): 74–101, here 77.

27. See James K. Aitken, Jeremy M. S. Clines and Christl N. Maier, eds., *Interested Readers: Essays on the Hebrew Bible in Honor of David J.A. Clines* (Atlanta: Society of Biblical Literature, 2013).

28. It is always dangerous to venture into the "no man's land" of someone else's intellectual conflicts, but I wandered into this debate before I spotted the warning signs. Nonetheless, I do believe that it has been an interesting walk.

29. Nick Salvatore, "Herbert Gutman's Narrative of the American Working Class: A Reevaluation," *International Journal of Politics, Culture, and Society* 12, no. 1 (1998): 43–80, here 64.

and life if we are not willing to investigate their lives—labour activities, church activities, newsletters—as opposed to the sociologists' articles in journals.[30] The "family resemblance" to Gold's recommendations of the kinds of "evidence" he is interested in, is hard to miss here. However, Salvatore's essay then became quite critical, and among Salvatore's concerns was the nature of the documentary evidence that Gutman cited, as Gutman had relied on editorials and speeches in the trade union newsletters to proclaim his "working-class Christianity." Salvatore's criticism becomes even more serious, however, when he suggests that Gutman himself did not try hard enough to get to some kind of assessment of the workers themselves, because Gutman emphasized community *leaders* in the newsletters (especially Union publications) but didn't get a good sense of the views "of the people." Furthermore, Salvatore accused Gutman of failing to recognize differences between Catholic and Protestant workers' cultures and contexts. Salvatore was therefore highly skeptical that Gutman's evidence was *representative* and refers to the conservative influences of Protestantism as well as the occasions for radical political activity and suggests that Gutman may well have exaggerated the extent of his "working-class Christianity" by the selectivity of his trade union sources. Even more serious, Salvatore did not believe that Gutman had a very good understanding of nineteenth-century American religious experiences.

Notably, one of Gutman's students, Leon Fink, offered a rather spirited response that acknowledged the limited "range" of Gutman's analysis yet still argued that Gutman's "treatment of popular religion, if limited in range, surely opened vistas that labour historians had previously utterly ignored."[31] Is this, then, an open and shut case of the abuse of evidence to intentionally create a misleading picture of history? Is Salvatore correct on this score?

Earlier in his critical essay, Salvatore introduces Gutman's own background in the following paragraph:

> Born in New York City to Jewish immigrant parents in 1928, Gutman's boyhood was framed by three major influences. First, he was a child of the Great Depression and witnessed first-hand the real suffering of everyday Americans as he experienced it in his Jewish immigrant world. Second, he grew to young manhood with a world view largely defined by the political parameters of the 1930s immigrant left. His parents were not Communists, but they remained sympathetic to that party and belonged to the International Workers Order, the Communist-led fraternal organization that provided medical and life insurance for its members. As a result, Gutman once recalled, 'I grew up in the Yiddish Old Left and spent many summers at Camp Kinderland, part of the closed little Left world of New York.' That particular left tradition assumed a certain prominence

---

30. Salvatore, "Herbert Gutman's Narrative," 65.

31. Leon Fink and Nick Salvatore (reply), "Herbert Gutman's Narrative of the American Working Class: A Reevaluation" [with Response], *International Journal of Politics, Culture, and Society* 12, no. 4 (1999): 662–70, here 663.

1. Wading in the "Streams" of a Methodological River Delta

in Gutman's life when, following his active support for Henry Wallace in 1948, he 'drifted about that time into a brief, intense if uneventful involvement with the orthodox communist movement.' While he eventually rejected the Communists for their narrowness of vision, he remained on the left, a socialist determined 'to redefine socialism, to free up socialism from the totalitarian shroud that it [had] lived in for fifty years ... '[32]

Salvatore proposed that Gutman basically did not understand American religion—especially *Christian* religion—the very topic that Gutman was proposing to be potentially important but nevertheless neglected—in labour studies and working-class life. For Salvatore, Gutman had "little understanding" of nineteenth-century American religious experience. This is because Gutman was especially interested in the progressives, rather than a survey of working-class attitudes as a whole.

The fact remains, however, that Gutman *did* provide an impressive amount of interesting evidence, and he certainly had not *concocted* his evidence—Salvatore rather attacked what Gutman thought it *meant* in terms of identifying large "movements." But does this mean that Gutman's evidence didn't mean anything important at all? I believe that Gutman had indeed located something significant, but perhaps overstated the meaning of it. A key to a different reading of Gutman's evidence is the biographical background of Gutman that Salvatore provided, but then seems to have missed an important implication of that background—namely Gutman's *Jewish/New York/Yiddishkeit* perspective.

If one may be patient with a certain "meta-analysis" of Gutman's article, I believe we then find that something interesting emerges in listing Gutman's many examples (from a single journal article!) and thus we can see more clearly the strikingly large number of citations in Union publications from the end of the nineteenth century. These are the very types of citations that Salvatore does not think are "representative." But what *do* they represent, then? And why was Gutman so impressed with this material? Consider the following examples:

(1) *Union Pacific Employee Magazine*, 1891, discusses the Crucifixion of Jesus.[33]
(2) *The Railway Times*, 1896, referring to God and His son, stated that labour's complaints had "the unequivocal indorsement of the Holy Writ."[34]
(3) *The Railway Times*, 1894, refers to the "energizing principles of the gospel of Christ."[35]

---

32. Salvatore, "Herbert Gutman's Narrative," 48.
33. Gutman, "Protestantism and the American Labor Movement," 80.
34. Gutman, "Protestantism and the American Labor Movement," 81.
35. Gutman, "Protestantism and the American Labor Movement," 83.

(4) *The United Mine Workers Journal*, 1894, featured a discussion of the Exodus accounts, quoted at length by Gutman.[36]
(5) *The United Mine Workers Journal*, 1897, Gutman quotes an even more extended passage referring to Adam and Eve, Noah, Moses and Aaron ("Walking delegates"), and finally the "Nazarene" …[37]
(6) *The Railway Times*, 1894, referring to Followers of Christ and the Kingdom.[38]
(7) *Journal of United Labour*, 1882, referring to Moses, "while fleeing from bondage and endeavoring to deliver his people from the hands of the Egyptian destroyer."[39]
(8) *Coast Seaman's Journal*, 1891, "Peter, James, and John … three sailors … "[40]
(9) *The Railway Times*, 1897, discusses Jesus as an: " … agitator such as the world has never seen before nor since … despised and finally murdered to appease the wrath of the ruling class of His time … "[41]
(10) *The Labour Leader*, 1895, cites Eugene Debs referring to Daniel's treatment by the Persians.[42]
(11) *Labor Standard*, 1876, where George McNeill asks: "Have the Pharaoh's descendants nothing to learn from Pharaoh's fate?"[43]
(12) *The Labour Leader*, 1890, features another commentary on Crucifixion.[44]
(13) *Knights of Labor*, 1886, quoting the passage of Jesus calling on the children.[45]
(14) *Locomotive Firemen's Magazine*, 1894, Gutman refers to "Paul's directive to Titus."[46]
(15) *The Railway Times*, 1895, features Moses analogies.[47]
(16) *Coast Seaman's Journal*, 1897, citing Samson and Delilah.[48]
(17) Finally, and perhaps most interesting of all, *The United Mine Workers Journal*, 1894, refers in passing to Moses, Mordecai, and Ehud,[49] that last reference to the book of Judges pushing textual awareness of the Bible rather firmly!

Presented in this manner, the evidence seems much clearer—and I would suggest—*very* important. What seems to have struck Herbert Gutman, the Jewish-American

---

36. Gutman, "Protestantism and the American Labor Movement," 84.
37. Gutman, "Protestantism and the American Labor Movement," 85.
38. Gutman, "Protestantism and the American Labor Movement," 85.
39. Gutman, "Protestantism and the American Labor Movement," 85.
40. Gutman, "Protestantism and the American Labor Movement," 86.
41. Gutman, "Protestantism and the American Labor Movement," 86.
42. Gutman, "Protestantism and the American Labor Movement," 88.
43. Gutman, "Protestantism and the American Labor Movement," 89.
44. Gutman, "Protestantism and the American Labor Movement," 89.
45. Gutman, "Protestantism and the American Labor Movement," 91.
46. Gutman, "Protestantism and the American Labor Movement," 92.
47. Gutman, "Protestantism and the American Labor Movement," 93.
48. Gutman, "Protestantism and the American Labor Movement," 96.
49. Gutman, "Protestantism and the American Labor Movement," 98.

historian raised in the context of Yiddishkeit and Left Jewish culture in New York, is was what one may call "textual" or even "*Biblical radicalism*"—or what I am calling "Proletarian Exegesis." In short—it is *the use of The Bible!* Arguably, Gutman was doing "Reception History" before the rise of this term! That these articles were the views of labour "leaders" and not necessarily the views of "the general working-class attitudes" *may* well be true (but this is far from certain), but surely this kind of Biblical imagery and language is taken up precisely because it is thought to be deeply *meaningful to the readership*? More to the point, Gutman is clearly impressed with arguments *that cite Biblical texts*, and not simply religious themes expressed more generally—noting particularly the frequent Hebrew Biblical analogies. Gutman suggested that this was indicative of at least some Protestant attitudes among religious working-class peoples in America—and surely this is not an unreasonably huge leap! Why would Salvatore think otherwise? I have a suggestion.

As we have stated, Salvatore also severely criticized Gutman for a lack of attention to *Catholic* working-class movements. But what is the common element in the material Gutman cites? The Bible. *And what is singularly absent from most Catholic articulations of theology before the 1950s? The Bible, of course.* The issue becomes particularly clear when considering the 2007 volume dedicated to a group of historians invited by the University of Notre Dame to discuss their personal relationship (and often upbringing) with Catholicism in relation to their work. It is a fascinating collection of essays, but from my perspective, it is also notable for one striking feature—there is but *one* single reference to Scripture in *all* the collected essays! And that reference is, somewhat ironically, in Salvatore's own essay. In his essay, however, Salvatore spoke of a sermon he was invited to give at Sage Chapel at Cornell. He preached on Ezekiel—but Salvatore clarifies that he based his Bible comments on one of Rev. C. L. Franklin's sermons on Ezekiel 37, the Protestant African American pastor (and father of the incomparable Aretha Franklin) who was the subject of his biographical research at the time.[50] Thus, the Biblical reference isn't even Salvatore's own use, it is Franklin's reference.

The point is that there is a very clear reason why a study of the use of the Bible by late nineteenth- and early twentieth-century religious radicals would include very few citations by and from Catholic activists—their form of expressing spirituality and political activism is not the instinctive Protestant—and Jewish—*appeal to Biblical images and motifs*. It is certainly not absent, but it is arguably not a primary "source" for Catholic progressive argumentation until well after World War II. Indeed, a significant expression of this can be clearly seen in the title of one of the essays from that same 2007 collection of essays by contemporary Catholic historians. In his reflections on the possible role of his Catholic upbringing on his later politics and historical research, James Barrett's essay is entitled: "The Blessed

---

50. Nick Salvatore, *Singing in a Strange Land: C. L. Franklin, the Black Church, and the Transformation of America* (New York: Little, Brown, and Company, 2005).

Virgin Made Me a Socialist,"[51] a thought that I would confidently challenge anyone to find in a *Protestant work*! Furthermore, it would be hard to imagine a gathering of American *Protestant* historians who are gathered both because their faith means something to them, and also to reflect on the influence of their Christian faith on their work as historians, without a single reference to the Bible. I would propose, then, that Gutman was clearly more comfortable with the Protestant-style *textual* references as indicative of a religious ethos, because of a Jewish-based "textual" recognition.

Stated another way—what Gutman has identified may not be a *widespread* "Protestant" working-class radicalism—*but he most certainly has identified the significant language in which such a Protestant radicalism would inevitably have been spoken!* In sum, I suggest that what Gutman had identified are examples of what I am here calling "Proletarian Exegesis" of the Bible. This is not to say that Catholic religious activism is not vitally significant and important,[52] but it is quite simply more commonly expressed in different theological terms than the Bible until well after the period we are interested in here. Nor is this a criticism of Salvatore's own work (whose 1982 biography of Eugene Debs, for example, is essential)—only to point to what I see as a potential blind spot in this debate, and one perhaps more obvious to a Protestant Bible scholar working for the Jesuits and Marymount Sisters for over thirty-five years now. The bottom line here is simply this: from the perspective of a project interested in reading the *Bible*, Gutman's 1966 essay is powerfully important, but perhaps not from the perspective important to Salvatore's concerns with a *representative* history. Furthermore, however, *representative* histories are rare! Most historical analyses are more selective—e.g., *which* group of poor, working-class, or small farmer Christians would be selected? Kelly Baker, for example, has examined the religious arguments (including limited comments on Biblical interpretation) for members of the Ku Klux Klan,[53] but how "representative" is this? Whatever other arguments Gutman was making, what he has identified is the potential for another program of investigation that has further inspired this present work—the role *of the Bible* for left-wing Christian activists, as particularly well illustrated in the case of Keir Hardie.

---

51. James R. Barrett, "The Blessed Virgin Made Me a Socialist: An Experiment in Catholic Autobiography and the Historical Understanding of Race and Class," in *Faith and the Historian: Catholic Perspectives*, ed. Nick Salvatore (Chicago: University of Illinois Press, 2007), 117–47.

52. Irish Catholic influence on especially Scottish labor organizing, for example, is well established and impressive and John Wheatley, for example, is nothing short of heroic as a Christian Labour leader in UK history, see Ian Wood's 1990 study, *John Wheatley* (Manchester: Manchester University Press).

53. Kelly Baker, *Gospel According to the Klan: The KKK's Appeal to Protestant America, 1915–1930*, CultureAmerica (Lawrence: University of Kansas Press, 2017).

The rise of studies in Christianity and labour movements

Finally, it is important to place the present project in context with a clear rise in interest in the twenty-first century in the role of Christian movements and leadership in the British and American labour movements. Most of this fascinating work is oriented on the recovery of historical movements and persons otherwise undervalued in history, which is important work. In most of this work, however, the role of the Bible is not a major element of investigation, suggesting that there is significant potential here if enough material can be gathered to make an argument.

In his foreword to the important 2016 collection of essays on Christian working-class movements, *The Pew and the Picket Line* (Christopher Cantwell, Heath W. Carter, and Janine Giordano Drake, eds.), Ken Fones-Wolf writes about how gratified he is with a wave of work by "young historians" who are looking seriously at "working-class popular Christianity." Fones-Wolf, himself the author of an important 1986 study in Christian labour organizing, *Trade Union Gospel*,[54] pointed out that a great deal of attention had previously been directed to studying the "Evangelical Right" and especially the rise of more assertive Protestant political conservatism since World War II. Among the best recent examples of this line of analysis is Darren Dochuk's 2012 work, *From Bible Belt to Sunbelt: Plain-Folk Religion, Grassroots Politics, and the Rise of Evangelical Conservatism*.[55] However, Fones-Wolf is surely correct in pointing out that many of these studies of the religious *right* have tended to focus almost entirely on leaders, institutions (churches and colleges), and increasing political organizing on the right in the twentieth century. Ironically, Nick Salvatore's question about Gutman's work still applies: how "representative" is this—and is this really the only valid goal for these studies?

It can be argued, however, that the more work that is being done by modern historians on Christianity and the working-class movements, the more we are recovering the perspectives of an increasingly large part of American religious life.[56]

---

54. Ken Fones-Wolf, *Trade Union Gospel: Christianity and Labor in Industrial Philadelphia, 1865–1915*, American Civilization (Philadelphia: Temple University Press, 1986).

55. Darren Dochuk, *From Bible Belt to Sunbelt: Plain-Folk Religion, Grassroots Politics, and the Rise of Evangelical Conservatism* (New York: W.W. Norton & Co., 2012).

56. Among these recent historical works, one is best advised to begin with the essays in *The Pew and the Picket Line: Christianity and the American Working Class*, Working Class in American History, ed. Christopher Cantwell, Heath W. Carter, and Janine Giordano Drake (Chicago: University of Illinois Press, 2016), but the interested reader then has impressive literature to look forward to reading, certainly to include Kyle G. Wilkison, *Yeoman, Sharecroppers, and Socialists* (College Station: Texas A&M University, 2008); Heath Carter, *Union Made: Working People and the Rise of Social Christianity in Chicago* (Oxford & New York: Oxford University Press, 2015); Richard J. Callahan, *Work and Faith in the Kentucky Coal Fields: Subject to Dust* (Bloomington: Indiana University Press, 2009);

Correspondingly, although not quite so prolific, recent work on *British* Christian Socialism has continued a steady interest in significant leaders and movements in that context.⁵⁷ In studies of UK Christian Socialism and Labour Studies generally, one frequently encounters the famous saying usually attributed to Labour secretary Morgan Philips (1902–1963), namely that British Socialism: "owes more to Methodism than Marx."⁵⁸ Finally, there are important works documenting

---

Robert Hunt Ferguson, *Remaking the Rural South: Interracialism, Christian Socialism, and Cooperative Farming in Jim Crow Mississippi* (Athens: University of Georgia Press, 2018); Jim Bissett, *Agrarian Socialism in American: Marx, Jefferson, and Jesus in Oklahoma Countryside, 1904–1920* (Norman: University of Oklahoma Press, 1999); Jarod Roll, *Spirit of Rebellion: Labor and Religion in the New Cotton South* (Urbana: University of Illinois Press, 2010); Jarod Roll and Erik S. Gellman, eds., *The Gospel of the Working Class: Labor's Southern Prophets in New Deal America* (Urbana: University of Illinois Press, 2011); and Matthew Pehl, *The Making of Working-Class Religion* (Urbana: University of Illinois Press, 2016). Finally, Gary Dorien continues a steady stream of important historical works closely related to this topic, the latest of which is *American Democratic Socialism: History, Politics, Religion, and Theory* (New Haven: Yale University Press, 2021). Older important works include James Dombrowski, *The Early Days of Christian Socialism in America* (New York: Octagon Books, 1966).

57. Here, one could start with a historical survey up to mid-nineteenth century, Eileen Groth Lyon's *Politicians in the Pulpit: Christian Radicalism in Britain from the Fall of the Bastille to the Disintegration of Chartism* (Aldershot: Ashgate, 1999); before considering John Oren's wonderful biography of one of the most colorful of the nineteenth-century Anglican Christian Socialists, Stewart Headlam: *Stewart Headlam's Radical Anglicanism: The Mass, the Masses, and the Music Hall* (Urbana: University of Illinois Press, 2003); and Mark Peel's recent biography of Donald Soper, the famous Methodist socialist preacher famed for his "Speaker's Corner" appearances in London, *The Last Wesleyan: A Life of Donald Soper* (Lancaster: Scotford, 2008); and the work I found particularly important, Peter Catterall's analysis: *Labour and the Free Churches, 1918–1939: Radicalism, Righteousness* (London: Bloomsbury, 2016), and then consider, for the Scotland "Free Church" context in the nineteenth century, Rev. Dr. Allan MacColl's masterful survey, *Land, Faith and the Crofting Community: Christianity and Social Criticism in the Highlands of Scotland, 1843–1893* (Edinburgh: University of Edinburgh Press, 2006). For the more "practical" experiments in British socialism, an excellent reference is still Philip Backstrom, *Christian Socialism and Cooperation in Victorian England* (London: Croom Helm, 1974).

58. Recent historical work is suggesting that this is a bit of an overstatement, especially if the reference to Methodism is taken too exclusively to refer to just that one religious denominational tradition (with the exception of so-called "Primitive Methodism" which certainly appears to have spawned more than its share of Christian socialists). If one expands that saying (which would unfortunately lose the clever alliteration on the letter "m") to suggest "independent/free churches and chapels" rather than simply "Methodism," then there is less argument about its value as a general observation. This is helpfully discussed in Peter Catterall's essential work, *Labour and the Free Churches*.

Continental movements, especially in traditionally Catholic European contexts.[59] I do not think it is being unfair to this marvelous body of work, however, to point out that the historical interests that (very impressively) drive this work have not included specific analysis of the use of the Bible. We have already noticed the lack of serious analysis of Woodbey's Biblical interpretation, for example. Further, although Jarod Roll and Erik Gellman discuss the maverick leader, Rev. Claude Williams, we await a full analysis of the Bible Study books he composed *for working with working-class leaders*, still unpublished and languishing in archive collections.[60] A similar observation can be made in relation to Latin American-driven Liberation Theology. Although strongly driven by Biblical discussions, these tend to be the work of impressively trained clergy, although it is important to take note of a "sub-set" of Liberation Theology works that does indeed concern itself with the "exegesis" of the poor or peasant. These specific works certainly do have a strong resemblance to this present project, although we are dependent on the oral reports of clergy in understanding the dynamics of this.[61]

---

59. This work continues to be led by Gerd-Rainer Horn, whose work on progressive "Left Catholicism" is essential reading. Horn's own monographs include *The Spirit of Vatican II: Western European Progressive Catholicism in the Long Sixties* (Oxford: Oxford University Press, 2015) examining intellectual and activist movements leading toward Vatican II, but also his wonderfully informative survey of European Christian Socialism, *Western European Liberation Theology (1924–1959): The First Wave* (Oxford: Oxford University Press, 2015). It is Horn and E. Gerard's edited collection, *Left Catholicism, 1943–1955: Catholics and Society in Western Europe at the Point of Liberation* (Leuven: University of Leuven Press, 2001), which forms an essential companion to the American survey mentioned above, *The Pew and the Picket Line*.

60. Roll and Gellman, *The Gospel of the Working Class*. At this writing, Jason Mikel, a PhD student at the University of Memphis, is soon completing a much anticipated dissertation on Williams, and in combination with Roll and Gellman's work, we will be released from being too dependent on Belfrage's endlessly entertaining hagiography that nonetheless often raises questions about its reliability as a source. Cedric Belfrage, *Let My People Go* (London: Victor Gollancz, 1940).

61. This "peasant reading" Biblical emphasis was led by Ernesto Cardenal's four-volume project, *The Gospel in Solentiname* (Maryknoll: Orbis, 1976), but helpfully discussed further in Carlos Mesters's *Defenseless Flower* (Maryknoll: Orbis Books, 1989). Nonetheless, it is hard to resist concluding that this particular emphasis on "people's readings" has never been a major driver of interest in Liberation Theology. Nonetheless, I continue to try to pay attention to moves in the direction of "culturally informed" readings of the Bible, even as I happily acknowledge that it is largely the work of scholars of color, see Smith-Christopher, "Cross-Cultural Interpretation of the Bible" in *Oxford Encyclopedia of Biblical Interpretation*, 2013: 128–50, as well as my essay: "Reading the Christian Old Testament in the Contemporary World," in *The Pentateuch: Fortress Bible Commentaries*, ed. Gale A. Yee, Hugh R. Page Jr., and Matthew J. M. Coomber (Minneapolis: Fortress Press, 2014), 43–66.

In most of the historical discussions of British "Christian Socialism," this emphasis on leaders and movements is also clear. The "first wave" Christian Socialists are associated with the interesting leadership of the High Church Anglican, F. D. Maurice. While these are endlessly fascinating figures to read about, Holman was surely correct to emphasize their rather elitist context and perspectives. Discussions, for example, about how "Trinitarian theology" can provide a conceptual foundation for social cohesion and political action may be quite fascinating to observe in Maurice,[62] but his work is thereby rarely built from a primary and sustained attention to Scripture. One of Hardie's recent biographers, the late Bob Holman, observes:

> They were usually middle-class Christians like F. D. Maurice and Charles Kingsley, who called themselves Christian socialists but who had little in common with the Christian poor. The Guild of St Matthew and the Church Socialist League made radical attacks on government and on the churches but had few working-class followers.[63]

I do not deny either its historical importance as a movement, nor its continued significance in the history of what may be called "Christian social theology" widely defined, but it was never an expression of explicitly and clearly "working class" Christianity, and occasionally revealed its middle-class aversions to more radical expressions of egalitarian, or even Christian, socialism. We can hear Michael Gold's voice in the background, "Not here, friend …."

A second "stream" of Christian Socialism in the UK that is also of serious interest even though not the central concern here, is expressed in many "practical" attempts and experiments in the UK to create alternative social projects in an effort to demonstrate an alternative socio-economic order even within emergent industrial capitalism. For example, Richard Owen's experiments (perhaps the most famous of such "practical" experiments) in Lanarkshire in Scotland were certainly not motivated by any Christian faith in Owen himself (who was indifferent, at best, to religion of any sort).[64]

---

62. Jones referred to "Sacramental Socialism" in this "High Church" context, Peter d'A. Jones, *The Christian Socialist Revival 1877–1914* (Princeton, NJ: Princeton University Press, 1968), 85–98.

63. Bob Holman, *Keir Hardie: Labour's Greatest Hero?* (London: Lion Hudson, 2010), 201.

64. There is a continued interest in Owen, but also a number of "practical socialism" experiments, see G. D. H. Cole, *The Life of Robert Owen*, Routledge Library Editions: The Labour Movement (London: Routledge, 2018). Many of Owen's supporters were committed Christians, including his Quaker business partner William Allen, with whom Owen eventually ended a business partnership because of Allen's insistence on Biblical education at New Lanark(!). I have noted that British experiments along these lines were often undertaken with a view of being more widely influential, even on Government policy. Many of the American experiments, however, were undertaken by religious groups seeking to live authentic Christian lives in response to the book of Acts. See Backstrom, *Christian Socialism*.

One endemic problem with this literature on "practical socialisms," including on Owen, by both American and British historians, is the constant emphasis on the exotic, and the failed. The ubiquitous use of the (often intended to be derogatory) term "Utopian," invariably suggests "ephemeral," "absurd," "misguided," or even the more damning insinuation of "impractical."[65] Combined with an almost voyeuristic emphasis on "deviant" sexualities in some of these communities, these are hardly studies that will provide much discussion of how some of the members seriously read their Bibles.

The sources for working-class Christian Socialism?

Finally, where does this wide-ranging discussion lead us? There is little disagreement that studies of Christian Socialism have not tended to feature serious analysis of how the Bible is read in these contexts. Michael Gold would suggest we are looking in the wrong places, but Herbert Gutman provided some serious clues. Ward knew it was "out there," and Woodbey provides powerful proof that discussions of Bible are to be found.

SUMMARY: The Miner's Bible: Keir Hardie and "Proletarian Exegesis"

Reflecting on all these foundations of thought, I finally settled on what is for me an obvious choice: J. (for "James," but rarely used) Keir Hardie. As I will briefly survey in subsequent chapters, historical assessments of Hardie, and especially the long-term importance of his contributions to the rise of Labour Party politics vary significantly. However, it should be clearly stated here that I am less concerned with the debates among socialist historians and political theorists, much less the biographers of Hardie himself, when they are concerned with Hardie's socialist "*bona fides*" (usually defined as the ability to write a clear, carefully referenced Marxist theoretical class-based analysis, such as Foner's discussions of Woodbey).

---

65. In the American context, these studies are deeply influenced by attention to John Humphrey Noyes (*The History of American Socialisms* (Philadelphia: J.B. Kippincott, 1870)), an odd character by any estimation. Because his was an early survey, his oddities tend to dominate analysis that is, at times, almost voyeuristic on groups with unusual sexual practices, which varies from Shaker celibacy to New Oneida free love ("complex marriage"). See Michael Robertson's survey of more recent experiments, *The Last Utopians: Four Late Nineteenth-Century Visionaries and Their Legacy* (Princeton and Oxford: Princeton University Press, 2019), which also contains helpful lists of literature. Even sympathetic treatments of more religious serious "socialist" groups like the Hutterites, however, tend not to discuss explicitly Biblical teachings; see the classic by John Hostetler, *Hutterite Society*, 2nd edn (Baltimore: Johns Hopkins University Press, 1997), whose sociological emphasis only lightly touches on the Bible.

Beyond this, there is at least one point upon which virtually all the biographies agree: Hardie's Christian commitments were by no means an insignificant part of his life and work. Thus far there is wide agreement. *What has not been the subject of serious analysis*, however, is specifically the question of Hardie as a reader, and especially interpreter, of his Bible.

On a final note, I wish to take seriously Nick Salvatore's insistence that we must be honest about the negatives as well as positives of "working-class/peasant readings" of the Bible. In my own search for "sources" (inspired, again, by Gold), for example, I have attempted to study European and European-American small farmer and/or working-class movements. I have been deeply discouraged by the persistence of racism. Time and again, the slow rise of class-consciousness and union organizing among white, poor, farming and labouring classes was *not* accompanied by re-thinking attitudes toward their obvious class allies among persons of color.[66] In many cases, this seriously weakened their viability—and there is clear evidence of powerful interests fanning the flames of racism to precisely (and frantically) prevent such an emerging solidarity across cultures. Even in Keir Hardie, I discovered, his slow movement toward an appropriately enlightened view of the struggles of Black South Africans and other peoples of color as *appropriately part of his politics* was painfully slow, *but he did get there, and significantly ahead of many others.*[67]

There is an obvious place to start on the question of "sources," and here Gold and Gutman's guidance does converge: There exists in the historical archives of labour movements, socialist activism, and union organizing, examples of activists (and their newspapers) whose writing most certainly includes profoundly interesting reflections on Scripture—reflections that were by no means tangential to otherwise "serious" social analysis. Rather, in many cases Scripture was at the very heart of their analysis because they were not only socialists, activists, and

---

66. A good analysis of this is certainly Tracy K'Meyer's study: *The Story of Koinonia Farm: Interracialism and Christian Community in the Postwar South* (Charlottesville: University of Virginia Press, 1997).

67. Hardie is often celebrated for his early feminism, but his racial views evolved more slowly, along with his support for native rights in British colonies. See Jonathan Hyslop, "The World Voyage of James Keir Hardie: Indian Nationalism, Zulu Insurgency and the British Labour Diaspora 1907-1908," *Journal of Global History* 1 (2006): 343-62; Prabha R. Shankar, "Socialist Labour Leader James Keir Hardie's (1856-1915) Contribution to India's Struggle for Freedom," *Proceedings of the Indian History Congress* 60 (1999): 675-83. Claire Hirschfield denies anti-Semitism in Hardie, "The British Left and the 'Jewish Conspiracy': A Case Study of Modern Antisemitism," *Jewish Social Studies* 43 (1981): 95-112. On Hardie's celebrated feminism, see Carolyn Stevens, "The Objections of 'Queer Hardie', 'Lily Bell' and the Suffragettes' Friend to Queen Victoria's Jubilee, 1897," *Victorian Periodicals Review* 21, no. 3 (1988): 108-14, and importantly, Deborah Mutch's study, *Women, Periodicals and Print Culture in Britain, 1830s-1900s: The Victorian Period* (Edinburgh: Edinburgh University Press, 2019).

radical journalists—but they were profoundly committed Christians—they were *Christian* Socialists, *Christian* activists, and radical *Christian* journalists.

Common to this project were a few considerations that helped me to finally select my subject for analysis. First, and obviously, there needed to be a sufficient body of data to be able to draw conclusions. That is why there were many cases where I chased down references to Christians in social histories, but I had to move on because I simply did not find enough writing and material. Second, I was interested in those voices that were not professional, nor professionally trained, Biblical theologians. Hardie is virtually entirely self-taught and minimally "formally" (that is, institutionally) educated, and a working-class activist. Third, I was focused on European, or Euro-American voices—not because other voices are not important—but because these *class-based* marginalized European and Euro-American voices have not received much attention at all from theologians—and especially Biblical theologians. Furthermore, as tempting as Woodbey's work certainly is—I happily pass this to interested colleagues of color.

Among my first explorations in Hardie's own writing was his famous 1901 pamphlet, *Can A Man Be a Christian on a Pound a Week?* In this short work, I was intrigued by his bold rhetoric, and it quickly became clear that the Bible was no mere "window dressing" in the life and rhetoric of the former miner. On the contrary, the Bible was arguably a central pillar in his life's dedication to socialism in the UK. Here is a case of a genuine "proletarian" reading of the Bible that seemed ready-made to fit a "proletarian" writing on the Bible.

As I will describe in more detail in the next chapter, Hardie was entirely self-taught (he started working odd jobs at age ten, some say as early as seven), and a self-described convert to Christianity from a struggling working-class family with little previous interest in religion. Christianity was not his "family tradition." By his twenties, he was an experienced miner. Within a few years, however, he was quickly blacklisted for his union activities with the miners, which then thrust him into full-time organizing and journalism to try to make a living. Is this a sufficient statement of "parameters" for why Keir Hardie deserves analysis in Reception History of the Bible? Not quite.

The fact is that Keir Hardie is not an otherwise anonymous worker who happened to write about the Bible. Such a subject would still be worth reading, of course, but James Keir Hardie is one of the founding fathers of the British Labour Party. In other words, in Hardie we are not speaking of a "fringe" or "incidental" figure of British history, and most certainly no mere "curiosity." More to the point, while his religious convictions have certainly not been ignored in the many biographies of Hardie, the *centrality of the Bible* in his thought and writing as a union organizer, labour advocate, radical journalist, and socialist agitator has not, in my view, received sufficient attention. Yet, as we shall see, there is certainly enough material to work with! As a journalist, Hardie has left us a wonderful legacy of writing—not the least because he founded his own newspaper, *The Miner*, which eventually evolved into *The Labour Leader*, one of the most important (but by no means the largest readership) among the many Labour newspapers in UK history. Reading through the archives of *The Labour Leader* is often profoundly interesting, especially for a Professor of Bible. In sum, in Hardie, we have a particularly striking example of what can without hesitation be called "working-class" exegesis of the Bible, or to propose the term he would certainly have heartily approved of: "Proletarian Exegesis" of the Bible.

This, then, brings me full circle, and I return to where this Introduction began. This is intended to be a work in Biblical Studies. I am interested in Keir Hardie as a reader of the Bible, and what we may learn from his exegetical patterns. Finally, I here attempt to hold Keir Hardie's work in a new light not merely because he is "poor white." Any book on the sermons of a fundamentalist preacher would be the same. I highlight Keir Hardie's reading of the Bible because it was in the context of a struggle for justice. Just as African-American scholars, for example, will tend to want to work on those historical figures whose hopes and work was/is for social progress rather than perpetuating damaging fundamentalist views,[68] I share that criterion for selection as well. This is not "history" pure and simple, and I hope that this is more than detrivializing a "neglected voice." I will here argue that Hardie's is a voice that must not be neglected because the times are gravely serious for those Christians who are both serious about Biblical Studies and serious about hopes for the progress of humanity. The reader, in the end, will have to decide if the project is successful in convincing anyone of this importance.

---

68. On precisely this danger, see Vincent Wimbush, *The Bible and African Americans: A History in Six Readings* (Minneapolis: Fortress, 2023). Of course, such selectivity raises questions about "representative" readings. This, however, is not an exercise in social survey and political polls. This is primarily an exercise in Biblical studies.

Figure 2.1 "Fallen Among Thieves," *The Labour Leader*, September 29, 1894.

Chapter 2

KEIR HARDIE: A LIFE AND CONTEXT

As we have tried to clarify in the opening section, one of the most important insights of recent Biblical Studies is the acknowledgment of context—not only for a better understanding of a text in its historical "context," but also the "context" of the researcher. Thus, even though this work is not intended to be a formal biography of Keir Hardie, if we are talking about reading the Bible "in context," then it is obvious that there is importance to placing Hardie's life (along with his close colleagues and allies) into some kind of context for his scriptural arguments. Although this chapter does not replace the major biographical works available on Hardie,[1] it is essential to establish some aspects of Hardie's life, by

---

1. The four most recent and detailed biographies are Kenneth O. Morgan's 1975 work *Keir Hardie: Radical and Socialist* (now considered the standard work), reprinted in 1997 by Phoenix, London; Caroline Benn's more recent and lengthier work: *Keir Hardie* (London: Richard Cohen Books, 1997); Iain McLean's biography *Keir Hardie* (London: St. Martin's Press, 1975) is already aware of Morgan's work despite being dated to the same year, and which helpfully provides details of specific events that do not presume extensive knowledge of British history; and Fred Reid's revised doctoral dissertation, *Keir Hardie: The Making of a Socialist* (London: Croom Helm, 1978). Benn's lengthy work, however, suffers from a lack of detailed bibliography and a somewhat erratic notation system (I am one to talk, of course). There is also an important and more recent shorter work by (the late) Bob Holman, *Keir Hardie: Labour's Greatest Hero?* (London: Lion Hudson, 2010). For the present project, it is notable that Holman's work includes a spirited defense of the importance of Hardie's Christianity, concluding (rightly, in my view) that Benn and Morgan have seriously exaggerated Hardie's "heterodoxy," thereby appearing to minimize (Benn, more than Morgan) the role of Hardie's Christian faith. On this, see my Chapter 3 below.

Older standards include the first great work, William Stewart's 1921 biography (authorized by the I.L.P., with a foreword by Ramsay MacDonald) entitled: *Keir Hardie: A Biography* (London: Cassell and Company, 1921). Only two years later David Lowe's 1923 work was published: *From Pit to Parliament: The Story of the Early Life of James Keir Hardie* (London: The Labour Publishing Company, 1923). Lowe is an author who, as he himself states in his introduction, "knew Hardie well" and worked with him for years (and is therefore wonderfully gossipy but also featuring numerous quotes from letters Hardie wrote to Lowe). Hamilton Fyfe's short volume for the "Great Lives" Series of Duckworth Press in London (1935) entitled simply: *Keir Hardie*, is too generalized to be very helpful. Emrys

featuring a stronger emphasis on the religious issues this book is focused on. As a Member of Parliament (hereafter "MP"), and also among the founders of the Labour Party of Britain, and finally as a journalist, we have mainly his editorials and pamphlets to draw upon with regard to his own religious ideas and ideals. But this project would never have begun if there was not a striking amount of Biblical discussion and argumentation present in Hardie's own writings.

Discussions of Biblical passages are not the *primary* mode of Hardie's communication, certainly, but neither are they the cynical proof-texts or side comments that Americans are used to from their own (typically conservative) politicians. We are not speaking here of a circus side-show like a recent American President who appeared to be stymied by a reporter's question to quote something—*anything*—from the Bible.[2] Quite to the contrary, Keir Hardie most certainly read, thought about, and discussed the Bible as a serious foundation upon which to think politically and socially.

Context for the life of Keir Hardie: A brief preliminary survey

For those more interested in the development of socialism in Britain, the biographies are quite helpful, as this seems to be the predominant interest for

---

Hughes, who married Hardie's daughter Agnes, wrote his biography which appeared in 1956 entitled: *Keir Hardie: A Pictorial Biography* (London: George Allen & Unwin). Besides including many insights from being a family member, it is also, among all the biographies (perhaps to be expected), the most richly illustrated with many photos. Finally, a very early yet significantly informative short pamphlet on Hardie's life was written by Canadian activist J. McArthur Conner (1917) and published in Toronto: Banner Press: *Jas. Keir Hardie's Life Story: From Pit Trapper to Parliament*, and rarely cited in modern biographies. There are popular works of less historical value, or intended for younger audiences, e.g., John Cockburn, *The Hungry Heart: A Romantic Biography of James Keir Hardie* (London: Jarrolds, 1956); Hyman Shapiro, *Keir Hardie and the Labour Party*, Then and There Series (London: Longman, 1971). There have also continued to appear collections of essays reflecting on Hardie's legacy, such as the two volumes edited by Pauline Bryan, including the 2015 volume, *What Would Keir Hardie Say?* and the 2019 volume, *Keir Hardie & the 21st Century Socialist Revival* (both by Edinburgh: Luath Press). Both of these volumes feature a variety of popularly written essays on various aspects of Hardie's life and concerns, the 2015 collection featuring Holman's contribution: "Christianity: Christian and Socialist" (35–48), which although interesting, consists of material covered already in his 2015 volume on Hardie.

2. Eugene Scott, "Trump says Bible is his Favorite Book, but Declines to Share Favorite Verse," CNN, August 27, 2015. This is the same President who concocted a major "media event" by holding up a Bible for the TV cameras (after tear-gassing any protesters who might ruin the moment); Katie Rogers, "Protesters Dispersed With Tear Gas So Trump Could Pose at Church," *New York Times*, June 1, 2020.

most of them.³ As a politician and writer, Hardie's circle of acquaintances was obviously large, and many of the biographies read like Hollywood-style surveys of the themes and historical personalities who weave in and out of the story, including discussions of the great personalities of political intrigue and activism whom Hardie met, and some he knew as friends, such as the pioneer (and controversial) feminists, the Pankhursts, Kropotkin the Russian anarchist, Louise Michel the heroine of the Paris Commune and her New Caledonia exile, Marx, and (especially) Friedrich Engels.

However, even more important for our concerns is the fact that the biographies provide resources for at least brief introductions to the many *Christian* Socialists who were friends and allies of Hardie—many of whom deserve serious consideration in their own right, especially if the present work is successful in convincing some readers of the value of this kind of "Reception History" of progressive Christian politicians' use of the Bible.

Thus, investigating the thoughts of Tom Mann, William Small, Frank Smith, and John Kenworthy, among many others, would be quite interesting since all of them described their work as characterized by their religious commitments. This doesn't work in all cases, of course, as my attempt to include John Trevor, founder of "The Labour Church" movement, in the next chapter (which considers some of Hardie's "allies" in Christian Socialism and their use of the Bible) foundered on the simple discovery that he considered his own heterodox faith to be "liberated" from taking the Bible seriously in any way, contrary to Hardie himself, and thus we have hardly any direct engagements by Trevor in regards to the Bible. Clearly, to try to force an analysis of Trevor's use of the Bible would run contrary to his own claims. In Hardie's case, however, his life and interest in Scripture is clear. Let us review elements of his biography that are important for our consideration in this project.

A nineteenth-century context in Western Scotland

It would be hard to overestimate the social, political, and religious significance of the fact that James Keir Hardie was not only born into poverty, in the middle of the nineteenth century (August 15, 1856), but also born a Scot. Each and every part of this first sentence about the life of Hardie is significant.

To set this in historical context, consider the comments in Burnett's edited collection of "Working People" writings from the 1820s to the 1920s, where Burnett himself helpfully summarizes the situation of the miner in British socio-economic context:

> A labourer of a very special kind – more akin, in some respects, to the skilled worker – was the miner. In the hierarchy of labour he defies classification; his

---

3. McLean's 1975 biography, for example, often includes comments on personalities, but when they are introduced in his narrative, it is typically accompanied by assessments such as: "by no means a socialist," "certainly not a socialist," etc.

earnings sometimes equalled those of the craftsman, in sturdy independence of thought and action he had no superior, yet down to 1914 the physical labour required of him was more intense, and the working conditions more dangerous, than in any other trade. The raw material of industrialization was dug out of the earth by the muscles of men aided only by pick and shovel, and as the demand continued to grow more and more men found their livings below ground. In the first reliable Census of 1851 coal-miners, at 216,000, were ninth in the occupational order: copper, tin, and lead-miners added another 53,000, and iron-miners 27,000. By 1881 the colliers numbered 382,000 and by 1911 they had reached their peak at 877,000 – as many now as the agricultural labourers; in that still prosperous year they raised the record total of 273,000,000 tons, and coal made up more than one-tenth of the value of all United Kingdom exports … Coal, it could be argued, rather than cotton, was king of the nineteenth century.[4]

To most Victorian observers coal-miners represented a strange almost half-human, stratum of the working class, pugnacious, brutalized by their lives of grimy toil, inhabiting isolated communities which, in leisure time, became dens of drunkenness and savage sports. A few praised the miner's courage and resourcefulness in a dangerous occupation where accidents were a daily occurrence, and the plight of women and young children in the mines early aroused humanitarian concerns.[5]

This was the century that was not, like the twentieth and twenty-first centuries, already hardened to many of the realities of destructive capitalism and the accompanying environmental and social devastation of industrialization. To the contrary, this was the century that experienced some of the greatest shocks, and developed some of the most radical responses, in European history and experience. As McLean helpfully pointed out, the many agrarian "utopias" written in the nineteenth century (e.g., Blatchford's "Merrie England" and various rural-based utopian proposals) make far more sense to twenty-first-century readers when it is remembered that: "Open moorlands and mountains could be seen at the end of even the most depressing street."[6] Thus, "Ruralist Populism" in this era came from recent and bitter experience. Scottish agricultural peasants saw large numbers of agriculture-dependent renters mercilessly evicted from lands on which their ancestors had worked and paid rent for generations in the aptly named "Highland clearances" (which continued from *c.* 1750 to 1860). The massive migrations to the cities—and some on to the "New World" (Australia, New Zealand, and North America)—would create a Scottish urbanized working class, but also a diaspora that would have consequences far beyond the United

---

4. John Burnett, ed., *Useful Toil: Autobiographies of Working People from the 1820s to the 1920s* (London: Allen Lane, 1974), 26 and 41.
5. Burnett, *Useful Toil*, 42–3.
6. McLean, *Hardie*, 57.

Kingdom. Ireland continued to suffer English colonization, especially symbolized by the (literally) manufactured crisis called a "Potato famine" (1845–1849)— when thousands of the poor starved while landowners in Ireland continued to export food, resulting in an Irish exodus that would also have implications for the UK and beyond (again, North America, Australia, New Zealand, and beyond), and reducing the homeland Irish population by nearly 25 percent. The use of desperate Irish labourers as "black leg" (strike breaking) labour in England and especially Scotland often meant that there were potential tensions between Scots, English, and even other Irish working men. Morgan also relates how resistant mine owners were to any activities of workers who might have hoped to organize for more consistent pay, often bringing in "black leg" labour from Ireland on those occasions when they tried to organize.[7] The policies of industrialization in England, too, would result in migration to the cities, providing cheap labour (including children) to support the beginnings of industrialization in the North of England. In the case of cotton and cloth production, for example, as many historians have observed, London "kept the books" and watched over the banking, and American slavery came to supply the high quality, and cheaply harvested, bulk cotton for the northern British mills.[8] The growing urban poverty was horrendous, but there were no governmental policies of compassionate care or response to the masses groaning under conditions that were already being described in mid-century publications but also through the rest of the century. These conditions gave rise to publications like Engels' 1845 work, *The Condition of the Working Class in England*, but equally influential was the later publication by the founder of the Salvation Army, "General" William Booth. Booth, with the help of Hardie's later political adviser and ally, Frank Smith, continued Engels' (and others) goals of describing the tremendous urban suffering brought on by the early industrialization and the horrific conditions that also fired the social commentary in the fictional work of Charles Dickens (1812–1870), and many others.

There were a number of important social responses to these nineteenth-century crisis conditions. The first half of the nineteenth century saw the rise of a series of political reform movements that became known as "Chartism" (*c.* 1837–1848). The Chartists sought to end the exclusive dominance of the wealthy classes in government. Contemporary to the last major actions of Chartism was the High Church Anglican "Socialism" of F. D. Maurice and Charles Kingsley, which continues to be appreciated in theological circles as theologically and socially innovative thinking, but it was a movement that hardly made an impression on actual working-class activism.[9] It was in the last quarter of the nineteenth century

---

7. Morgan, *Keir Hardie: Radical and Socialist*, 6.

8. Edward Baptist, *Half has Never Been Told: Slavery and the Making of American Capitalism* (New York: Basic Books, 2014). See David Brion Davis, *Inhuman Bondage: The Rise and Fall of Slavery in the New World* (Oxford: Oxford University Press, 2008), esp. 80–99.

9. Lyon, *Politicians in the Pulpit*.

that we see the rise of labour activism, and especially "socialism" (in many forms, both Marxist and non-Marxist), as a coalition of radical proposals to respond to the suffering engendered by the industrial revolution and unmitigated cruelties toward the poor and working people.

These issues not only gave rise to new social and political movements and proposals, but also unprecedented responses on the part of those (few) Christians not convinced that their wealth was a blessing of God, or that the poverty of the masses was simply some form of God's judgment on the sins of the poor. In the first half of the twentieth century, the Swiss theologian Karl Barth famously advised theologians to read the Bible in one hand with the newspaper in the other—the late nineteenth century saw many examples of Christians who not only read *about* subordinated people's suffering but those also who actually experienced it, and they kept reading their Bibles for some guidance on making progress against such unprecedented suffering. Among them was Keir Hardie.

Keir Hardie: A brief survey of his life

Recent biographies of Hardie locate his birthplace as the village of Legbrannock, North Lanarkshire, which sits between Holytown and Motherwell, today just south of the M8 highway running between Glasgow and Edinburgh. Hardie's mother was Mary Keir, but the identity of the biological father of Keir Hardie is still disputed. In any case he was born without a "legal" father.[10]

The location was obviously significant. Reid points out that this area was heavily populated with no less than sixty-six coal mines.[11] Irish immigrants had also arrived looking for work in the mines, and the environmental impact on the local geography was severe. Reid writes, "Black smoke by day and the lurid glow of furnaces by night hung over the whole district, giving it a hellish appearance which visitors often commented on."[12] Morgan adds, "By any standards Hardie's early years were scarred by poverty and distress."[13]

In 1859, Mary married David Hardie, a "ship's carpenter" and dockworker, whose last name James Keir Hardie adopted. Hardie's mother worked on occasion as a domestic servant, but the economic situations in southwestern Scotland only worsened in the final quarter of the nineteenth century, and Hardie's father had to face extended periods of unemployment. The frustrations of not finding work weighed heavily on him, and David Hardie drank heavily. Morgan refers to David Hardie's drinking problems and suggests that Hardie's life-long interest in temperance issues and anti-drink movements reasonably stem from his own experiences of a household cursed by frequent drunkenness.[14] Indeed, many of the

---

10. McLean, *Hardie*, actually begins his biography with this issue, 1–2.
11. Reid, *Keir Hardie: The Making of a Socialist*, 13.
12. Reid, *Keir Hardie: The Making of a Socialist*, 13.
13. Morgan, *Keir Hardie: Radical and Socialist*, 5.
14. Morgan, *Keir Hardie: Radical and Socialist*, 4.

biographies agree that the temperance movements that Hardie was involved with early in his life may have also had a role in helping to maintain Hardie's religious interests over his parent's "agnosticism."[15] On the other hand, overly psychological attempts to suggest that Hardie's "illegitimacy" also played a significant element in Hardie's own thinking seem strained, and not only because most biographers fail to convince *how* this impacted him,[16] but this is surely not to be overlooked as yet another element of the poverty-stricken circumstances of the Scottish industrial workers in the nineteenth century, and hardly unique to Hardie's own life.

The economic pressures on the family were serious enough that Hardie began working in 1865 just a few months short of nine years old,[17] taking a number of odd jobs working for a printing office, brass-finishing shop, and as a "rivet heater" in a boatyard.[18] Nevertheless, despite the need for Keir to contribute to family finances, his mother also encouraged reading, since formal schooling was virtually impossible for young Hardie. Morgan notes the dedication with which he approached reading at an early age, with a particular emphasis on reading Burns and Scottish folklore, and many of the biographies speak of young Hardie practicing writing on the sides of mine walls, drawing with his fingers in the coal dust and reading cast-off news sheets.[19]

He continued to work odd jobs to help with the family economy, but the biographies virtually all focus on an episode that Hardie himself recounts from 1866, when he had been working as a messenger boy for a local Glasgow baker at ten years of age (already passing into "Hardie lore" soon after his death).[20] Given how often it is referred to, we repeat the story here in full. The family moved in 1866 to Glasgow so that Hardie's father could find work with Napier's Shipbuilding Yard on the Clyde, but a lock-out prevented David Hardie from significant employment. Young Keir had been working 12.5-hour days for the baker in Glasgow, and during a period of time that coincided with the last week of one of his mother's pregnancies with a future brother, Hardie describes the events that left an indelible mark on his memory. Hardie recalls that his father had been away for three days looking for work, and at the time he had another younger brother with a fever, and his mother was also doing poorly with the pregnancy. Having been up for most of the night, he arrived at work fifteen minutes late the next morning. He was warned by another employee that he would be in trouble if this happened again. However, the very next day, in pouring rain, he arrived soaked

---

15. Morgan, *Keir Hardie: Radical and Socialist*, 4.

16. Reid, *Keir Hardie: The Making of a Socialist*, 40, but esp. 185–92; cf. Benn, *Hardie*, 4–5.

17. Conner, *Jas. Keir Hardie's Life Story*, 3.

18. Morgan, *Keir Hardie: Radical and Socialist*, 5, although Lowe suggests that Hardie was running errands at six years old; Lowe, *From Pit to Parliament*, 10.

19. Reid, *Keir Hardie: The Making of a Socialist*, 18; Morgan, *Keir Hardie: Radical and Socialist*, 7; Lowe, *From Pit to Parliament*, 11.

20. Conner, *Jas. Keir Hardie's Life Story*, 3–4.

and was again fifteen minutes late, without having had breakfast at home. Hardie recalled it was payday, and he was hopeful of bringing something home. Here is Hardie's own description of what occurred:

> 'You are wanted upstairs by the master,' said the girl behind the counter, and my heart almost stopped beating. Outside the dining room a servant bade me wait till 'master had finished prayers' (he was most noted for his piety). At length the girl opened the door, and the sight of that room is fresh in my memory even as I write, nearly fifty years after. Round a great mahogany table sat the members of the family, with the father at the top. In front of him a very wonderful looking coffee boiler, in the great glass bowl of which the coffee was bubbling. The table was loaded with dainties. My master looked at me over his glasses, and said, in a quite pleasant tone of voice – 'Boy, this is the second morning you have been late, and my customers leave me if they are kept waiting for their hot breakfast rolls. I therefore dismiss you, and to make you more careful in the future, I have decided to fine you a week's wages. And now you may go!'

> … I knew my mother was waiting for my wages. As the afternoon was drawing to a close I ventured home, and told her what had happened. It seemed to be the last blow … That night the baby was born, and the sun rose soon on the first of January, 1867 over a home in which there was neither fire nor food … the memory of these early days abides with me, and makes me doubt the sincerity of those who make pretense in their prayers. For such things still abound in our midst.[21]

Holman, characteristically, makes a strong connection between Hardie's own Christian faith and the intensity of his recollections of this early experience, writing that: "The incident planted in Hardie a venomous scorn of hypocritical wealthy Christians."[22] Similarly, Shapiro agrees that Hardie looked on that master-baker as typical of the many who preached Christianity but failed to practice it, and Shapiro believes that this may have contributed to Hardie's decision to join one of the smaller churches where he found more "sincerity."[23]

In the same year, 1866, Hardie first went to work in the mines (Monkland Iron Company) as a "trapper"—a position for younger people that involved opening and closing a door during a ten-hour shift in order to maintain the air supply for miners in a given section. He worked from 6.00 a.m.–5.30 p.m., six days a week, and four hours on Sunday. The walk to work and home was three miles each way.

---

21. Lowe, *From Pit to Parliament*, 11–12; Shapiro, *Keir Hardie and the Labour Party*, 4–5; Morgan, *Keir Hardie: Radical and Socialist*, 5; Stewart, *Keir Hardie: A Biography*, 5; Reid, *Keir Hardie: The Making of a Socialist*, 15; Hughes, *Keir Hardie: A Pictorial Biography*, 16–17; McLean, *Hardie*, 2–3.

22. Holman, *Keir Hardie: Labour's Greatest Hero?*, 18.

23. Shapiro, *Keir Hardie and the Labour Party*, 5.

Hardie also began to attend night school in Holytown at this time, but this formal schooling was short-lived. He later went to work as a pony driver at the mines, working his way into the pits as a "hewer," which is, as McLean describes: "as near as it was possible to get to a skilled and 'respectable' position in the Scottish pits of the period."[24] In the December 23, 1882 edition of Hardie's early column in the *Ardrossan and Saltcoats Herald*, he began a special Christmas "ghost story" with a description clearly drawn from his own life as a "trapper":

> In the month of December 18XX [Hardie did not reveal the year] I, a boy of ten years of age, was engaged to keep a trap-door in a pit in Lanarkshire, belonging to the Monkland Iron Company – my wage being 1s a day. The door was situated about the middle of a rather "stay brae" [steep road] where the hutches [load of coal] were all double snibbled [fastened with two sets of brakes or ropes]. Here also were the stables for the horses, of which there were six, and which it was part of my duties to clean out each day, a job that pleased me well, as it helped to relieve the monotony of my job. That this monotony was not a joke may be gathered from the fact that only eight "rake" [loads of coal] passed through the door each day, and that only when all the men were at work, some days there not being more than three or four. The main air course, strange to say, passed at the back of the stables from an old shaft which aired the pit I was in: hence the necessity for the door to prevent the air ... from rushing out and up the shaft, instead of going into the working places ...
>
> ... A water trough stood at the end of the stables, and was kept full by means of a pipe laid ... which ran along the air course before mentioned ... Let my reader try to imagine my position in this place day after day, sitting all alone, only seeing a human face as the driver passed and re-passed with his rake [carriage load]; no sound except the trickling of the water into the trough before mentioned, or the tick ticking sound occasioned by continuous droppings from the roof, or the occasional scamper of a mouse frightened in the midst of a meal which it would be making with the corn in the horses stables. I tried to beguile the time with reading, of which I was very fond; still the position was anything but a cheery one, especially to a boy of ten years of age with a firm belief in ghosts.

Major accident

At age twelve Hardie was involved in a cave-in that cut off the normal entryway, and a lift normally used to bring up workers was wedged into its shaft. After breaking the wedged lift into pieces and allowing the pieces to fall through the shaft, the mine workers above ground managed to get a smaller improvised container that could still descend through the shaft, and the men were brought up a few at a time. Still deep

---

24. McLean, *Hardie*, 3.

in the mine, however, young Hardie himself had fallen asleep near his pony, and two workers had to return down the shaft to find the sleeping boy near his horse.[25]

Hardie also worked in above-ground quarries, and by the time he was twenty, he had become what many of the biographers refer to as a "skilled practical miner." By 1871, the family moved back to their home area, and Keir's father and Keir's two brothers along with him, were all again hired for mine work. Reid proposes that wages rose in this period, and the family realized some relief from previous stresses.[26] It was during this time, also, that Mary opened a small food shop to compete with the monopolies of the mine-owned shops. Keir's father, David, was then threatened by his employers over the shop, but rather than force his wife to close the shop, he quit. Mary carried on her work and the small shop was said to be relatively successful.

The brief raise in prices noted by Reid, however, did not last long. The years 1873–1887 saw a severe depression in the price of coal, and it was accompanied by early attempts to organize labour in Scotland in the 1870s. It was after he was blacklisted that Hardie became an organizing "secretary" for the fledgling local mine worker unions. When the cautious approach to reform from older labour organizers like Alexander MacDonald were rejected in the Hamilton district of the Lanarkshire Miner's Union—largely because of the workers' dissatisfaction with the deals MacDonald was trying to negotiate with factory and mine owners—it was young Hardie, among the younger workers, who was encouraged to move into some levels of leadership in 1878. Hardie's Hamilton branch voted to strike, against MacDonald's advice. Hardie was already showing a stubborn independence, and he also disagreed with MacDonald's cautious approach. Hardie supported the local workers in their desire for a strike in August and September of 1879. It was known as the "tattie strike," because of the dependence of many union families on potatoes given by sympathetic local grocers that sustained them in difficult economic times.[27] Reid and Hughes, in fact, state that it was among Hardie's duties to organize the supply of potatoes for workers.[28] At this stage, however, the mine owners were too powerful, and the strike action failed miserably.

A further result, however, was that Hardie was not only blacklisted by the local mine owners but gained a reputation for his organizing. Hughes tells the story of Hardie and his two brothers heading down a pit when the cage stopped and headed back to surface. When it reached the surface again, the manager was there to meet them, stating: "We'll hae nae [have no] damned Hardies in this pit,"[29] and the Hardies were all sent off. The family, living in mine company-owned housing, had to also move.

---

25. Lowe, *From Pit to Parliament*, 13–14; Morgan, *Keir Hardie: Radical and Socialist*, 6.
26. Reid, *Keir Hardie: The Making of a Socialist*, 21.
27. Morgan, *Keir Hardie: Radical and Socialist*, 10.
28. Reid, *Keir Hardie: The Making of a Socialist*, 50–1; Hughes, *Keir Hardie: A Pictorial Biography*, 26–7.
29. Hughes, *Keir Hardie: A Pictorial Biography*, 26.

At this stage, Hardie was able to accept the invitation to become a secretary for the Ayrshire Miners (who were "more than willing to have him as their paid organizer"[30]) and moved to Cumnock to be closer to the workers he was representing. Hughes explains that this was a different region from Lanarkshire, since Ayrshire miners lived in smaller and isolated villages, and it was Hardie's job to try and build up union membership until they were in a position to demand higher wages.[31] Hughes further recounts, no doubt based on Hardie's own recollections, that there were times when miners were threatened for even offering Hardie meals or accommodations in his travels between villages.[32] Reid points out that Cumnock was a town far less controlled by local industry because of a wider variety of businesses and the significance of Cumnock as a market town,[33] but McLean adds the significant detail that Cumnock also afforded the advantages of living in housing not owned by local industrialists—removing the threat of losing housing at the whim of the owners.[34]

At this tumultuous time, Hardie was also married in 1879 (age twenty-three) to Lily Wilson, a young woman whom many of the biographers believe was unsuited for Hardie's political career. Benn, for example, proposes that Lily may have expected Hardie to be a more "respectable" Liberal leader like MacDonald,[35] but nonetheless honors Lily for working hard at keeping the family together on the modest support that Hardie managed to earn.[36] Hughes, perhaps understandably as a family member, staunchly defends Lily as a woman Hardie was "lucky to have," who faced the task of raising a family on what little Hardie could send to her long after he left the area, as she was still living in Old Cumnock. Thus, Lily often lived apart from Hardie during his busiest campaigning years, and Reid outlines how Lily was often not entirely sympathetic to her husband's growing involvement in Union activities.[37]

In 1881, Hardie was involved in another major strike. Hardie again organized soup kitchens, and the strike lasted ten weeks before the workers were forced by hunger to return to work. However, the company did determine that they should offer the workers a raise—no doubt surprised at the successful strike that they believed would not last longer than one week,[38] and the owners actually raised wages after the strike had ostensibly failed.

---

30. Benn, *Hardie*, 25.
31. Hughes, *Keir Hardie: A Pictorial Biography*, 27.
32. Hughes, *Keir Hardie: A Pictorial Biography*, 27–30.
33. Reid, *Keir Hardie: The Making of a Socialist*, 55.
34. McLean, *Hardie*, 10.
35. Benn, *Hardie*, 22.
36. Benn, *Hardie*, 79; Lily is particularly honored in Stewart's early work, *Keir Hardie: A Biography*, 14–15.
   37. Reid, *Keir Hardie: The Making of a Socialist*, 54–6.
   38. Hughes, *Keir Hardie: A Pictorial Biography*, 28.

Hardie, however, often faced economic challenges in feeding his family—the union work was not sufficient to support him. Notably, it was Hardie's church involvements that would rescue the family finances. Hardie had joined the local Congregational Church in Cumnock, and the minister had been a writer for the Cumnock district edition of the *Ardrossan and Saltcoats Herald*, a traditionally Liberal-perspective paper. When the minister could no longer continue with his writing, Hardie assumed the position which was his first work as a regular journalist. The announcement of a new regular column by an authentic "miner" was printed in the April 15, 1882 edition. It became a regular feature under the heading "Black Diamonds: Mining Notes Worth Minding," and Hardie wrote under the pen-name "Trapper." Only after Hardie quit his regular responsibilities with the *Herald* (December 30, 1887) was it routinely written in the pages that "Trapper" was in fact Keir Hardie. Beginning with the *Herald* column, Hardie would never again be without a printed voice, and it became one of his main concerns in his life. Morgan writes: "His major lifeline ... proved to be journalism. Entirely self-taught, he had made himself more than a competent writer. Earnestness and passion compensated for any lack of polish."[39]

Although clearly sympathetic to workers' suffering, and mindful of his own economic difficulties, Morgan states that Hardie was not especially drawn to socialism in the first thirty years of his life.[40] He was still supporting the "left wing" of the Liberal party in his published columns in the mid-1880s.

It was during this time, however, that Hardie also became involved not only in the Congregational Church, where he engaged in lay preaching and leadership, but also the "Good Templar's Lodge," a temperance organization. Reid summarizes a number of biographers who believe that Hardie was not the radical he would later become in these years living in Cumnock: " ... this rebellious and discontented young miner's leader fell into an uneasy compromise with middle-class radicalism and evangelicalism ... a young married man with a growing family, he shrank from the life of a miner's agitator."[41] However, church life wasn't so quiet, either.

In 1884, there was controversy in the local church where he was active. Hardie sided with a young minister, Andrew Scott, when he refused to discipline a lay member who had a drinking problem, especially with the kind of heavy-handed discipline that some prominent members of the church had demanded. So frustrated with the behavior of the wealthier and more powerful lay leaders of the church, Hardie withdrew from church involvement, noting in his diary "Principles to be thrown aside to suit Mammon. This may be Christianity but I will have none of it."[42] Before leaving, however, the biographers note that Hardie delivered a sermon which (not insignificantly) drew on the Epistle of James, ch. 2, a New Testament book that is famously fiery in its denunciation of bigotry and preferential treatment given to the wealthy in the early Christian gatherings:

39. Morgan, *Keir Hardie: Radical and Socialist*, 12.
40. Morgan, *Keir Hardie: Radical and Socialist*, 14.
41. Reid, *Keir Hardie: The Making of a Socialist*, 68.
42. Cited in Reid, *Keir Hardie: The Making of a Socialist*, 75.

James 2:1–10 – My brothers and sisters, do you with your acts of favoritism really believe in our glorious Lord Jesus Christ? 2 For if a person with gold rings and in fine clothes comes into your assembly, and if a poor person in dirty clothes also comes in, 3 and if you take notice of the one wearing the fine clothes and say, "Have a seat here, please," while to the one who is poor you say, "Stand there," or, "Sit at my feet," 4 have you not made distinctions among yourselves, and become judges with evil thoughts? 5 Listen, my beloved brothers and sisters. Has not God chosen the poor in the world to be rich in faith and to be heirs of the kingdom that he has promised to those who love him? 6 But you have dishonored the poor. Is it not the rich who oppress you? Is it not they who drag you into court? 7 Is it not they who blaspheme the excellent name that was invoked over you? 8 You do well if you really fulfill the royal law according to the scripture, "You shall love your neighbor as yourself." 9 But if you show partiality, you commit sin and are convicted by the law as transgressors. 10 For whoever keeps the whole law but fails in one point has become accountable for all of it.

The Epistle of James, it must be recalled, is a writing which ends with the following warnings (which Hardie would indeed cite in later editorials):

James 5:1–6 – ¹ Come now, you rich people, weep and wail for the miseries that are coming to you. ² Your riches have rotted, and your clothes are moth-eaten. ³ Your gold and silver have rusted, and their rust will be evidence against you, and it will eat your flesh like fire. You have laid up treasure for the last days. ⁴ Listen! The wages of the laborers who mowed your fields, which you kept back by fraud, cry out, and the cries of the harvesters have reached the ears of the Lord of hosts. ⁵ You have lived on the earth in luxury and in pleasure; you have fattened your hearts in a day of slaughter. ⁶ You have condemned and murdered the righteous one, who does not resist you …

Although Benn characteristically exaggerates the significance of Hardie's leaving the Congregational Church by claiming it was "an important step in his conversion to socialism,"[43] we will see that Hardie's Christian commitments remained throughout his life and reading a passage like James ch. 2 would suggest that this makes clear sense. Yet it was also certainly true that Hardie's condemnation of "Churchianity" would be frequent in his writing, but crucially—it was a criticism from "within" a commitment to what Hardie saw as a truly *Biblical* Christian faith.

During this same period, Hardie seemed to believe that workers' rights would be strengthened by a Liberal Party victory, but he became frustrated with the lack of any progress of political reforms that he believed would be a natural compensation of workers' support for the Liberal Party. In his work for Ayrshire miners, Hardie agitated for issues like free primary education, and reforms of colliery inspection

---

43. Benn, *Hardie*, 35.

to further prevent the frequent, and deadly, accidents. McLean comments that: " … earlier radicals would have called these matters none of the state's business: a comforting doctrine for industrialists, less so for working men."[44] Hardie also showed interests in issues beyond the confines of Scotland itself (as his column in the *Herald* also proves). A particularly strong issue at the time was serious consideration of Home Rule for Ireland, and Hardie supported it, also thinking that home rule in Ireland might strengthen the Irish economy such that it might actually slow the number of Irish workers coming to Scotland and often providing strike-breaking "black leg" (or more common now, the slang term "scab") labour.

In 1886, the Liberal Party lost considerable support and a Conservative government came to power with the support of those Liberals who were opposed to Irish Home Rule. Hardie, it seems, was now seriously questioning whether he could trust even the left-wing of the Liberal party. Among his written attacks, notes McLean, are the earliest of Hardie's exposé articles on industrial conditions for workers—often revealing hypocritically awful conditions in industries supported by Liberal Party officials.[45] Hardie was becoming convinced: workers needed their own representation. Reid believes that Hardie had many supporters in this anger toward the Liberal Party: "Hardie was caught up in a socialist agitation among the Ayrshire and Lanarkshire miners which helped to change his political consciousness."[46]

Although still not yet an avowed "socialist," Reid summarizes Hardie's ideas as generally similar to "Cooperative utopianism."[47] This is generally thought to be a set of ideas that were hopeful of finding a means of cooperation between sympathetic persons of various class backgrounds. It is certainly true that Hardie was often engaged in calling for cooperation among political ideologies, but Hardie was also at this time beginning to move toward a serious questioning of private ownership of means of production as inevitably corrupting and untrustworthy, and also toward the idea that workers must be represented by their own political party voice—a "Labour" party.

In the crisis years of 1886–1887, industrial owners, in response to a strike, again brought in black leg labour to try to break the strike. When strikers tried to prevent them from entering the workplaces, the owners called in militia forces from Glasgow. Inevitably, violence broke out—and Hardie began to see the owners' actions as a threat to any right of workers to organize at all. During this same turbulent time, however, Hardie was also meeting important socialist thinkers in London circles at the time, including Tom Mann and Friedrich Engels. Finally, Hardie launched his own newspaper, *The Miner*, in 1887, although he continued to write for the *Ardrossan and Saltcoats Herald* until 1887, and thereafter only occasionally until 1890. It is significant to get a "reading" on Hardie's attitudes at

---

44. McLean, *Hardie*, 13.
45. McLean, *Hardie*, 19.
46. Reid, *Keir Hardie: The Making of a Socialist*, 79.
47. Reid, *Keir Hardie: The Making of a Socialist*, 86.

this time, and his 1887 announcement that he will end his regular column in the *Herald* is worth quoting at length:

> Five years have now come and gone since I first made the acquaintance of your readers ... The evils which I have sought to attack were not to be put down by smooth words and silken phrases. That I have given offence betimes, 'twere useless to deny; but no man can espouse the cause of the poor without giving offence to some, and it is not always possible to keep within the bounds of moderation when seeing evils done and suffered enough to make an angel weep and Satan blush for shame ... Now, however, the time has come when, as far as these notes are concerned, I must say farewell. Not that all the evils of the miner have disappeared, or that I have grown weary in well-doing; but other duties have come to monopolize my time, and other fields of usefulness are opening out before me ...
>
> I have without wavering, sought to be a friend of the poor, the needy, and they who have no helper, and I have no higher ambition than to continue such. Whether in teaching the truths of Christianity, in enforcing by precept and example the beauties of temperance, in trying to lead men in the paths of wisdom toward organization, or in writing "Black Diamonds" my aim has ever been the same—the overthrow of evil, and the upbuilding of Good. It cannot be charged against me that I have been actuated by sordid motives, since my temperance and evangelistic work have always been given without thought of, or for, reward.[48]

Thus, Reid is surely correct to emphasize a significant change in Hardie's thinking during the violent industrial actions of 1887, despite the doubts of a biographer like Morgan who nonetheless agrees that there were some important changes in Hardie's worldview. Morgan argues that these events hardly created the conditions for Hardie to have a "Damascus road" conversion to radical socialism, declaring that Hardie was still a "left-wing Liberal."[49] Interestingly, Morgan wants to insist that it was Hardie's religious experiences of 1878, rather than his political "conversions" of 1887, that remained "the dominant experience of his life to that time."[50] Reid, on the other hand, argues that:

> This volte-face is so sudden and dramatic that it seems to justify the term "conversion." The strike of 1887 forced Hardie to drop the mental habit of deference towards the susceptibilities of middle-class allies ... His pent-up resentment at the lowly position allotted to him and his class boiled over in 1887 into a fierce, righteous anger against the Mammon-worshippers who blocked

48. *Herald*, December 30, 1887.
49. Morgan, *Keir Hardie: Radical and Socialist*, 15.
50. Morgan, *Keir Hardie: Radical and Socialist*, 22.

the path of Progress. Henceforth he would be the heroic leader of his class heading its crusade for a new moral world in which the ethic of cooperation would replace the ethic of competition.[51]

The period of time between 1887 and 1892 is a time, states Reid, when we have little information from Hardie himself. Further, *The Miner* collapsed already in 1889 after a difficult two-year run, and *The Labour Leader*, one of the main sources for our analysis, would not start regular publication until 1893–1894. What is to be observed at this point, however, is that the biographies exert considerable energy tracing the evolution of Hardie's political "doctrines"—was he "socialist" yet or not?—which may be of interest to political historians, but as we have already clarified, this is not our *primary* interest. Most of the Biblical writings that we will consider from Hardie come from *The Labour Leader*, for example, and thus from the period when his decision to call himself a socialist is clearly certain. Further changes in Hardie's life, however, are even more significant—namely his entry into Government.

Hardie the parliamentarian

Hughes suggests that Hardie's serious interest in Parliament began in Scotland with his friendship with a man; a more colorful character can hardly be imagined. Robert Bontine Cunninghame-Graham was half-Scot and half-Spanish and descended from Scottish aristocracy[52] and a man who had spent time on the South American pampas and American Western plains. Cunninghame-Graham's social conscience led him to be a "natural rebel ... and reliable ally in the Parliamentary fight for the miners' Eight Hour Day,"[53] and indeed the "first socialist to be elected to Parliament."[54] Finally, it was Cunninghame-Graham who also introduced Hardie to the world of Parliamentary debate. Hardie attended Cunninghame-Graham's maiden speech as a (brief) Member of Parliament. Parliamentary "maiden speeches" were traditionally intended to be non-controversial. Cunninghame-Graham, however, threw tradition to the wind with his attacks on privilege and wealth among Parliamentarians, and Hughes humorously notes that Cunninghame-Graham recalled—in this same speech—the story of Carlyle hosting Ralph Emerson for a visit to Parliament, and after a half-hour of watching deliberations from the gallery, leaned toward his American guest and asked, "Do you believe in the Devil, *now*?"[55]

---

51. Reid, *Keir Hardie: The Making of a Socialist*, 98.

52. Benn claims he was known by some as "the uncrowned King of Scotland" owing to his privileged descent, Benn, *Hardie*, 45.

53. Hughes, *Keir Hardie: A Pictorial Biography*, 33.

54. Benn, *Hardie*, 46.

55. Hughes, *Keir Hardie: A Pictorial Biography*, 33. This, of course, is why we read multiple biographies so as not to miss gems like this one.

From Cunninghame-Graham's strong and friendly encouragement, Hardie determined that political involvement would be part of his efforts for change in Britain. Hardie first ran for Parliament as a "labourer's candidate" in April 1888 at the Mid-Lanarkshire (Scotland) by-election, but lost by a significant margin. He was, suggests Morgan: "truculent and unconciliatory, all too prone to indulge in unprofitable and gratuitous attacks on the clergy or the royal family."[56] Yet, Morgan assesses that even though he lost badly, he "gained new stature as the symbol of working-class revolt."[57] Hughes speaks of the fact that both Cunninghame-Graham and Hardie become well-known speakers in the area despite the election's loss.

As an indication of Hardie's commitment to working for change in government, Hardie was also involved in the formation of a "Scottish Labour Party" in 1888, which assembled a coalition of sympathetic groups, including the crusading Scottish journalist John Murdoch, whose fiery (and deeply Biblical) writings in his newspaper *The Highlander* could not fail to have impressed Hardie,[58] even though Hardie does not discuss Murdoch directly (Hughes, for example, does not even mention his presence, while others state that Murdoch *chaired* the meetings). Stewart, writing within six years of Hardie's death, believed that this contact with Murdoch in the same year as his first Parliamentary campaign was significant:

> On May 19th (1888) twenty-seven men met in Glasgow. Mr. John Murdoch, a man well known in connection with the Highland Crofters' agitation, sturdy in frame as in opinions, presided, and Hardie explained the object for which the meeting had been called, viz., the formation of a bona fide Labour Party for Scotland. A Committee was formed to arrange for a conference to be held without delay to form such a Party.[59]

Reid also confirms the significance of the "Christian" element of this Scottish Labour Party:

---

56. Morgan, *Keir Hardie: Radical and Socialist*, 29.
57. Morgan, *Keir Hardie: Radical and Socialist*, 31.
58. Reading the editorials of Murdoch in his crusading newspaper, *The Highlander*, will stir any soul. This indefatigable defender of Highlanders' rights, and Scottish Christian radical, must soon have his academic champion to analyze his fiery reading of the Bible. In the meantime, we have James Hunter, ed., *For the People's Cause: From the Writings of John Murdoch, Highland and Irish Land Reformer (1818–1903)* (Edinburgh: Crofters Commission, 1986), whose interests were more general. Many editions of *The Highlander* (which pre-date Hardie's journalism) are available for careful perusal at the Mitchell Library in Glasgow but be prepared for outrageous photocopying charges and a ban on making your own photographic records.
59. Stewart, *Keir Hardie: A Biography*, 43.

Hardie had compensated for his quarrels with Scottish trade union leaders by attracting a new Christian socialist type of activist to the party. By the end of 1893 they held leading positions and were loyal in the main to Hardie with whose politics they sympathized.[60]

The potential significance of this work with Murdoch becomes more intriguing when reading editorials in *The Highlander*, which regularly featured Murdoch's writings detailing the implications, for example, of the Levitical "Jubilee Year" (Lev. 25) for policy in Scotland, among other Biblically-based editorials.[61]

McLean, also, considered that Hardie's involvement with Scottish political activist groups—including both the Scottish Land and Labour League and the Scottish Home Rule Association: "played a part in advancing the next stage of Hardie's political career."[62] Along these lines, Reid also emphasized, in particular, the involvement of Archie McArthur, an avowed Christian Socialist who would later work on the concept of youth education for socialism in the "Socialist Sunday School" movement that Hardie (with Caroline Martyn, see Chapter 4 below) were also keenly interested in supporting.[63]

However, another emerging interest for Hardie in this period was his growing conviction about the importance of making international connections on workers' issues, and we have already noted his growing contact throughout Britain, as well as beyond, among socialist organizations.[64] Hardie attended the Second Socialist International in Paris in 1889, where Morgan carefully notes that Hardie characteristically attended sessions of both the "Marxists" and the "non-Marxists"—indicating his open mindedness to a variety of perspectives and his interest in building cooperative coalitions in politics. One of the sticking points for Hardie in fully identifying with any of the socialist "camps," however, was the role of violence. Hardie was early and consistently opposed to violence in defense of workers' rights—a pacifism that would characterize his politics throughout his life.[65]

---

60. Reid, *Keir Hardie: The Making of a Socialist*, 138.

61. Murdoch's *Highlander* editorials featured observations such as "British laws of primogeniture intend to keep millions off the land, whilst the Mosaic laws were bars to keep the millions in possession of the land" (*Highlander*, September 13, 1873); "What the Gospel has most to fear is from the character and conduct of those who profess to believe it … " (September 5, 1874); "preach matter-of-fact Gospel to the people as the Apostles did. Let any one read the Acts of the Apostles and compare the discourses of Peter, of Stephan, and of Paul with the 'Gospel Sermons' generally discoursed to perishing men, and he will perceive a difference which should at least account for the absence of hope of the Gospel … Go to people with the Gospel and protest against existing land laws, they will have a brave people to lead into Canaan … " (March 23, 1878).

62. McLean, *Hardie*, 27.

63. Reid, *Keir Hardie: The Making of a Socialist*, 138.

64. Morgan, *Keir Hardie: Radical and Socialist*, 39.

65. Morgan, *Keir Hardie: Radical and Socialist*, 40.

After his initial loss in the Parliamentary election in Scotland, Hardie would go on to serve as a Member of Parliament representing other constituencies for nearly eighteen years, between the years 1892 and 1895, representing the "West Ham South" district of London; and then again during four terms beginning in 1900 until his death in 1915 (coming second behind the Liberal candidates in 1900, 1906, January 1910, and then December 1910 in a "double" constituency that sent the first *two* persons in the results), sharing representation with Liberal party candidates representing Merthyr in South Wales. This constituency was divided into separate one-person constituencies soon after Hardie's death in 1915.

American readers need to be reminded that British political parties can call any candidate to contest a local constituency election for Parliament, even from outside their local "home" area if they so wish, contrary to American Congressional representation that requires at least some semblance of residential connection to the states that they "represent" (however strained, or recent, this connection "of convenience" can sometimes be). Hardie's growing fame as a spokesperson for workers' issues would have led to his "name recognition" outside of Scotland, both in London, but also in Wales.

Hardie first visited the London constituency of "West Ham South" in 1890, an area of growing labour activism with a population characterized, Morgan states, by: "dockers, gasworkers, and Irishmen—all of them influenced by the new unionism."[66] Soon, talk of Hardie entering the election became serious (Cunninghame-Graham was again involved in advocating for Hardie)—and a fortuitous division between two Liberal candidates likely settled the vote in Hardie's favor.

Although Hardie did not have a strong personal connection to London, he quite fortunately met—and made fast friends with—a former "Salvationist" (e.g., former member of the Salvation Army) and Christian socialist by the name of Frank Smith, who had broken with the Salvationists. Benn notes that Smith had been at the head of a "social wing" of the Salvation Army, which "General" Booth worried would become too much of an emphasis within the religious denomination. Frank Smith left rather than give up his interest in political agitation, even trying to start a "Socialist Army" with its own publication called "The Worker's Cry" (in answer to the Salvationist "War Cry"[67]). It is important to also recall that Smith had assisted "General" William Booth in writing the famous Salvationist critical manifesto, *In Darkest England and the Way Back* (1890) which detailed some of the worst sufferings of urban Britain, and especially London, at the end of the nineteenth century.[68] Modern readers may fail to fully grasp the full impact of Booth's title without being reminded that a wildly popular account by Henry Stanley about his last adventure in Africa looking for the famous missionary, Dr. Livingston, was

---

66. Morgan, *Keir Hardie: Radical and Socialist*, 44.
67. Benn, *Hardie*, 96.
68. Lowe, *From Pit to Parliament*, 65–6.

entitled, *In Darkest Africa*, and was also published in 1890. Therefore, Booth's book was a sardonic comment against arrogantly pointing beyond England's shores for examples of suffering and social "darkness."

Smith's London-based activism, therefore, created many local contacts and he campaigned vigorously for his new friend and political ally, Keir Hardie. It is also notable, states both Lowe and later Benn, that Hardie often had positive things to say about Salvationist work. Indeed, Hardie was always hopeful that Booth, and many other Salvationists, would embrace socialism as a logical step forward from his otherwise laudable concerns for the poor in England, and especially the destitute of the cities. Such a step was, of course, one that Smith himself clearly and frequently encouraged.[69] In London, Hardie was competing against the Conservative Party candidate, and Hardie won: 5,268 votes to 4,036. In an interesting note, McLean mentions that one of his opponents tried to smear Hardie as an "atheist," and Hardie was easily able to solicit testimonials from "elderly Scottish ministers who had known him in his youth" to testify otherwise.[70]

Upon taking his seat in Parliament on August 3, 1892, Hardie famously refused to wear the "parliamentary uniform" of black frock coat, black silk top hat, and starched wing collar that even other working-class MPs wore for the occasion. Instead, Hardie wore a plain tweed suit, a red tie, and a deerstalker. Although the deerstalker hat was the correct and matching apparel for his suit, he was nevertheless lambasted in the press, and was accused of wearing a flat cap, headgear associated with the common working man, e.g., a "cloth cap in Parliament." Morgan adds that a brass horn player played the "Marseillaise" as he rode a carriage toward Parliament. The "Member for the Unemployed" had arrived, as illustrated in one of the most famous political cartoons from the time (see Figure 2.2).

As a Parliamentarian, Hardie advocated an eight-hour workday, Irish Home Rule, a graduated income tax, free schooling, pensions, the abolition of the House of Lords, and supported women's right to vote, but also nationalization of land, banks, mines, railways, docks, waterways, and tramways. McLean believes that Hardie was not yet calling himself a socialist even in 1889, but Reid writes that Hardie's manifesto of 1890 "suggests that Hardie had been taking socialism even more seriously since coming to London."[71] Surely McLean is right, however, when suspecting that Hardie would hardly have made socialism a major public issue in West Ham, given the large Irish population in his constituency, and the Catholic hierarchy's hostility to socialism: "Only once in his first spell as an M.P. did Hardie claim in Parliament that socialism was the only solution to the unemployment problem."[72]

McLean states that the years 1888–1892 are "marked by Hardie's final abandonment of the Liberal Party."[73] In 1893, Hardie and others formally initiated

69. Benn, *Hardie*, 95–7, 181; Lowe, *From Pit to Parliament*, 65–7.
70. McLean, *Hardie*, 37.
71. McLean, *Hardie*, 42; Reid, *Keir Hardie: The Making of a Socialist*, 131.
72. McLean, *Hardie*, 43, 46.
73. McLean, *Hardie*, 41.

He carried the plight of the unemployed to the House of Commons. Cartoon by 'Jordie' from 'The Labour Leader', 1894.

Figure 2.2 Famous image of Hardie the new MP, "carrying" the unemployed.

the "Independent Labour Party" (ILP), an action that clearly worried the Liberal Party members, who were afraid that this new organization might well, at some point in the future, win the working-class votes that they traditionally received. That was, of course, precisely the hope. Hardie spent the next five years of his life building up this Parliamentary Labour movement and speaking at various public meetings; he was arrested at a women's suffrage meeting in London, but the Home Secretary, concerned about arresting the leader of the ILP, ordered his release. At its inauguration, the ILP advocated:

> Abolition of child labour under 14 years of age; a legal eight-hour maximum working day; State provision for aged, sick and disabled workers, and for widows

and orphans; abolition of indirect taxation, and taxation to extinction of all unearned incomes; work for the unemployed; every proposal for extending political rights and democratizing the system of government.[74]

The other major involvement by Hardie in activism besides his speaking, and his role as a Member of Parliament, was his journalism. As noted, Hardie had launched his newspaper, *The Labour Leader*, in 1889 as a successor to *The Miner* which he published in Ayrshire, but it was not on economically stable ground until 1893–1894. *The Labour Leader*, it has been said, was characterized by an editorial line that featured Hardie's "familiar evangelical style; the first issue was headed with a poem by Tennyson on the theme of 'the Christ that is to be.'"[75] Morgan proposes that *The Labour Leader* "lacked the earthy humanism and the good humor of Robert Blatchford's *Clarion*. It was far more earnest, without being dogmatic. Hardie himself supplied most of the copy …,"[76] even declaring that Hardie himself was "Lily Bell" writing in the women's section as well.[77]

Notably, however, when Morgan states that Hardie the journalist: " … was an evangelist proclaiming a secular religion,"[78] it is an odd comment given the fact that *actual* religion was much more than an occasional topic of debate and discussion in the pages of *The Labour Leader* (or this book could not have been written!). The circulation was reputed to be as high as 50,000 in 1894,[79] and not surprisingly, it will be *The Labour Leader* that will provide most of our examples of Hardie's Biblical exegesis in Chapter 5.

Hardie "the Parliamentarian" is often criticized by the biographers with regard to his first term as an MP for a "lack of diplomacy." This is often illustrated by his reaction to the government's lack of response to a mine disaster in Wales at Albion Colliery, at Cilfynydd in South Wales, where over 250 men and boys were killed. The main news of the days during and after this disaster, however, were far more concerned with covering the assassination of President Carnot in France, and especially the birth of the son to the Duke of York, the child who would become Edward VIII. Hardie was furious with the media coverage that preferred the child over the disaster, and bitterly condemned Britain even having a monarchy. Benn writes that Hardie's complaints about attention to issues and events like the Queen's death, the birth of a prince, instead of death at mining disasters: " … was rather straight Old Testament rage against kings …."[80] Other biographers have also

---

74. Hughes, *Keir Hardie: A Pictorial Biography*, 66.
75. Morgan, *Keir Hardie: Radical and Socialist*, 42.
76. Morgan, *Keir Hardie: Radical and Socialist*, 66, echoed by McLean, *Hardie*, 106.
77. For a further appreciation of Hardie's feminist writing, including as "Lily Bell," see Hamish W. Fraser, "Keir Hardie: Radical, Socialist, Feminist," *Études écossaises* 10 (2005): 103–15.
78. Morgan, *Keir Hardie: Radical and Socialist*, 67.
79. Morgan, *Keir Hardie: Radical and Socialist*, 67.
80. Benn, *Hardie*, 123.

taken up this discussion, and Stewart writes, in his earlier biography of Hardie, of these important events:

> On June 23rd a terrible explosion occurred at the Albion Colliery, Cilfynydd, South Wales, by which two hundred and sixty men and boys lost their lives. On the same day a child was born to the Duchess of York. On the following day, June 24th, M. Carnot, the President of the French Republic, was assassinated. On June 26th, 70,000 Scottish miners came out on strike against a reduction of wages. Now turn to the House of Commons. On June 25th, William Harcourt moved a vote of condolence with French people. On June 28th, the same Cabinet Minister moved an address of congratulation to the Queen on the birth of the aforesaid royal infant. Never a word of sympathy for the relatives of the miners who had been killed: never a word of reference to the serious state of affairs in the Scottish coalfield. Only one man protested. That man was Keir Hardie.[81]

Hardie's insistence that a financial payment to the royal family be instead diverted to the suffering families of the miners invoked an enraged response. McLean, however, calls Hardie's protests on this occasion "memorable and courageous."[82] Despite his efforts on behalf of the unemployed, and his good work on "The Select Committee on Unemployment," his doctrinal "impurities" (from a Marxist perspective) led many of his contemporaries on the left, including Engels, to be pleased with Hardie's defeat in 1895.[83] Yet it was not Hardie's Parliamentary successes that made him famous, but his speeches and activism. By 1895, Hardie had become a well-known national figure. Speaking of this period of Hardie's life, including the years out of Parliament (1895–1900), McLean writes:

> Hardie's life during these years was an unending round of speeches, railway journeys, trips to London for Parliament and the Labour Leader, and infrequent journeys to Cumnock to see his family ... Hardie was a missionary, a revivalist, and not an economist or any sort of precise or analytical speaker ...[84]

Even during dark times for the prospects of a serious labour representation in Parliament, much less a time for legislative victories, Hardie was determined to "stay the course," and McLean notes particularly that during these years between Parliamentary terms, Hardie was unusual in his determination to keep hand to plow in the advancing of political and labourers' concerns.[85]

In 1900, just before his second successful run for Parliament, this time representing Merthyr in South Wales, Hardie organized a meeting of various

81. Stewart, *Keir Hardie: A Biography*, 88.
82. McLean, *Hardie*, 47.
83. Morgan, *Keir Hardie: Radical and Socialist*, 81.
84. McLean, *Hardie*, 56.
85. McLean, *Hardie*, 66–7.

trade unions and socialist groups with Parliamentary representatives and they agreed to form a "Labour Representation Committee" (LRC), which is normally seen as the direct pre-cursor to the Labour Party (as opposed to the more diverse interests behind the earlier "Scottish Labour Party"). Later that same year Hardie, representing Labour, was elected as the junior MP for the dual-member constituency of Merthyr Tydfil and Aberdare in the South Wales Valleys.

In his introduction to a 2015 reissue of Hardie's autobiographical sketches from 1907 entitled "From Serfdom to Socialism," John Callow summarizes Hardie's Parliamentary years in general, observing:

> He was the first man from the midst of the working class who completely understood them, completely sympathized with them, completely championed them. He was the first working man who, having entered Parliament, never deserted them, never turned his back on a single principle which he had professed, never drifted away from his class in thought, in feeling or in faith. When he came there was no Labour representation in our country ... The Working Class had no political mind of their own. Parliament was no more theirs than was the workshop or the factory. Their masters ruled in both.[86]

After his defeat in 1895, Hardie decided to go to the United States, with Frank Smith. The initial reason was to give an address at the Labor Congress in Chicago on September 2, but Morgan points out that this was an era of particularly harsh financial crises in the USA, with the Pullman Strike of 1894, and the jailing of Eugene Debs, who was a leading figure in Railway union activism (and eventually the most successful Socialist candidate for President of the United States before Bernie Sanders). This was also the time of the march of Joseph Coxey's "Army" on Washington, DC which tried to pressure the US Government to make good on promises of financial assistance for the unemployed by marching across the entire US toward Washington. Through his visits, and his written observations, Morgan considered Hardie an apt observer of American disunity in the working classes.[87]

Morgan further writes that during these years, 1895–1896, Hardie's *generalized* socialist sympathies caused problems among those who wanted more "doctrinal socialist purity"—and thus there were often conflicts with various Marxist and socialist factions.[88] Benn also writes that Hardie was considered "ideologically unstable" by other socialists.[89] What characterized Hardie, and thus the ILP more generally, however, was what Morgan refers to as "flexible radicalism."[90]

---

86. John Callow, ed., *Keir Hardie, From Serfdom to Socialism* (London: Lawrence & Wishart, 2015), 41.
87. Morgan, *Keir Hardie: Radical and Socialist*, 87.
88. Morgan, *Keir Hardie: Radical and Socialist*, 87–9.
89. Benn, *Hardie*, 134.
90. Morgan, *Keir Hardie: Radical and Socialist*, 88–9.

2. Keir Hardie: A Life and Context

This period is often considered a time when Hardie's various attempts at building support and coalitions meant that it was difficult to identify a clear and consistent "party line." Morgan writes of Hardie's "erratic" attempts to promote a socialist coalition, but also that: "He himself was now almost wholly detached from the trade union world,"[91] and the ILP itself had leaders who were "middle class idealists," like Ramsay MacDonald (a pharmacist), Bruce Glasier (artist and designer), and Philip Snowden (a civil servant). Nevertheless, it is acknowledged that throughout this time, Hardie was giving speeches and encouraging Labour unity and authentic workers' representation in Parliament.

It was during this time outside Parliament that Hardie's newspaper also engaged in Upton Sinclair-like "exposés" of industrial cruelties—the most famous of which was a series of articles attacking the chemical works at Shawfield, Scotland, owned by J. Campbell White, or "Lord Overtoun," a philanthropic Scots Presbyterian, prominent in the Sunday Observance Society. As Morgan observes, Overtoun had worked his men at the Shawfield chemical works at a horrific pace, including a:

> ... seven-day week at a wage of barely threepence an hour and at grave cost to their health ... The Overtoun horrors roused widespread excitement. Hardie's brilliantly effective series of tracts on Overtoun, entitled "White Slaves" stirred up the same passions as did W. T. Stead's more lurid Babylonish exposures, or the "muckraking" journalists in the American magazine press ...[92]

There is little doubt that what particularly infuriated Hardie,[93] was the public persona of Overtoun as a pious Christian man who supported church causes such as "The Sunday Observance Society." The latter involvement was especially galling for Hardie, given that Overtoun himself did not give his own workers a weekend break, and therefore no Sunday break for his workers to attend church. "Ruthless streak" or not, even McLean, however, agreed with the bitter irony pointed out by Hardie in his description of Lord Overtoun presiding over a meeting of the "United Evangelistic Association" under a banner reading, "Come unto Me all ye that labour and are heavy laden, and I will give you rest ...."[94] Because this was both theologically as well as politically significant for Hardie, Hardie marshalled the Bible heavily in his attacks on Overtoun, so these articles will be among Hardie's writings of particular interest for further consideration in Chapter 5. Indeed, Holman's 2010 biography (the volume with the most serious interest, so far, in discussing Hardie's Christian faith), actually begins with a discussion of the Overtoun affair. Overtoun, however, was hardly the lone victim of Hardie's unwanted attention—there were many others, and a similar attack, but with less sustained attention in the newspaper, were those written against Lord Penryn in Wales against the slate workers. Stewart writes of the Overtoun controversies:

---

91. Morgan, *Keir Hardie: Radical and Socialist*, 96.
92. Morgan, *Keir Hardie: Radical and Socialist*, 96.
93. McLean even speaks of Hardie's "ruthless streak," *Hardie*, 74–5.
94. McLean, *Hardie*, 75.

The vindication of the exposure was found in the fact that as the controversy went on the conditions inside Shawfield Works kept improving. Sunday labour was reduced to the absolute minimum necessitated by the nature of the trade, better sanitary arrangements were introduced and wages in some degree increased.[95]

To note other matters with which Hardie was concerned, we note the conflict in South Africa, 1899–1902, known as "The Boer War," which was staunchly denounced by Hardie, and a good indication of what Morgan calls Hardie's "Anti-War credentials." Hardie's vociferous opposition to all violence was particularly evident here, but would be equally visible in his later life, and courageous opposition to World War I, where he tried to encourage workers in Europe to unify together in opposition to their countries engaging in war with each other.

Around 1900, Morgan reports that Hardie was "restless," and although he was replaced as ILP chairman, he wanted to return to Parliament. Eventually, as we previously noted, it was determined that he should represent the constituency in South Wales known as Merthyr Tydfil. It was, Morgan states, a good location for Hardie's particular orientation, as it was an area with an: " … old radical Chartist tradition; it had returned the Welsh pacifist Henry Richard, in the momentous election of 1868. It boasted a vigorous Trades Council …," and Morgan further notes that Hardie had written "compassionate articles about the Welsh workers conditions" in 1898.[96] His campaign was helped by the Quaker industrialist, and famous chocolatier, George Cadbury, who donated 150 pounds toward the campaign. Here again, however, there is also the element of Christian faith—Wales historically being a particularly strong center of independent churches.

In the event, similar to West Ham South in London, the Liberals were divided between rival Liberal candidates at Merthyr—and Hardie was in. Although not terribly familiar with Welsh issues and traditions in the beginning of his representation there, Hardie invested himself seriously in his representative duties.[97] Soon after this, Hardie wrote one of his most famous pamphlets, entitled *Can a Man Be a Christian on a Pound a Week?* (1901), which made "a powerful appeal to the national conscience on behalf of the under-paid and the over-worked."[98] It is also a not insignificant occasion for Hardie to reflect on Biblical passages yet again, and so will be one of the important writings featured in our analysis in Chapter 5.

Stewart honors April 23, 1901 as the date of the "first complete Socialist declaration ever made in the British House of Commons"[99] when Hardie introduced a resolution in favor of common ownership of land and capital in Britain. Still, Morgan writes that 1902–1903 were "difficult days" for Hardie, with his daughter

---

95. Stewart, *Keir Hardie: A Biography*, 140–2.
96. Morgan, *Keir Hardie: Radical and Socialist*, 114–15.
97. Morgan, *Keir Hardie: Radical and Socialist*, 118.
98. Morgan, *Keir Hardie: Radical and Socialist*, 122.
99. Stewart, *Keir Hardie: A Biography*, 180.

ill and the death of his mother and father.[100] Furthermore, in a difficult transition for him, Hardie was asked to step aside as editor of *The Labour Leader* in 1903.[101]

There were changes coming, however, for the better. In 1906, Hardie had won a difficult election to return to Parliament from Merthyr. It was also in 1906–1907 that the name of the political coalition that Hardie participated in developing had changed, officially, to "The Labour Party." But 1906 also saw a significant legislative victory. In 1900, a dispute between railway workers and the owner of the Welsh "Taff Vale Railway" became serious. When the owner brought in black leg labour to break the strike, the union leafleted the incoming workers to get them to join in the industrial action. The owner of the Railway then sought financial compensation for the loss to his business, but the eventual decision in favor of the owner, and against the union, threatened union organizing throughout Britain—opening them up to charges of lost revenue and potentially breaking the financial ability of unions to organize or engage in strikes and pressure tactics in any fashion whatsoever. But during the Liberal government of 1906, the Taff-Vale decision of 1901 was overturned by the Trades Disputes Act. Noting the potentially devastating impact of the precedent established by the Taff-Vale decision (including even the preventing of the printing of leaflets!), McLean comments:

> … It is customary to decry Hardie's abilities as leader of the Parliamentary Labour Party, but it is worth bearing in mind that there was never a legislative success remotely comparable to the Trades Disputes Act under the leadership of any of his successors up to 1915.[102]

Throughout this time, Hardie also maintained his international interests, and Morgan states that Hardie's "Christian beliefs in brotherhood informed his internationalist interests."[103] He left on another world tour in 1907. He made controversial stops in both India (where he supported the more radical nationalist Tilak over the gradualist policies of Gandhi) and South Africa and continued to speak in support of home rule for British colonies abroad; women's rights—especially to vote; anti-militarism; union rights, and even appealed to the Japanese royal family on behalf of jailed Japanese socialists.

There have been some important observations with regard to Hardie's attitudes toward race issues. Certainly, there are offensive illustrations in *The Labour Leader* depicting black Africans—but it must be stated that Hardie made progress on this issue, and McLean quotes Hardie's strong opinions in favor of equal pay and equal citizenship for black South Africans as much as white South African colonists, and McLean is even stronger when he states:

---

100. Morgan, *Keir Hardie: Radical and Socialist*, 124.
101. Morgan, *Keir Hardie: Radical and Socialist*, 140–1.
102. McLean, *Hardie*, 120.
103. Morgan, *Keir Hardie: Radical and Socialist*, 169.

On colonial and Indian affairs Hardie was many years ahead of his time. He was almost the only British politician of his day to protest the treatment of black South Africans. And his views on India were thought so scandalous that they provoked a tremendous uproar – yet only forty years later India was given sovereign independence.[104]

Hardie wrote: "There is room to spare for both races in South Africa, but if the white workman is to retain his footing he must not connive at the exploitation of the coloured man. That way ruin lies."[105] Although advocating for home rule for virtually all British colonies, Hardie never took the position on these issues that is more common in the twenty-first century—namely that such colonies should never have existed in the first place. Still, Stewart also cites Hardie's observations of South Africa to suggest that a labour movement there should never allow natives to be reduced to "a landless proletariat at the mercy of their exploiters for all time."[106]

Holman, especially, points to comments Hardie made in Liverpool, during a Railway Strike in 1910. Looking at the glorious scenery in a local parkway, he said:

> There is joy, beauty, peace, and prosperity everywhere, except in the homes and lives of the common people. Oh men and women, in the name of that God whom you profess to believe in, in the name of Jesus Christ of Nazareth who died to save your souls, how long do you intend to submit to a system which is defacing God's image upon you ... which is blurring and marring God's handiwork, which is destroying the lives of men, women and children? ... fight for the coming day when in body, soul and spirit you will be free to live your own lives and give glory to your Creator.[107]

Holman notes that Hardie sat down to "long and prolonged cheering."

His international speaking, domestic speaking, and preaching, however, do not salvage his reputation among the doctrinaire socialists. Morgan cites the opinion of G. D. H. Cole to the effect that Hardie was a: "wooly minded romantic who contributed nothing to the intellectual content of the labour movement."[108] But in his own evaluation, Morgan expresses Hardie's "flexible radicalism" by stating that Hardie "Created a Marx, as he created a Christ, in his own image."[109] Morgan expands on this:

> Hardie's vague vision of founding 'Christ's Kingdom on Earth' with Jesus, the working-class son of Joseph the Carpenter, as 'the elder brother and the Great

---

104. McLean, *Hardie*, 171.
105. Noted in Hughes, *Keir Hardie: A Pictorial Biography*, 160.
106. Stewart, *Keir Hardie: A Biography*, 258; cf. Shankar, "Socialist Labour Leader," 675–83.
107. Cited in Holman, *Keir Hardie: Labour's Greatest Hero?*, 167.
108. Morgan, *Keir Hardie: Radical and Socialist*, 201.
109. Morgan, *Keir Hardie: Radical and Socialist*, 203.

Comrade', was inspirational. It fired the imagination of thousands of working men of nonconformist background caught up in the economic depression and the class warfare of the late Victorian and Edwardian eras. But the vision was subordinate to the reality of creating a self-conscious party of the workers and their middle-class sympathizers.[110]

Crushed by the realities of World War 1, Shapiro writes that Hardie believed that "Socialism and Christianity had both failed … in preventing WWI."[111] Hardie was also likely weakened by his tireless speaking and traveling schedule, and after an illness, Hardie died September 26, 1915, at age fifty-nine. Though young and not even sixty, photos of Hardie portray a man looking gray and elderly.

Hardie's legacy

Although I note that Hardie was praised by colleagues, even before his death as "the old man" of the movement, it is interesting how much debate there is among biographers about Hardie's political legacy. I leave these evaluative statements to the historians and political scientists and take note of the following important summaries. The ambiguity of these summaries is best indicated by the last sentence of Benn's 1997 biography: "Despite all his failure and failings, his life was successful."[112]

In fact, this kind of ambiguity is evident throughout all the biographies. Already when Hughes published his biography in 1956, it was often suggested that Hardie's political career was not "successful." Hughes, however, objected (in terms, it must be said, that reflect a more optimistic 1950s that sounds quaint in the twenty-first century):

> if we have arrived at a 'mainly middle-class society' from which grinding poverty and grime in Britain have largely disappeared it is due mainly to the influence that the Labour Party, which Hardie fought so doggedly to bring into being, has exerted on British politics … when Keir Hardie first brought the plight of the unemployed to the attention of the House of Commons, Mr. Gladstone thought that this was not a subject with which Parliament should concern itself.[113] Indeed, if Mr. Gladstone could come back to survey the political scene today, he would have to come to the conclusion that Keir Hardie had been extraordinarily successful …[114]

110. Morgan, *Keir Hardie: Radical and Socialist*, 217.
111. Shapiro, *Keir Hardie and the Labour Party*, 86.
112. Benn, *Hardie*, 434.
113. See Benn, *Hardie*, 102, on this.
114. Hughes, *Keir Hardie: A Pictorial Biography*, 7.

More recently, Callow writes:

> He was the first man from the midst of the working class who completely understood them, completely sympathized with them, completely championed them. He was the first working man who, having entered Parliament, never deserted them, never turned his back on a single principle which he had professed, never drifted away from his class in thought, in feeling or in faith. When he came there was no Labour representation in our country. The Trade Union movement was in feudal knights' Fee to the Liberal Party. The Working Class had no political mind of their own. Parliament was no more theirs than was the workshop or the factory. Their masters ruled in both.[115]

Benn writes that socialist partisan disappointment with Hardie's first Parliamentary term is unfair—noting that socialist critics expected "too much from one man," but also noting that Hardie himself had expected too much from "one institution," but Hardie's rhetoric that terrified the wealthy classes nevertheless provided great "hope" for millions of workers at the time.[116] Keir Hardie was voted the Labour Party's "greatest hero" in a straw poll of delegates at the 2008 Labour conference in Manchester. Over thirty streets in Britain are named for him, and there is even a "Keir Hardie Methodist Church" in London. Shapiro wrote in his 1971 biography:

> From time to time the history of a nation – and even of the world – is made a different place, for better or worse, by the efforts of one man. Such a man was Keir Hardie, the founder of the Labour Party in Britain, and so of modern 'social democracy.'[117]

McLean summarizes as follows:

> In 1893 Keir Hardie did more than anyone else to found the I.L.P., and in 1900 he did more than anyone else to found the Labour Party. These are his greatest political achievements, and are unquestionably his, whatever claims others may have to share in them ... Hardie had considerable ability both as a propagandist and as an organizer. But, first, last, and always, he had staying power. This was his greatest strength, and it sprang from his personality ... He could brush off an amount of failure and ridicule that would deter almost anybody else ...[118]

With this context of his life briefly summarized, let us turn to more direct reflections on the role of religion and especially the Bible in Hardie's life and writing, and his close allies, which represents the major burden of this study.

---

115. Callow, *Keir Hardie, From Serfdom to Socialism*, 41.
116. Benn, *Hardie*, 125.
117. Shapiro, *Keir Hardie and the Labour Party*, v.
118. McLean, *Hardie*, 168–9.

Figure 3.1 "Covet Not thy Neighbour's Goods," *The Labour Leader*, 1894.

Chapter 3

HARDIE (AND HIS BIOGRAPHERS) ON HARDIE'S RELIGION

In this chapter, I once again draw heavily from the excellent biographies, but this time with an eye toward engaging in more critical dialogue with the existing writing on Hardie. Although it is only when we begin the focused attention to Hardie's *reading of the Bible* that we will largely part company with virtually *all* Hardie's biographers, here we have reason to take issue with assessments of Hardie's religious contexts. There are four issues I will raise in this chapter. First, I wish to add to the discussions about Hardie's early involvement with a small Scottish Church movement founded by James Morison, known as the "Morisonians." Second, I will discuss Hardie's commitment to temperance. Third, I will re-examine the issue of Hardie's "eccentric" or "unorthodox" religious interests. Fourth, and finally, I will argue that a particular event late in Hardie's career, a speech he made in Lille, France in 1910, that has been (almost) universally *neglected*, was a singularly important indication of Hardie's own faith and values. Before these four discussions, however, it is helpful to begin by getting our first look at a sample of Hardie's actual performances as a speaker, considering a speech from 1892.

The new MP: Hardie "In the Field" (1892)

This speech was delivered in Swindon, on December 12, 1892, at the Inaugural Meeting of the "Wiltshire General and Agricultural Workers' Union" (North Wilts Herald – Friday 16 December 1892). As is often (helpfully) the case with published notes from delivered speeches in this era, reactions from the crowd are often noted. In his remarks, Hardie called for unity among workers:

> … the interests of one class of workers are bound up in those of another. You cannot separate what is called the "unskilled" labourer (though that is a contradiction of terms) from the trained mechanic (applause). They must stand or fall together, and it is largely because of the division which has existed between different sections of labour in the past that the combination of workers has been made less effective than it would have been otherwise …

Among the more interesting features in this address is Hardie's arguments against those who suggest that charity from the wealthier classes—or the church—is the way forward for dealing with the poverty of the working people:

> What steps, I will ask, do you propose to take to alleviate the evil you see around you? Some people will tell you that the workers are poor because they do not exercise enough thrift, and that if they would only live on a little less than they earn our troubles would be at an end. Well, I can understand preaching thrift to some people. My neighbour in Scotland is the Marquis of Bute, and his income is over £1,000 a day (laughter). Now, if I had an income like that I think I could struggle along on eight or nine hundred (renewed laughter), and store up the rest for the inevitable rainy day. But when it comes to preaching thrift to people who are scarcely in receipt of enough wages to enable them to keep body and soul together it is adding insult to injury (hear, hear). As a Scotchman born and bred, 1 think I can be relied on to keep a firm grip on the 'siller' [= money] when I have it, but I do protest against the habit of people assuming that the improvidence of the working classes is the cause of all the misery from which they are suffering (cheers). There is another class of people who say that the workers want more religion (laughter) I do not believe that (cheers). They want more practical Christianity, it is true; but if they are to rely on the pulpit for leading and guidance in this matter I must say I think the day of their emancipation is a good way ahead (laughter). Who today are the men with the chief seats in our synagogues but those who have the most money. These are the "pillars"— "caterpillars" I have heard them called—of the Church; these are the men she loves to honour and respect I am told, the true inculcation of Christian duty is to teach the rich to give of their wealth for the alleviation of the misery of the poor, and it is said the parable of the Good Samaritan carries that meaning. I do not believe it. To say that it does is equivalent to saying that if the robbers who fell upon the man going from Jerusalem to Jericho and despoiled him, afterwards devoted ten per cent of the proceeds of the robbery to buying the oil and wine to pour into the wounds they had caused, they would have been fulfilling the whole law and the Scriptures (laughter). When wealthy landlord or employer gives back in charity to the workers a tithe of that of which he has sweated them he is acting in the same manner as those robbers I have spoken of (hear, hear and laughter). No; I believe the Church will only fall into line with the workers when the workers will be able to get along without the Church; they must rely on no outside organization (hear, hear). It is hinted that it is possible either of the parties in the State will help you Politicians, like the Church, will help you when you can help yourselves, and not before I have no faith whatever in either Liberal or Conservative party to do anything for the working classes until they are compelled to do so by the people. I don't blame them for this. They cannot legislate in advance of public opinion; and it is your duty to enlist that opinion on your side, and that you can only do by organization (applause). There are men in Parliament, as there are in the Church, who are sincerely desirous of doing all in their power to help the labouring classes, but they do not know what is wanted, nor how to begin, nor by what method to secure it. Others are ignorant,

prejudiced and self-interested, and they cannot be expected to be anxious for any change which will make life less pleasant or less comfortable for them ...

Here, then, is how Hardie concludes this speech—giving a good idea of the emotive style of Hardie's speechmaking, but also his continued appeals to religious themes and motifs, including his concluding recitation of the final stanzas of Lord Tennyson's poem, *In Memoriam*:

> And when I think that there are in these country districts millions of acres of good land lying idle and wanting cultivation and that in other parts there are thousands and tens of thousands of people also lying idle, l am impelled to say that it is the duty of the State to bring the two into contact, and to give those who are unemployed an opportunity of getting an honest living (applause). If I am told the reason of the land lying idle is that it will not pay the landlord to cultivate it, I say that the first duty of the land is to grow bread for the workers, that if that is not done it is not being put to a proper use, and that if that is done, though not a penny is paid for rent, it is performing good service (applause). We want to concentrate attention on this point—that men and women are of more value than property; and we want, moreover, to mould our constitution to our new circumstances. In times past the landlords were supreme, and they moulded the constitution to suit their own selfish ends; in later times the commercial classes came into power, and they pursued a policy of extending trade and commerce; now the time has come when the workers are becoming dominant, and if they are wise they will shape their constitution so as to bring the greatest good to the greatest number, so as to act for the whole and not for the class, so as to give people the opportunity of developing that which is best and noblest in them, and so as to restore the full meaning of Christ's teaching that 'Life is more than meat, and the body than raiment' (applause). I trust that you will help to build up and strengthen trade unionism in every form, and will lend a hand, in a spirit of true and unselfish brotherhood, to help this new movement to improve the position of the agricultural labourers in this county. In doing so, you will be helping in a work which may be described in the lines of the dead poet:—
>
> Ring out a slowly dying cause,
> And ancient forms of party strife;
> Ring in a nobler mode of life,
> With sweeter manners, purer laws.
> Ring in the valiant man, and free
> The larger heart, the kindlier hand;
> Ring out the darkness of the land;
> Ring in the Christ that is to be.

To be clear, this is not among the most "Biblical" of Hardie's speeches or writings (as we shall soon see), but it is nonetheless a good introduction to a chapter focused more on Hardie's "religious ideas" discussed more broadly before turning to a specific examination of Hardie's "exegesis." This is, however, a very good example of what has often been referred to as Hardie's "evangelical" or "missionary" style of presentation, a "religious" style which McLean claims "never made an impact" on Anglican or Catholic listeners, and especially not in "godless London,"[1] other than the fact of his *being elected to Parliament* precisely in the very same section of "godless London," presumably. This is among many examples of a notable tendency among Hardie biographers who work very hard indeed at minimizing the significance of Hardie's Christianity, to which Holman (2010) has, in my view, quite rightly taken great exception.

This speech, however, is also sufficient evidence in itself to raise serious questions about assessments of Hardie's religious ideas and ideals such as McLean's statement that Hardie's religious "principles" were pretty simple, "in so far as he professed them in public—which was not very far,"[2] yet this speech suggests, quite to the contrary, that those religious principles were rather assertively professed.

I call attention to this because of the tendency in the (especially recent) biographies to argue that Hardie's religious ideas should mainly be discussed (albeit briefly) as part of a description of Hardie's *early* life, suggesting that as his political views and involvement matured, religion began to mean less. This tendency has contributed to the underestimation of the importance of religion in Hardie's later life. This clear tendency, then, provoked the spirited "response" by Holman in his 2010 biography, where he sought to "balance the scales" in the direction of *emphasizing* Hardie's religious interests.

There are some issues upon which the biographies largely agree. For example, Hardie's Christianity was surely not an influence from his parents, who were normally considered to be under the influence of "secular" thinking. With regard to David Hardie, Reid argues that:

> The harsh experiences of the Glasgow years had turned him towards secularism and the republican movement with which it was closely associated. The anti-clerical propaganda of Charles Bradlaugh's National Secular Society had spread into Scotland and David Hardie had become a reader of his paper, the *National Reformer*. A copy of Tom Paine's *The Age of Reason* is said to have stood on the bookshelf in his house, alongside the Bible and *The Pilgrim's Progress*.[3]

It is therefore not to be overlooked that Hardie's decision to declare himself a Christian was not the easily dismissed result of a pious family upbringing. He did not, so to speak, simply "learn to use the lingo." It is important to note that recent debate on the role of religion in late nineteenth-century socialism in the UK also recognizes that Hardie's religious commitments are not easily dismissed as either

---

1. McLean, *Hardie*, 167.

2. McLean, *Hardie*, 164; see Lowe on Hardie's religion, expressed in "few words," *From Pit to Parliament*, 76.

3. Reid, *Keir Hardie: The Making of a Socialist*, 23.

insincere, nor simply to be dismissed as using religious "language" to speak of otherwise decidedly political and social realities. This last point is *not* insignificant.

Note, for example, the brief debates in the late 1970s in the pages of *History Workshop Journal* raised by Stephen Yeo's provocative 1977 article, "A New Life: The Religion of Socialism in Britain, 1883–1896." Yeo was mainly interested in the religious language used by a variety of advocates of socialism and the importance of understanding this language: " ... if 'religious' elements were at the centre of socialism of these years, they were not, on the face of it, associated with ... passivity or frustrated political initiative ...."[4] Notably, however, in citing many examples of religious-like language in many socialist activists in this time period, Yeo clearly *differentiated* Hardie's Christianity from religious flavored rhetorical flourish in many others:

> A language and style of religiosity surrounded such altruism in these years. The words 'evangelists,' 'apostles,' 'disciples,' 'new birth,' 'preachment,' 'street preaching,' and 'gospel' recurred in the anti-'religious' Morris as much as in the 'religious' Hardie ...[5]

Yet Yeo is compelled to write: "Even in its unreformed state, however, labour leaders like Tom Mann, Keir Hardie and Ben Tillett showed considerable interest in denominational Christianity."[6] Despite such affirmations, a number of issues still persist in the most recent biographies.

James Morison and the "Evangelical Union"

All the biographies note Hardie's early involvement with the "Evangelical Union," a splinter movement led by the Scottish theologian James Morison (1816–1893). Although the significance of this is typically only briefly considered, we will illustrate why this is worthy of a bit more than casual consideration.

All agree that in Hardie's early years in Scotland, he became a member of the Evangelical Union Church, Park Street, Hamilton. Morgan writes that Hardie's early years were "impacted" by his embrace of the "twin causes" of evangelical Christianity and of temperance.[7] His conversion to Christianity was dated in his own diary to 1877. Thus, at age twenty-one, Hardie wrote in his diary: "Today I have given my life to Jesus Christ." Of course, "giving my life to Jesus" means entirely different things, depending on the denominational and theological context within which this kind of statement is made. At the outset, there is no doubt that even using

---

4. Stephen Yeo, "A New Life: The Religion of Socialism in Britain, 1883–1896," *History Workshop* 4 (1977): 5–56, here 8.
5. Yeo, "A New Life," 17.
6. Yeo, "A New Life," 18.
7. Morgan, *Keir Hardie: Radical and Socialist*, 8–10.

this kind of language suggests a more "evangelical Protestant" context, because it would be rare indeed for Roman Catholics (for example) to speak of a conversion in precisely these terms. Therefore, it is important to consider the particular theological context for Hardie's conversion in relation to the "Evangelical Union." This context ought not be quickly skipped over in a perfunctory manner, but that has been the general practice in the biographies. McLean, for example, wants to say that it was significant that Hardie was raised among "puritan ideals of the Covenanters,"[8] no doubt intending to refer to a kind of "generic" Scottish Calvinist context. Combined with the number of occasions when he refers to Hardie as a "missionary" or, with other biographers, an "evangelist," these generalizations run the distinct danger of overlooking the significance of Hardie's *specific choice* of theological affiliation. Yet, anyone reading Scottish Church history would be quickly dissuaded from any ill-conceived notion that large numbers of Scots cared little about the nuances separating different theological traditions. None of the biographers treat this as entirely incidental, but neither have they appeared to have spent much time investigating the further significance of the Morisonians themselves.

The Christian movement in Scotland known as the "Evangelical Union," also known colloquially as "The Morisonians" began, as previously noted, with the founder, Dr. James Morison, and was thus a splinter group from the larger Scottish Presbyterian Church movements. This is a particularly interesting episode for our concerns, and Morgan is not unaware of at least some of the significance of Hardie's exposure to this rather unique Christian theology (especially for a Scot) precisely because Morisonians challenged some of the central tenets of the (otherwise often quite harsh) expressions of Calvinist orthodoxy often typical of Scottish Calvinism in the eighteenth and nineteenth centuries. Morgan did note that he believed that Morison's "gospel" had certain radical "tendencies" although Morison himself was "no socialist." Morgan calls Morisonianism "Universalist" in creed, meaning that Morison taught that Christ's atoning death was for everyone, not merely an "elect." Furthermore, the polity of the church was "intensely democratic" in ethos.[9] These are valid enough observations, as far as they go, but much more can be said on this topic.

Stewart, in his early biography, already believed that it was the "simplicity" of the Evangelical Union's Gospel that appealed to Hardie,[10] but this is itself still too much of a simplification. In Kenneth Roxburgh's recent summary of the thought and work of the Revd. James Morison, he notes that Morison lived: "in a social and political context in which the rights of individuals were stressed … "[11] and in this context referred to the Chartist movements in the lifetime of Morison, and

---

8. McLean, *Hardie*, 5.

9. Morgan, *Keir Hardie: Radical and Socialist*, 8.

10. Stewart, *Keir Hardie: A Biography*, 8.

11. Kenneth Roxburgh, "James Morison (1816–1893)," *Scottish Church History* 32, no. 1 (2002): 115–41, here 119.

their demands of universal (usually, however, only male) suffrage. However, Roxburgh also cites the nineteenth-century Scottish Church historian Fergus Ferguson, who already had written in 1876 about Morison's Evangelical Union and noted that Ferguson was already making interesting comments about the political implications of Morison's ideas, while Morison was still very much alive and active. Ferguson has observed that the times were calling for: " ... untaxed bread for all; liberty for all; a suffrage for all" and noted that Ferguson had already proposed that Morison's ideas and movement were: " ... a protest against religious conservatism, and in harmony with the liberal and liberalising spirit of the age."[12] Finally, Roxburgh also notes that there was an interesting comment made by a speaker during a celebration of Morison's ministry, that: "The Doctor just wanted that every man should have a Christ to vote for ...."[13] Clearly, in reference to using the term "vote," the political implications of Morison's theology, while not explicitly developed by Morison himself, were not lost on observers already in the nineteenth century.

It is perhaps important to consider what Morison was reacting *against*, as well. Readers unfamiliar with the extremes of Calvinist "predestination" may be forgiven for not immediately understanding the serious social implications of such a religious doctrine. These extremes emerge more clearly when one realizes that, at least for some, Calvin's pre-destination meant that God's love is *not* for every person, and many people are "pre-ordained" by God for eternal punishment, with no chance of ever responding positively to the Gospel message of God's redeeming love in Christ—and thus—no chance of being "saved" and "dwelling in heaven with God eternally." Therefore, Christ did not die for the salvation of those "pre-destined sinners" and sufferers. Whatever the theological merits of the argument (and the present writer considers them without merit, nor the Anselmian roots they are built upon), it is significant only to note that one of the potential social implications of such ideas is clear: there is an inescapable divide in the human condition between the saved and the lost, a divide which can never be bridged. An obvious next step, however, would be for an industrial middle class (especially) but also a sufficiently pious wealthy class, to assure themselves of their own *positive* status before God precisely on the "evidence" of their social and economic successes—and what their views of the struggling poor would be under these terms can only be surmised by their actions, as an outraged Hardie frequently pointed out.

Morison's *universality* had the immediate implication that *any and all can respond to God* ... and Christ's atoning work was therefore potentially for *every* human being. No human is cursed *by God*—rather they are "on their own"—free to respond and acknowledge God's love, or not. Nothing is "predetermined" by God, and God's love is not "limited," nor is Christ's suffering only for "some." It seems easy to imagine the joyous response to Morison's reassuring Gospel message for

---

12. Fergus Ferguson, cited in Roxburgh, "James Morison (1816–1893)," 133–4.
13. Roxburgh, "James Morison (1816–1893)," 134.

people who were otherwise raised on a rigid Calvinist doctrine potentially mixed with class resentments,[14] and William Adamson's 1898 biography of Morison already stressed, as Roxburgh has more recently reaffirmed, that evangelism—namely the enthusiastic sharing of this message and speaking widely throughout Scotland—was a major concern of Morison's own work, proclaiming that God "loved all men [sic] without exception or distinction."[15] Morison wrote with some fire about any who would proclaim to people their eternal damnation, yet at the same time proclaim that there was nothing they could do about it! Morison writes—again with clear disdain—about those who:

> ... go to these reprobates for whom Christ never tasted death, and invite and exhort and implore them to accept a Saviour that never died for them, and a pardon that never was provided for them. Oh this tender mercy is indeed cruel. But they add cruelty to cruelty. They threaten the poor reprobates with a sorer punishment if they will not avail themselves of the inaccessible and wholly unattainable salvation. All other cruelties are mercies compared to this. Such preaching of the gospel is the deepest depth of mercilessness ...[16]

With this sample of Morison's rhetorical flourish, we begin to see one final aspect of Hardie's early attraction to the Evangelical Union. Adamson's lengthy biography of Morison describes *at length and in great detail* the trials and expulsions of Morison from Scottish Calvinist church leaders who examined him in detail and rejected his ideas as "heresy." To detail these tribulations of a man who spoke endlessly of God's unlimited love would surely appeal to a man like Hardie who would be later dedicated to pronouncing Socialism as a *Christian-inspired* political message of justice and compassion in the face of suffering, irrespective of his own setbacks and failures, even among the successes, throughout his career. In other words—the *persecutions of Morison* would have been among the Evangelical Union's more serious appeals to those seeking to grow a social movement that encountered such spirited resistance in British society.

By way of comparison, any serious student of Anabaptist theology (the family of originally Swiss, Dutch, and Germanic Christian traditions including the traditionalist Amish and Hutterites, and the more modern Mennonites and Church of the Brethren) would recognize important historical and ideological themes at work here. If one, for example, takes note of the abuse in American popular culture (especially in televised programs) that pillories and often mercilessly ridicules the lifestyle decisions of the Amish in America (the Hutterites seem spared only because they are less well known, and rarely drive visibly distinctive horse-drawn carriages), then one cannot fail to understand the impact of a book

---

14. William Adamson, *The Life Of The Rev. James Morison, D. D., Principal Of The Evangelical Union Theological Hall, Glasgow* (London: Hodder and Stoughton, 1898), 84.
15. Adamson, *The Life Of The Rev. James Morison*, 215.
16. Morison cited in Adamson, *The Life Of The Rev. James Morison*, 346.

known as *Martyr's Mirror* (usually occupying pride of place on an Amish shelf next to the Bible). The book is *the* traditional Anabaptist classic that outlines and explains (with accompanying illustrations) the excruciating torture and suffering of early Anabaptist leaders, often brutally massacred by Catholic and Lutheran/Protestant alike in the sixteenth century. Already first published in 1660, and often republished since that time, any person raised on *Martyr's Mirror* will surely be theologically, and also psychologically, more prepared to "stand against the tide" of social traditions and even expect social abuse. The Morisonian tradition, as evident already in Adamson's 1898 book, including remembering (at great length) the trials of Morison himself, standing before severe examination when his main message was the universality of God's love for humanity, can therefore be seen as bracing stuff indeed.

Hardie's preference for a Morisonian Gospel would therefore suggest three areas of particular appeal and influence—(1) a compassionate universalism that emphasized God's "democratic" love for all, as well as (2) an emphasis on the importance of speaking, evangelizing, and "spreading the word." Both influences are obvious in Hardie's own life as a tireless "evangelist" (the word is used constantly in the biographies) for Christian socialism. But finally, (3) a sense of righteousness in the face of adversity. That these issues remained of interest to Hardie may be indicated in his later reproduction of the following delightfully irreverent satirical verse in his editorial column in *The Labour Leader*, entitled simply "Calvinism":

We are the saved elected few
Let all the rest be damned
There's room enough in hell for you,
We can't have Heaven crammed[17]

We have already had occasion to mention the serious disagreement that Hardie had with other members of the Congregational Church that he and Lily Hardie had joined. When Hardie agreed with the Church pastor, Rev. Scott, that a member struggling with drink should not be severely disciplined, the middle-class lay members, especially a certain Mr. Adam Drummond, sought to dismiss the pastor.

In his diary entry of February 20, 1884, Hardie notes that he

... was asked to take the weekly Prayer Meeting for Mr S. who is ill, the abuse he received on Sunday having been too much for him. A.D. was present and I read Second Chapter James which it seemed had formed the subject of dispute between him and Elliot though I knew it not. Then I spoke of going forward in brotherly love and kindness and he seemed to think from the way I looked that I

---

17. *Labour Leader*, May 3, 1902, repeated December 27, 1907.

meant him and I got agitated and made matters worse by stopping at this point. Of course it will be said that the whole thing was planned, but it was not.[18]

What we know is that Hardie left the church in disgust, and this was only one of many occasions when Hardie would clearly differentiate between what he saw as authentic "Christianity" as opposed to what he often called (as did many others) hypocritical "Churchianity." The latter term would be used again and again in Hardie's later journalistic rhetoric.

Hardie, temperance, and the "Order of Good Templars"

It is also important to briefly discuss the interest Hardie always exhibited in issues of "self-improvement," which may have been stronger in his earlier years but was never far away from his comments on workers taking care of themselves. Already in his early column for the *Ardrossan and Saltcoat Herald*, for example, Hardie approvingly wrote for a March 1885 contribution, the following lengthy discussion:

> Rev. J. S. Robertson, of Cumnock, has just published an address to working-men, being a sermon delivered in the Parish Church on Sunday, 8th February. The address is, on the whole, worthy of a wide circulation, and is fitted to do much good. All through the discourse runs a line of thought clearly recognizing that all men are brethren in the great family of God, and nothing tends more to raise the fallen than this same thought that, no matter how low or degraded a person may have become, God loves such a one with all a father's love, and desires nothing more than the return of such a one to all the rights and privileges of those who are of the household of faith. Here is a sad truth put in small compass: 'A fallen man can never respect himself, and life becomes to him a thing of eating and drinking, toiling and resting, and the man as lost is the animal.' These few words convey only too true a picture of what the existence of only too many of our working people really is. Speaking of the effect of working in the mine has on the mind, he says, 'That there is a tendency in this work to lead men to forget who they are, is evident from the fact that very many of their number are living far below their proper level ... Low down in the bowels of the earth you toil, shut out from God's pure light, in work which is both dirty and dangerous; and it is not perhaps to be wondered at that many of you forget who you are, and so lose your self-respect: 'Only a miner!' Say that, and believe that, and you will become only a miner, and lose all your self-respect. What I wish you to feel now and always is that you are more; in fact, you are not miners at all, and he who says of you 'only a miner' is probably not living his own free self either. You are God's child, you work is mining, but the blackest work to which a man may put his hands can never disguise or blot out the Image of Him in whose likeness he was

---

18. Reid, *Keir Hardie: The Making of a Socialist*, 74.

made and as you pick away at the seam of stone at which you are employed, you can do so in the blessed and soul elevating consciousness that He who curiously places it in the depth of the earth is your Father. Let that idea get possession of your souls and it will redeem your work from insignificance. If it were not beneath God your Father to form that material at first, it cannot be beneath you to bring to light his hidden power, wisdom and love. Your work is honourable if the workman is in right relations with his God; and though I would not choose to work that work, yet when I meet you, blackened almost past recognition, as you return from your labours, do I not know that your work is as honourable as my own, and that you too are God's child? That self-respect which springs from the consciousness of man's true relations to God is not that the sources of true elevation of the working classes? Oh, what a charm your daily work would have for you if done in this spirit.' Speaking of Intemperance, Mr. Robertson says – 'Without sobriety therefore you cannot respect yourself, and without self respect you cannot be brave men; and power is always dangerous in the hands of those who have no consciousness of their own personal dignity – no self-respect.' To this it may be added that so long as the liquor traffic exists in our midst, so long will we have intemperance among the working-classes and therefore it clearly becomes the duty of those who are afraid of the 'new found democracy' to work for the overthrow of the drink shop, and thus rob the people of the dangerous element. Here is another item worth quoting: 'A cessation of this expenditure (on drink) would be equivalent to raising the savings of every poor man's family throughout Great Britain by £10 a year, or 4s a week. It is therefore desirable in the best interest of the working classes that they should realize the terrible obstacle which intemperance presents to their true advancement and progress.' The quotations will help to give an idea of what the whole is like. No man can read the sermon without feeling benefited, and while I am not prepared to say amen to everything contained in it, still I have no hesitation in affirming that the working-men of the district have been placed under a debt of gratitude to Mr. Robertson, and this they can best show by seeking to confirm their lives to the principles which he has laid down for their guidance.[19]

Thus, among the issues Hardie frequently addressed was the danger of drink. Reid, for example, believes that Hardie was deeply influenced, especially earlier in his life, by a line of thinking that held that workers should seek to improve their lives and especially their personal consumption habits, so that their own drinking and lack of thrift would not make their poverty even worse[20] and proposes that Hardie may well have been influenced by certain attitudes typical of evangelical Protestants, lower "middle-class" attitudes toward the significance of "self-improvement." Hardie's other young adult interest, of course, was the temperance movement. He joined a temperance organization called the "Independent Order of Good

19. *Ardrossan and Saltcoat Herald*, March 6, 1885.
20. Reid, *Keir Hardie: The Making of a Socialist*, 36–9.

Templars," a "lodge" type organization dedicated to promoting temperance issues. The organization was, in fact, quite large, and recent historical interest seems entirely justified:

> In the 1870s and 1880s, among groups hostile to alcoholic drink, the Templars were the world's most numerous and most militant. In addition to being a teetotal organization, the Independent Order of Good Templars was one of the world's largest fraternal societies. A mixture of lodge ritual, wholesome companionship, and denunciation of drink attracted a youthful membership in North America, Britain and its Empire, and other parts of the world. Millions of men and women joined the Templars after the Civil War, most of them white, a few of them black. Their motto was 'Faith, Hope, and Charity.'[21]

Hardie was, in fact, secretary of the local branch of the organization by 1877. Many biographers have suggested that his involvement in this organization would have given Hardie a good "training" in organizational structures and "democratic organization," Reid stating that the Church and the temperance movements would have given Hardie "reassurance" and this, with the Evangelical Union particularly, gave him:

> ... a socially acceptable role as a lay preacher and temperance organiser, and the esteem of ministers, newspaper editors, shopkeepers and others who welcomed him, though a humble miner, into their congregation ... British workers of the nineteenth century often found in evangelical religion the assurance of dignity in the sight of God which compensated for the low esteem in which their secular calling was held.[22]

An important element of the temperance movement must not be missed—the proto-feminist nature of the movement in both the UK and the USA. Women were thought to suffer the severest consequences of male drunkenness, and thus temperance and anti-alcohol activism went hand-in-hand with struggles for the right to vote and other support for women's social and economic advancement. Hardie's later advocacy of women's rights (often against the advice of others) surely had some roots in his involvement and agreements with the concerns of temperance movements as much as his later friendship with the Pankhurst family and their allies. Arguably, on this issue alone, it is timely for a reconsideration of Hardie's temperance concerns. Fahey writes:

> Connections with other topics, notably women's history, make temperance a respectable subject for research today, although in a secular age religiously

---

21. David Fahey, *Temperance and Racism: John Bull, Johnny Reb, and the Good Templars* (Lexington: University Press of Kentucky, 1996), 5.
22. Reid, *Keir Hardie: The Making of a Socialist*, 40.

motivated teetotalers and prohibitionists arouse a derision that diminishes the importance historians assign the temperance movement. To an even greater extent, intellectual snickers handicap the study of the fraternal movement as part of popular culture. Images of boisterous Shriner parades and smoky poker games at the Elks lodge make it easy to dismiss fraternal societies as ephemeral.[23]

Reid notes that there was a confluence of temperance movements and the Evangelical Union in some cities, and in Hamilton, Hardie came under the influence of Rev. Dan Craig. Reid explains:

> Craig was himself a model of working-class self-improvement. The son of an Ayrshire weaver, he had begun life as a joiner. After some years as a lay preacher in the Evangelical Union, he had been sent to its theological college in Glasgow and had become the ordained pastor of the Hamilton congregation in 1871. His eloquent preaching filled the church and the grateful congregation raised his salary in the first six months from eighty pounds to one hundred and sixty pounds. His sudden accidental death in 1874 was a shock for Hardie, who recalled: 'He took a great interest in me and completely changed the course of my religious thought, which, up till then, about my nineteenth year, had been of a very negative character!'[24]

With regard to Hardie's involvement in temperance organizations, however, there is yet again little serious interest among Hardie biographers in the wider implications of the temperance movement in late nineteenth-century England. In an article dealing with Liberal Party concerns with alcoholism at the end of the nineteenth century, Fahey notes a number of reasons why the temperance issue became increasingly serious in Britain in this time:

- increasing scientific evidence of the health implications of alcoholism;
- the obvious impact on the people when volunteers were sought for the Boer War, and so many men failed minimal health expectations;
- worries about economic efficiency in "an increasingly competitive world";
- growing consciousness of the conditions of poverty, with their attendant vice, disorder, and disease;
- the defense of respectability and the validity of traditional values;
- fear of race "degeneracy";
- the anger over the rising political influence of the drink trade and its alliance with reactionary politicians;
- concern with women's drunkenness and propriety;

---

23. Fahey, *Temperance and Racism*, 6.
24. Reid, *Keir Hardie: The Making of a Socialist*, 36–8.

- the suspicion of the profit motive in matters of public interest which the agitation for disinterested management sometimes expressed.[25]

Fahey also noted the impact of Joseph Rowntree and Arthur Sherwell's work: *The Temperance Problem and Social Reform*, published in April, 1899 (90,000 copies sold).[26] Further, in her 2008 essay delightfully (and quite descriptively) entitled: "Intemperate Narratives: Tory Tipplers, Liberal Abstainers, and Victorian British Socialist Fiction," Deborah Mutch draws a very significant contrast between the descriptions of drink in the writings of Blatchford and Hyndmann's more secular (and what Mutch calls their "Tory-socialist" middle-class backgrounds) publications such as the *Clarion*, and Hardie's "evangelical" *Labour Leader*:

> ... the image of voluntary abstinence fed into the Unlike the Tory-socialist promotion of the healthful and cheerful nature of moderation, Liberal-socialist authors could rely on the power of the temperance debate to suggest the superiority of their perspective rather than have to argue their case ... The Liberal-socialist embrace of teetotalism was not simply the promotion of individual health and welfare but, as high profile socialists such as John Burns and Ben Tillett argued, the sober worker would be able to stand up to employers and to organise themselves economically and politically ... for the Liberal-socialist teetotalism would enable the workers to succeed both individually and collectively ...[27]

In summary, then, attempts to "explain" Hardie's religious interests as either (a) limited to his earlier life, or (b) more associated with the social value of the temperance movement and the camaraderie offered there and church, are insufficient. Holman was surely right to point out that Hardie's interest in religion has rarely been seen as an important aspect of Hardie's life in biographies, even if noted briefly by all of them.[28] Holman further notes that the Hardies joined the Cumnock Church on July 19, 1882. It was the minister here who found Keir Hardie his first job in journalism when the minister himself retired because of ill health.[29] There was controversy, however. When the pastor, a certain Andrew Noble Scott, was in trouble for his (apparently overzealous) evangelistic activity, some of the influential congregation members moved to dismiss him, and Hardie

---

25. David Fahey, "Temperance and the Liberal Party—Lord Peel's Report, 1899," *Journal of British Studies* 10 (1971): 132–59, here 132–3.

26. Fahey, "Temperance and the Liberal Party," 158.

27. Deborah Mutch, "Intemperate Narratives: Tory Tipplers, Liberal Abstainers, and Victorian British Socialist Fiction," *Victorian Literature and Culture* 36 (2008): 471–87, here 483.

28. Holman, *Keir Hardie: Labour's Greatest Hero?*, 34–5.

29. Holman, *Keir Hardie: Labour's Greatest Hero?*, 35, cf. Stewart, *Keir Hardie: A Biography*, 8.

3. Hardie (and his Biographers) on Hardie's Religion

resigned in solidarity. As Morgan states it, Hardie was "never a regular churchgoer again," and states:

> His Christianity was highly flexible, a religion of humanity with little doctrinal content, utopian, romantic, outward-looking, democratic and egalitarian ... on such a basis, rather than on hard-headed economic analysis, was Hardie's socialism to be founded.[30]

This is only the first of a number of significant simplifications in the biographies of Hardie, particularly from Benn and Morgan. More attuned to socialist history and theory, both biographers also seem clearly sympathetic to attempts to distance Hardie from any kind of "Christian orthodoxy." It must be said that such a "tin ear" to theological issues, and more importantly the socio-political implications of these theological issues, is part of the problem of coming to grips with Hardie's Christianity, and more particularly his reading of the Bible. In sum, the biographers, in the main (with the notable exception of Holman's work), seem unable to interpret Hardie as interested in serious theology, and even more seriously interested in interpretation of the Bible. In an observation that effectively summarizes what this entire project clearly seeks to overturn, Benn even ventured to say that Hardie was *not*:

> ... particularly grounded in the Scriptures ... in later years he mentions the New Testament as having been influential in his life but in all his writing and speaking there is little evidence of the widespread familiarity with it that thoroughly religious churchgoers in the nineteenth century would have had ... Hardie, brought up politically, became attracted to religion as an extension of an already formed social conscience ...[31]

Yet Holman responds, appropriately, that Hardie's "propensities" were to turn to Scripture rather than Marx, and Hardie had commented that Jesus was more important to his thinking than all other sources combined,[32] and Holman noted Fenner Brockway's comment that when he asked Hardie about his life, Brockway had said:

> Towards the end of his life he said that were he to live it again he would devote it to the advocacy of the gospel of Christ ... This was not a statement of despair. He always recognized that Christianity was about hope and resurrection ... He was a remarkable politician and mainly so because he was rooted in Christianity ...[33]

---

30. Morgan, *Keir Hardie: Radical and Socialist*, 9.
31. Benn, *Hardie*, 17.
32. Holman, *Keir Hardie: Labour's Greatest Hero?*, 198–204.
33. Cited in Holman, *Keir Hardie: Labour's Greatest Hero?*, 204.

Clearly, *both* Benn and Holman's perspectives cannot *both* be true. And since Benn's work (nor any other of the otherwise interesting biographies) shows little interest in actually discussing this claim that Hardie was "not grounded in Scriptures" or that there was "little evidence of the widespread familiarity" typical of "churchgoers," we will respond to show her perspective quite limited indeed on precisely this issue. Christian radicalism, in short, seems not to have been on the radar for many biographers of Hardie, even though Hardie himself indicated a familiarity with precisely these traditions within Christian history. On this, Callow is especially attentive to Hardie's place among a wider theological tradition of Christian radicalism:

> His impetus was rooted in 'the Christianity of 'Christ', as distinct from the 'Christianity' of organized religion, where he found much hypocrisy,' and its inspiration lay in the pages of Renan's historicized life of Jesus. This attempt to reclaim the historical 'reality' of Jesus as a man, and political actor, had an enormous personal appeal for Hardie. As a result, his pursuit of a religious ideal was hallmarked by a doctrine of resistance to temporal powers. The subsequent ossification of Low Church Protestantism, and its failure to engage with the Liberation Theology championed by a section of the Roman Catholic Church in Latin America—as encapsulated in the writings and careers of the Boff brothers, Dom Helder Camara and Ernesto Cardenal—should not obscure the revolutionary current that was inherent in the Protestant Reformation. It was precisely this strain of religious radicalism—as expressed by John Ball during the Peasants' Revolt; Jan Hus and Jan Zelivsky during the Hussite Revolution; and by Thomas Muntzer at the height of the Peasants' War in Germany—that was being eagerly rediscovered and celebrated across late nineteenth-century Europe by historians and statesmen as different as Frederick Engels, Frantisek Palacky, Belfort Bax and Tomas Masaryk.[34]

Certainly, there is discussion of Hardie's lack of interest in particular Christian orthodoxies and extensive Church involvements. But this can be read more as exasperation with the lack of support from clergy, on the whole, for the early socialist movements.

At this point, we simply note that Keir Hardie, as we shall see in subsequent chapters, certainly did maintain an interest in the Bible, and especially the message of Jesus, even as he engaged in spirited attacks on what he saw as the hypocrisy of the churches' support for an industrial system that resulted in so much suffering.

Hardie and "heterodoxy"

In his 1999 article outlining various aspects of Christianity and Socialism in "Edwardian Britain," Geoghegan repeats the notion that Hardie, an "idiosyncratic

---

34. Callow, *Keir Hardie, From Serfdom to Socialism*, 32–3.

figure"³⁵ lived a faith that "commentators have found ... difficult to pin down" because of Hardie's "eclectic, even esoteric, religious beliefs" and specifically notes "spiritualism and reincarnation."³⁶ For this, he cites Morgan. In an article that is otherwise quite helpful, it is unfortunate that the influence of Benn's and Morgan's ideas about Hardie's supposed unorthodox and eccentric views persist.

In his (brief) assessments of Hardie's religious faith, Morgan seems unable to resist returning a few times to his insistence on Hardie's religious oddities, apparently intending to insulate Hardie, one presumes, from being claimed by Christians of any orthodox persuasion? Morgan writes:

> His religious mysticism, his concern with spiritualism and thought transference, his belief in a previous incarnation for humans and for beasts alike, his attachment to old folk myths, to the Druids, to oral tradition, to the sustaining force of mother earth – these were facets of the essential Hardie, too.³⁷

Benn, too, gleefully lists Hardie's "oddities" as including: " ... sun signs, omens, lucky days, and psychic manifestations, horoscopes, palmistry ...."³⁸ This is quite a list, and it is important to examine these kinds of breezy claims. There are a variety of incidents that Reid, Morgan, and Benn (particularly) cite for the heterodoxy of Hardie. Before turning to spiritualism specifically, let us consider another example of what Morgan believes to be Hardie's "oddities."

Morgan wants to say that readers would have found Hardie's interests in "naturalism" to be strange. However, when one checks the reference Morgan provides for Hardie's "surprising" attacks on city life³⁹ we find Hardie citing the Salvationist William Booth's criticism of the poverty and ill-health of city living for the poor, and Hardie acknowledging the healing qualities, especially for children, of country living. These are hardly "strange ideas," especially when placed in the context of Booth's criticism of urban poverty. This, however, is only a mild exaggeration compared to the discussions specifically about "Spiritualism."

To begin, we will have occasion to point out that modern "Cultural Studies" approaches to religious history have resulted in a significantly deepened interest in examining Spiritualism as a movement in its *fin de siècle* British social context, but also as a movement that in some contexts had lent itself to political leftism.⁴⁰

---

35. Vincent Geoghegan, "Socialism and Christianity in Edwardian Britain: A Utopian Perspective," *Utopian Studies* 10 (1999): 40–69, here 56.
36. Geoghegan, "Socialism and Christianity," 56.
37. Morgan, *Keir Hardie: Radical and Socialist*, 289.
38. Benn, *Hardie*, 262.
39. Hardie, "Between Ourselves," *The Labour Leader*, July 18, 1903.
40. Besides the classic work of Braude, two further works emphasize potential left-wing associations with Spiritualism. See Ann Braude, *Radical Spirits: Spiritualism and Women's Rights in Nineteenth-Century America*, 2nd edn (Bloomington: Indiana University Press, 1989/2001); Melissa Daggett, *Spiritualism in Nineteenth-Century New Orleans: The Life*

To be fair, Benn already admitted in her 1997 biography that Spiritualism was not as "déclassé" in Hardie's time, noting Conan Doyle's interests.[41] Doyle, however, was hardly a significant allowance by Benn in Hardie's favor, it must be said, given Conan Doyle's equal defense of the existence of forest faeries.

More significantly, since the work of Ann Braude however, there has been a significant sea change in historical interest and analysis of "Spiritualism." Before briefly taking this up, however, let us consider the main sources for these evaluations of Hardie's "strange" ideas. Morgan's evaluation of former Salvationist Frank Smith's friendship with Hardie, starting with Smith's role in the first successful Parliamentary campaign in West Ham, South London in 1892, includes his suspicion that much of the rather unorthodox religious and spiritual interests mentioned by Hardie derived largely from Smith's influence. As we have noted, by all accounts the former Salvationist was certainly an interesting character in Hardie's life as well as a major assistance to him (providing housing and financial assistance in London), and Smith's interest in "spiritualism," states Morgan: "powerfully influenced Hardie's political philosophy." Morgan makes the strongest statements along these lines—but suspicion is raised here because these stronger claims are not footnoted, yet Morgan will continue to argue that Hardie's friendship with Smith: "takes us to nearly the core of his personality."[42] But what is his basis from making such a sweeping evaluation of Hardie's heterodox Christian thought?

Morgan, and other biographers, comment on two specific occasions, and Morgan writes (again, of Hardie and Smith) that: "Their interest in spiritualism and the supernatural was intensified, Hardie even attended a séance which was supposed to determine his vote on the 1886 Irish Home Rule Bill …."[43] This is one of the most frequently cited events, and therefore is worthy of some careful consideration—but also because the discussion of this is an unfortunate case of exaggeration on Morgan's part. I am not alone is noting this pattern in the biographers. Barrow's 1980 study notes that "Keir Hardie was not vocal about spiritualism" (already raising suspicions about Morgan's sweeping generalizations), and Barrow points out that: " … there has grown up a commonplace among biographers that he occasionally attended seances and that his religious beliefs included a virtual acceptance of spiritualism."[44] Barrow is not at all certain about this, clearly, but Barrow is certainly correct about the way this particular incident is discussed.

Consider, for example, the somewhat strained reporting of this incident in Reid's biography, where Reid proposes that because (in the early 1900s) there "were few

and Times of Henry Louis Rey (Jackson: University Press of Mississippi, 2017); and Emily Suzanne Clark, *A Luminous Brotherhood: Afro-Creole Spiritualism in Nineteenth-Century New Orleans* (Chapel Hill: University of North Carolina Press, 2016).

41. Benn, *Hardie*, 105.
42. Morgan, *Keir Hardie: Radical and Socialist*, 46.
43. Morgan, *Keir Hardie: Radical and Socialist*, 56–7.
44. Logie Barrow, "Socialism in Eternity: The Ideology of Plebeian Spiritualists, 1853–1913," *History Workshop* 9 (1980): 37–69, here 51.

in the movement in whom he felt able to confide," he follows this with: "He even tried going to a spiritualist séance to converse with Parnell and Robert Burns ..." and although acknowledging it to have been a "hoax," Reid clearly implied that Hardie took the matter quite seriously.[45] Similarly, Morgan writes that 1902–1903 were "difficult days" for Hardie, with his daughter ill and the death of his mother and father,[46] and that it was during this time that Hardie revealed an interest in "quasi-religious activities as palmistry and astrology during these difficult years."[47] But once again, Hardie's actual discussions of these activities suggest something other than Hardie as a "devoted disciple" of "Spiritualism." He does write that he attended a dinner party some years before, where someone read his palm, and someone else asked Hardie if they could have their astrologer draw up a horoscope (in other words, emphasizing that these were not Hardie's own ideas), and he does mention that both activities revealed that he would have difficulties in his forty-eighth year. But when Hardie actually reports this in his column, he states that he mentions these things both for the interesting "coincidence" (!), but also to be: " ... fair to those who believe in Palmistry and Astrology to make these facts known ...."[48] This is hardly the basis for identifying Hardie as a devotee.

When one consults the issue of *The Labour Leader* that is the main source for the biographers in their discussions of spiritualism itself,[49] Hardie's own words give quite a different impression of the matter. Here, Hardie writes that he was actually recalling a previous incident when people tried to convince him to vote against Irish Home Rule. All this "lobbying" of Hardie reminded him, he said, of:

> ... a very amusing incident of the same period, at which an artist invited me to his study to have a talk with Robert Burns through a well-known spiritualist medium. I took the precaution of taking half a dozen friends with me, amongst whom, by the way, was Bruce Wallace, Frank Smith, S. G. Hobson, and other well-known people in the movement in those days, and the medium delivered messages from Parnell, Bradlaugh, Bright, and others, including Robert Burns, all of whom asked me to vote against the Irish Home Rule Bill! The thing was very amusing, and exceedingly well planned. I never got to the bottom of who was responsible for the séance, but there is no question about it that the whole incident was prearranged, and I was very glad indeed that I had taken the precaution to have a number of friends present.[50]

---

45. Reid, *Keir Hardie: The Making of a Socialist*, 171.
46. Morgan, *Keir Hardie: Radical and Socialist*, 124.
47. Morgan, *Keir Hardie: Radical and Socialist*, 125-6. Clearly the story is growing.
48. *Labour Leader*, February 26, 1914.
49. E.g., Stewart, *Keir Hardie: A Biography*, 70; Morgan, *Keir Hardie: Radical and Socialist*, 46, 57; McLean, *Hardie*, 165; Reid, *Keir Hardie: The Making of a Socialist*, 171. Reid at least acknowledges Hardie's good humor over the incident.
50. *Labour Leader*, February 26, 1914.

However unintentional it may have been, Morgan and other biographers' discussions of this incident—making more serious what Hardie himself clearly dismissed as an "amusing incident"—is arguably misleading. The problem is, however, that there is a clear consistency to many of these misrepresentations of specifically religious ideas. This is not to say that in other circumstances Hardie may well have taken Spiritualism seriously, but these particular incidents do not support Morgan (and Benn) in their sweeping conclusions. McLean, however, supplies the final main "source" for Hardie's "serious" interest in Spiritualism—namely the autobiography of Philip Snowden, where Snowden makes a brief passing comment to Hardie's belief in reincarnation,[51] but appearing on the same page was also Snowden's more detailed conviction that Hardie maintained Church membership to the end, and that throughout, Hardie's life expressed "a deep religious faith."[52]

An important point to make, however, is this: should it be convincingly argued that Hardie took Spiritualism seriously—is this the basis for a criticism of his own Christian conviction? More recent work on Spiritualism has rather significantly changed how we view this phenomenon. In other words, Hardie would hardly have found himself in some crazy "fringe group" (precisely where Benn wants to locate him, it seems) in the late nineteenth century, and Morgan and Benn's arguments suffer from the fact that more recent and serious historical analysis of Spiritualism as a movement (and especially the role of women and women's rights in that movement) had not yet been available to Morgan, and although available, was not consulted by Benn. But we have no such excuse in the twenty-first century.

The modern classic on reconsidering the historic, and especially social, significance of Spiritualism is Ann Braude's *Radical Spirits*, where Braude clarifies the radical political implications of Spiritualism as a movement. The movement, which quickly spread from the USA to the UK and beyond, had its origins in 1848, but was already on the wane in the 1890s. If one is able to look past the modern rationalist sniggering at beliefs taken quite seriously in the nineteenth century, but often embarrassing to contemporary readers, one is then able to appreciate some of the *social implications* of this movement, however dismissive one might be about the realities of the alleged "manifestations" thought to be at the heart of the movement. Similar analysis of the social contexts for the belief and practice of "magic," alchemy, and even "scientific" agricultural "truths" that now

---

51. Philip Snowden, *An Autobiography* (London: Nicholson and Watson, 1934). The incident is discussed in vol. 1: 317–18.

52. Snowden's *Autobiography*, incidentally, is more interesting for its contrasts with Hardie's writing. Although Snowden claims his knowledge of the Bible was "above average" (vol. 1: 22), he rarely discusses Scripture in the massive two-volume work, but we certainly have his testimony that the Socialist movement in Great Britain: " … derived its inspiration far more from the Sermon on the Mount than from the teachings of the economists" (vol. 1: 63).

are understood to have contributed later to environmental disaster, all come to mind, not to mention the topic of religion in general—as Braude points out when she discusses the "squeamishness" of social historians unwilling to acknowledge the role of religion in radical politics.[53]

Concerning Spiritualism, the obvious and immediate appeal was not only contact with the dead as "evidence and proof" of an afterlife for the recently bereaved—although this is not to be taken lightly. If death is the ultimate threat of power that the wealthy and powerful have over histories' poor masses, not to the mention the constant accompaniment of realities of poor health, housing, and food, then somehow breaking the "final separation" of death is already clearly a potentially radical notion—and frankly a notion that cuts to the very heart of the meaning of the Christian cross as a symbol of earliest Christianity's defiance of the Roman occupation forces in Palestine. Secondly, however, there is the matter of "direct access." Not only was the movement founded on a radically "democratic" idea of direct access to spiritual truths and experience unmediated by institutional leadership or constraints (it is no accident that among the earliest adherents to Spiritualism were Quakers), this connection becomes clearer when it is established by the evidence that radical politics and Spiritualism were often very closely associated. Braude's work focused on the significance of women in leadership in Spiritualism, making serious contributions to women's status in wider society. Following Braude's work, Daggett (2016) and Clark's (2017) studies of Spiritualism among people of color in New Orleans also focused on the obvious fact that the *politics* of Spiritualism would clearly be affected by one's emphasis on the particular "spirits" that are called upon for guidance. In sum, it is one thing to wish to speak to your grandmother, but becomes something else when a group of African-Americans seek to speak to Haitian revolutionary leaders like Toussaint L'Ouverture.

Thus, we can make two observations. First, these two rare discussions by Hardie have been clearly exaggerated in significance by the biographers in order to emphasize Hardie's "heterodox" character—clearly aiming to remove Hardie as much as possible from the "stains" of a serious Christian faith. Even more significantly, however, we can now point out that such interests would hardly be an indication of Hardie being somehow distracted from the serious work of socialism—these religious interests were arguably, and especially in nineteenth-century Britain, *part and parcel of his radical politics*. In short, the nineteenth-century context of practices like Spiritualism are found to be unusually consistent with Hardie's involvement with the "democratic" spirit of the Scottish "Morisonian" critique of Calvinist orthodoxy of "limited salvation," and entirely consistent with religious political radicalism. These (rare) expressions of interest in what is now seen as "eccentricities" do not, in fact, detract from the otherwise overwhelming confirmation of Hardie's commitments to a profoundly *Christian* Socialism.

---

53. Braude, *Radical Spirits*, xvii.

The need to emphasize this in the face of the best biographies (that nonetheless fail us on this topic) is clear when we cite Benn's rare acknowledgments of the importance of religion to Hardie:

> Some in the socialist movement saw a ... danger in the supernatural views of men like Hardie and Smith – in their allegiance to the unreason of religion ... Many rationalists and secular socialists never understood, and therefore distrusted, the Christian and temperance tradition in which so many working people had been raised. This was a split at least as great – and certainly as enduring – as that between Marxist and non-Marxists, which Labour historians make so much of retrospectively. Many Marxists were secularists, but so also were hard-headed journalists like Blatchford, and many Fabians. And within the SDF there were still those with religious views – like [Tom] Mann. Hyndman wrote scornfully of Mann's and Hardie's 'queer jumble of Asiatic mysticism and supernatural juggling ... called Christianity.'[54]

However, based on even a cursory consideration of the overwhelming evidence of Hardie's frequent interest in Biblical discussion in the pages of Hardie's newspapers, and especially *The Labour Leader*, Benn is clearly exaggerating when she claims:

> Although Hardie was firmly rooted in the religious tradition, his own commitment to religion – in the organized form of its earlier days – was declining. He particularly disliked the nonconformist churches, dominated, as he had experienced, by professional and trades people. The popular myth may have grown since Methodism and not Marxism fuelled British socialism, but Wesley's tradition, peopled by wealthy industrialists, had grown respectable by the middle of the nineteenth century ... it was this establishment that became Hardie's main political target.[55]

Here again, I believe Holman was entirely justified in responding to these same overstatements. Referring to Benn's similar tendency to want to emphasize Hardie's unorthodox views,[56] Holman objects: "Yet his statements showed that his Christianity remained rooted in traditional beliefs. He often cited verses from the Bible and accepted them as truth."[57]

The fact remains, Hardie's international speaking and organizing, domestic speaking and preaching, and service in Parliament, however, do not entirely salvage his reputation among the doctrinaire Marxists. Although Morgan cites the

---

54. Benn, *Hardie*, 106.
55. Benn, *Hardie*, 106-107.
56. Echoed by Reid, *Keir Hardie: The Making of a Socialist*, 183, and one begins to suspect if Reid isn't a source of some of this line of reasoning on Hardie in Benn's work.
57. Holman, *Keir Hardie: Labour's Greatest Hero?*, 198.

opinion of G. D. H. Cole to the effect that Hardie was a: "woolly minded romantic who contributed nothing to the intellectual content of the labour movement,"[58] in his own evaluation, Morgan expresses Hardie's "flexible radicalism" by stating that Hardie "Created a Marx, as he created a Christ, in his own image."[59] Morgan expands on this:

> Hardie's vague vision of founding 'Christ's Kingdom on Earth' with Jesus, the working-class son of Joseph the Carpenter, as 'the elder brother and the Great Comrade', was inspirational. It fired the imagination of thousands of working men of nonconformist background caught up in the economic depression and the class warfare of the late Victorian and Edwardian eras. But the vision was subordinate to the reality of creating a self-conscious party of the workers and their middle-class sympathizers.[60]

Similarly, while Benn admits that Hardie " ... did not abandon Christianity ... " she wants to emphasize that he " ... began a crusade against 'churchianity', claiming that 'the rich and comfortable classes have annexed Jesus' and made him a 'symbol of respectability rather than a force to combat social evils.'"[61] This, however, is not to comment on whether Hardie's Christianity was important to him or not—but rather his critique of *majority church life* in Britain. Benn more helpfully describes the fact that Hardie had a great deal of company in this period, although seriously misreads John Trevor's theological ideas when she claims that Hardie's:

> ... development was parallel in the Labour Church movement, where various clergy began establishing religious centres to link working-class politics and religion. One of the first was John Trevor's Church in Bradford, established in 1891. Inside Labour Churches, class-conscious arguments from preachers like Ben Tillett were heard, criticizing existing nonconformity for excluding working people. Services were indistinguishable from political meetings; when Christ's name was introduced into one of Tillett's addresses, there was prolonged applause. The doctrine was simple, God had a "divine plan" which people had to implement in society, like a political manifesto. Carlyle, Ruskin, Walt Whitman and Morris were "teachers and prophets" along with Isaiah and Christ.[62]

Benn continues, somewhat awkwardly, to suggest that:

> Hardie did not reject orthodox Christianity any more than he rejected orthodox Marxism. He ignored them both and concentrated on the socialism that he

---

58. Morgan, *Keir Hardie: Radical and Socialist*, 201.
59. Morgan, *Keir Hardie: Radical and Socialist*, 203.
60. Morgan, *Keir Hardie: Radical and Socialist*, 217.
61. Benn, *Hardie*, 107.
62. Benn, *Hardie*, 107.

perceived to be common to both. What gave his emerging views coherence was his passion to preach the gospel of socialism, not as ideology but as religion: 'Socialism is the modern word for Christianity' he claimed. Morgan sees Hardie's earlier religious conversion preceding the later socialism. In fact, they were one and the same, the first now absorbed into the second until they were virtually indistinguishable ... In a growing commitment to socialism Hardie also rediscovered the faith he had found in religion as a young man ...[63]

With respect, these are the observations of non-theologians—but if we are expected to pay close attention to the niceties of differing forms of Marxist analysis—orthodox or heterodox—it doesn't seem out of line to expect attention to details of theology.

The issue at stake here can be simply stated: If Hardie can be safely distanced from Christianity by exaggerating his unorthodox, fringe, or eccentric notions, then it is even easier for secularists to dismiss *all* of Hardie's religious ideas as equally peripheral to Hardie's historic importance to socialism and labour organizing. It would obviously follow, then, that any attention paid to Hardie's reading of the Bible would be as meaningless a distraction as religion itself. Yet the amount of evidence in Hardie's own life and work that must be dismissed or overlooked to arrive at this conclusion is breathtaking.

There is simply no evidence in reading through the pages of *The Labour Leader*, evidence so prolific that even this work focusing on Hardie's discussion of Bible can only summarize the extent of it, that Christianity and the Bible was ever of less interest to Hardie (and many of his readers, judging from the letters sent in). Furthermore, the preoccupations of "orthodox" or "unorthodox" are more reflective, it seems, of intra-Marxist arguments as much as, if not more than, comments on the Christianity of Hardie. Benn, as others, seems to presume a form of Christian "orthodoxy" that doesn't allow for interpretation, nuance, or change. That is to say, if you differ from some pre-determined "orthodoxy" (defined, one presumes, by majority Anglican, Scottish Calvinist, or Methodist Confessions of Faith), then you are somehow "leaving" Christianity. One is constantly reading in the biographies, for example statements such as Benn (and here partially citing Morgan) stating that Hardie's socialism "cannot be termed Marxist," but then gratuitously adding: "nor would many say his religion could be termed Christianity."[64] This is wooden thinking, and particularly ill-informed given Hardie's occasional references to a much wider variety of Christian interpretations in history—including his awareness of Anabaptist movements and other Christian radicalism. Yet, Benn captures moments that should have cautioned her about proposing any kind of diminution of Hardie's faith—such as the occasion when walking with friends around Norwich Cathedral in the evening, when Hardie's

---

63. Benn, *Hardie*, 107.
64. Benn, *Hardie*, 260.

booming voice was heard over the crowd starting a recitation of Psalm 23.[65] Finally we consider a speaking engagement later in Hardie's life that is now emerging as much more significant than all the biographers have supposed, not only for Hardie, but for Christian Socialism in France.

In Lille, France, 1910

There is one final example in this series of arguments about the significance of Hardie's Biblical Socialism and his Christianity, and thus its centrality to his political work. The later biographers all cite what appear to be Hardie's "offbeat" interests and then simply miss the significance of some events. An excellent example is Hardie's invited attendance at a special conference in Lille, France in 1910, representing the British "National Council of the Pleasant Sunday Afternoon" (started by Congregational Protestants in UK). Even an earlier biographer like Stewart, simply concluded that this visit was "another opportunity for preaching Socialism and international good will …."[66] But Stewart goes on to note that Hardie delivered a speech which:

> made him even more than ever a man of mystery to the scientific Socialists who found in the materialist conception of history the only key to the explanation of every problem. What kind of a Socialist could he be who said, 'Behind nature there is a Power, unseen but felt. Beyond death there is a Something, else were life on earth a mere wastage,' and who declared, 'I myself have found in the Christianity of Christ the inspiration which first of all drove me into the movement and has carried me on in it.' Yet this man was an advocate of the general strike. They could not understand him. Nor could the commercialized professors of Christianity. To both he was an enigma.[67]

Once again—there is much more to this—and an interest in theology would have led biographers to pursue this a bit further. In recent studies, thankfully, we do have considerable light shed on the significance of this visit.

In Chalamet's excellent 2018 analysis of French Christian socialism, this event in Lille is given its due appreciation.[68] As Chalamet argues, an important number of leaders among Protestant French Christians were moving in directions very similar to Hardie—namely Christian Socialism—and among these movements was the one that led to the "Foyer du peuple" (The People's Hall) in Lille, precisely the movement that had invited Hardie to come and speak. "The People's Hall" was

---

65. Benn, *Hardie*, 120.
66. Stewart, *Keir Hardie: A Biography*, 303.
67. Stewart, *Keir Hardie: A Biography*, 303.
68. Christophe Chalamet, *Revivalism and Social Christianity: The Prophetic Faith of Henri Nick and André Trocmé* (Cambridge: Lutterworth Press, 2017), 32–6.

founded by French Christian Socialist Henri Nick, and already by 1900, Nick's movement incorporated both Bible studies for local workers, but also many social activities and meetings, and was a ministry " … that did not hide its sympathies with socialist ideals."[69]

In fact, Chalamet clarifies that the invitation to Hardie to address the large gathering in Lille in 1910 was "one of the highlights of the life of the Foyer du Peuple before the first World War."[70] Furthermore, Chalamet explains that the mundane sounding "Pleasant Sunday Afternoon" Society (a group dedicated to rest, especially for workers, which was invited to send delegates to the same event) boasted 2,000 different chapters and half a million members, and 300 chapters in London alone.[71] Among the other speakers was Professor Paul Passy, an outspoken French Christian Socialist who later grew impatient with the moderation of some French Christian Socialists and formed the more assertive group based in France: "The Union of Socialist Christians."[72] Chalamet notes that this 1910 event was considered a "very successful gathering," reported widely in European newspapers, and even came to the attention of the influential American Social Gospeler, Walter Rauchenbusch.[73] Finally, Chalamet explains that the people engaged in these French movements, including the main organizers of the 1910 event, would go on to have a profound influence on the ideas of the young André Trocmé, the famous pastor of "Le Chambon," who has gained considerable notoriety for leading his village's provision of safe houses that saved over 3,500 French Jews in defiance of officials in Nazi-Occupied France. Trocmé, of course, is today justifiably famous among Protestant Christians for his courage and writings, and Chalamet has also clarified his lesser known, but equally firm commitment, as a Christian *Socialist*.

In sum, Chalamet's study brings an entire movement, French Protestant "Christian Socialism" (called "Social Christianity" for most of its early twentiety-century existence), into the light for English readers, and sheds light on the ramifications of Hardie's involvement. The founder of "Social Christianity," namely Tommy Fallot, wrote:

> Socialism has drawn a good deal of its program from the Gospel. It seeks to build society on the pillars of justice, something the Gospel seeks to do as well. In that regard, a condemnation of socialism would represent a condemnation of the Gospel and the prophets.[74]

Hardie's own involvement takes on added significance in the light of this recent research and adds more to the perfunctory observations in the biographies such as

69. Chalamet, *Revivalism and Social Christianity*, 27.
70. Chalamet, *Revivalism and Social Christianity*, 32.
71. Chalamet, *Revivalism and Social Christianity*, 32.
72. Chalamet, *Revivalism and Social Christianity*, 33.
73. Chalamet, *Revivalism and Social Christianity*, 34.
74. Citing Fallot, in Chalamet, *Revivalism and Social Christianity*, 15.

Morgan's that throughout this time, Hardie maintained "his international interests," and summarizes that Hardie's "Christian beliefs in brotherhood informed his internationalist interests."[75] Nevertheless, Chalamet's study clearly places Hardie in dialogue with the movement involving a figure like André Trocmé, and perhaps suggests a more significant assessment of Hardie's "international interests."

We have particularly interesting sources about Hardie's involvement. The first is an article in *The Labour Leader*, June 3, 1910; the second is Conner's 1917 pamphlet on the life of Hardie, which chooses to highlight this event among those he selected for a 26-page biography, and a 1912 report written by the President of the "Brotherhood Movement."[76]

The article in *The Labour Leader* signed "W.W." is undoubtedly to be identified as William Ward, the president of the National Council of Pleasant Sunday Afternoons, who himself appealed to Hardie to speak. When the meetings were determined to be located in Lille, a significant manufacturing district, it was determined that Hardie would be the obvious choice. As Conner reports, Hardie was paraded

> not to the palaces and mansions of the rich but following the example of the Master, to the headquarters of the workers where the poor dwell. They were to meet at Bourse du Travail where the working class organizations of the district were waiting to receive them.[77]

The most significant pronouncement of the day was made by Hardie when he declared that the impetus which directed him in his life's work had been derived more from the teachings of Jesus Christ than all other sources combined and he finished up with the remarkable statement, "we have sown on this continent the seed of the Gospel of Jesus Christ. It may have to be watered with tears and even made wet with blood but a bountiful harvest is sure to be reaped."[78]

Conner reports the observations of Professor Passy (who is identified by Chalamet as "a well-known professor at the Ecole des Hautes Etudes and a militant socialist as well as a Christian," who reported in L'Espoir du Monde on the event[79]) that one might have doubted whether the workers gathered there were willing to listen to words about Jesus Christ and the Gospel, but (stated Passy):

> … They were soon reassured, however. This man with the strenuous and yet kindly aspect was it not their Keir Hardie, the old collier whose devotion to the working classes had been affirmed a thousand times? Were not those who

---

75. Morgan, *Keir Hardie: Radical and Socialist*, 179.
76. P. W. Wilson, "The Brotherhood Movement," *The Contemporary Review* 102 (1912): 680–7.
77. Conner, *Jas. Keir Hardie's Life Story*, 20.
78. Chalamet, *Revivalism and Social Christianity*, 33–4.
79. Chalamet, *Revivalism and Social Christianity*, 33–4.

gathered round him Delory and Ghesqmere their own socialist members of parliament ... there was no need to fear a trap, they might rest assured that their own impressions would guide them correctly ... Then the interest turned to approval which gradually became more and more ardent, and towards the end of Keir Hardie's speech it was with stampings of enthusiasm that these men who both call themselves and believe themselves to be materialists cheered the words of the old Scotch tribune on the fatherhood of God and the work of Jesus Christ. For a moment it seemed as if the people had rediscovered their Saviour. However, I feel that I am perfectly right in saying that a breach has been made in the thick ramparts of prejudice that separates our people from the true gospel. All those who applauded the orator at Lille can now say in all sincerity: it is not true that a man who believes in God, who loves Jesus Christ, is necessarily a participant in exploitation and tyranny. All can say, as Keir Hardie said, that it was the spirit of Christ which leads men to take up the cause of the oppressed without being a hypocrite or imbecile.[80]

In Ward's lengthy report in the June 3 (1910) edition of *The Labour Leader*, a fuller account of Hardie's message is provided. Ward writes:

Mr. Hardie described the Brotherhood movement as an association for the promotion of fellowship, whose aim was to unite all who accept the social teachings of Jesus. It does not recognize any particular creed, nor is it attached to any particular church. Taking the teachings of Jesus as set forth in the four gospels it seeks to interpret and apply the spirit of these to the problems of modern life.

Hardie, writes Ward, "frankly acknowledged the spirit of materialism that was a dominant factor of the early Socialist movement ...," but this was a response to "clericalism" which was "but a misrepresentation of Christianity." Lately, however, there has been a "remarkable and gratifying" change:

It is now becoming more clearly recognized that Socialism is at the bottom not merely an economic, but a moral question. It stood for the bringing about of right relationships among men for an equal opportunity for all to develop their God-given faculties, and live a full, free, and glorious life ... to the Socialist and Labour men who clearly apprehend this, Christ's teaching should appeal with irresistible power. He did not merely denounce those that were rich: Christ's Gospel teaches us that life is the only thing of value, and that the possession of property comes between a man and the development of his life ... Christianity on its social side can never be realized if it is to be interpreted in the light of Christ's teaching, until there is full, free Communism, and the very idea of private property has disappeared from men's minds. It is true that Christ founded no

---

80. Conner, *Jas. Keir Hardie's Life Story*, 21.

party. He formulated no economic doctrine, but He laid down principles so broad and deep that when these come to be applied, as one day they will be applied when the world grows wider, not only will poverty due to lack of bread have disappeared, but poverty due to the accumulation of riches shall also have disappeared from the world. The broadening concepts of Christianity, which were becoming more common every day, were an important factor in the case. It was now being recognized that religion sweetens, purifies, and hallows every relationship. The rich and comfortable classes had annexed Jesus and perverted His Gospel. And yet He belongs to the workers in a special degree, and the Brotherhood movement is tending to restore Jesus to His rightful place as the Friend and Saviour of the poor. 'I am here,' added Mr. Keir Hardie, 'to ask you as a Socialist and Labour man not to rule out the principles of Christianity. I myself have found in the Christianity of Christ the inspiration which first of all drove me into the Movement, and which has carried me on in it.'

A remarkable demonstration followed the conclusion of the speech. The large audience, composed mostly of French Socialists, with a sprinkling of Belgian and Dutch comrades, cheered vociferously. Then, at the instigation of M. Ghesquiere, Socialist Deputy of Lille, three verses of 'L'Internationale' were sung by the French, in which many of the English joined, followed by three verses of 'All Hail the Power of Jesus' Name' by the English, joined by several Frenchmen. Thus terminated one of the most remarkable meetings ever held on the continent.[81]

We need only briefly cite Wilson's 1912 report of the same event:

At whitsuntide, 1910, there occurred at Lille in France an event, the significance of which can scarcely be exaggerated. A British Brotherhood Deputation visited the city, accompany by Mr. Keir Hardie. In a great hall, 2000 French workman – materialist, agnostic, and atheist – heard from Mr. Keir Hardie an address which they regarded as absolutely sensational. He declared that 'the impetus which directed him to his life's work, and the inspiration which has carried him on it have been derived more from the teachings of Jesus Christ than from any other source. A test question for men and movements is: What think ye of Christ?' An extraordinary scene followed. The audience sang 'L'Internationale' and afterwards the British delegates responded with 'All Hail the Power of Jesus' Name,' which the French Socialists encored.[82]

Such events in the life of Hardie raise serious questions about biographers who frequently attempt to minimize the significance of both Scripture and Christian

---

81. Ward, *The Labour Leader*, June 3, 1910
82. Wilson, "The Brotherhood Movement," 687.

faith in the life of Hardie, whether early or late in his life. This chapter has, I believe, built a reasonable case that a study of Hardie's use of the Bible is a fair way to assess part of his life and impact.

SUMMARY

While there is no doubt that "heterodox" material is rare in his writing, the very fact that it is raised so often suggests that the idea here, to put it crudely, seems to be that biographers want to say to British Christians, in so many words, "Well, he certainly wasn't YOUR kind of Christian!" Such suggestions, however, only beg further (theological!) questions. For starters, this is a highly questionable approach because it typically ends up comparing Hardie's working-class context for his version of Christianity against mainline notions—typically represented by academic or fundamentalist religious literature. Yet, we have seen that Hardie himself frequently contrasts his faith against official versions of the churches.

Furthermore, if interest in culture/ethnic mythology (e.g., Celtic stories, indigenous Scottish mythologies and traditions, etc.), Spiritualism (including "ghost stories"), or other unusual mystical notions would question one's full commitment to Christianity, a class-based analysis of the religious interests of many European working-class populations would soon disabuse anyone from believing that these were rare ideas among the faithful! Indeed, if the Bible *itself* is subject to such an analysis, it reveals that there are passages that reveal the "beliefs" and "practices" of Israelites themselves often included the decidedly unorthodox! (1 Sam. 28; Jer. 44, etc.).

In short, to note the difference between the Christianity of the academy and the Christianity of the factories and mines is not to observe how "less Christian" the working classes are—it is rather to observe that their Christianity is interestingly made functional for themselves—or in other words—precisely the point of this study in attempting to identify "Proletarian Exegesis." It is also precisely the point of this study to show how Hardie's use of Scripture reveals not merely a creative person at work, but a person that obviously and undeniably sees Scripture as central to what he is doing. I acknowledge that Benn was not always entirely antagonistic to Hardie's faith, as when she proposes that:

> What gave Hardie his strength as an agitator was his ethical perspective. Capitalism was epitomized by the 'selfish greed of each for himself,' while socialism was an 'instinct' in each of us, 'that highest impulse to share.' The ring of religion was always heard. 'Faith without works is dead' and capitalism 'in the end is bound to work its own overthrow,' equivalent messages he found in all major world religions. Hardie believed each such religion (however subsequently commandeered by the state or by power-seekers) had started with the plight of the common people, and was a political movement; just as he believed scientific socialism was an ethical commandment ... His flexible, humanitarian, but

essentially cultural socialism, long thought to be so outdated, today assumes a new importance in a world where millions of people's politics are still confined to expression through their religion.[83]

Before we turn to a more direct consideration of Hardie's reading of the Bible, I will leave the last words of this chapter on "Hardie and Religion" to the Reverend Rowland Jones of Troedyrhiw, in South Wales, paying tribute to Hardie after his death, in the October 2, 1915 edition of *The Merthyr Pioneer*, which featured a number of "Letters in Memory of Hardie." Jones, recalling his attendance at a political speech of Hardie's, wrote:

> I remember Hardie's stirring speech. I can recall now his serious furrowed face, his stentorian voice, and impassioned appeals. I have never been able, although young at the time, to forget that event … The people who called Hardie an atheist never made a greater mistake. It is true that Hardie never made a loud profession of religion like many of his detractors, but if ever a truly religious man lived in this country, that man was Keir Hardie. That night he spoke to me like a seer about God. Jesus Christ, Eternity, and Prayer. I can assure you I felt quite astonished, because Hardie never displayed the inner sanctities of his soul. 'I believe in God,' he said, 'And I believe in prayer.' … Hardie's attitude towards the Christian Church was greatly misunderstood by a large section of the public. I have no doubt that he himself was responsible, to a large degree, for this misunderstanding. I told him once about some of his indiscriminate utterances about the churches and ministers and he replied with some heat that he was a friend to every church that lived the Christian Gospel, and to every minister who had courage enough to preach against the evils that destroyed the lives of men. He was not ashamed he said, to be the uncompromising enemy of every Laodicean Church that kept Christ outside its doors and allowed pride and bigotry and ignorance to reign within.

The very reference to a "Laodicean Church" in Hardie's rhetoric is itself an indication of the sophistication of his Biblical knowledge—referring to the "lukewarm" status of one of the churches in the book of Revelation (3:14–15)—in other words, decidedly "in house" language.

Before we turn to a survey of Hardie's scriptural arguments, we need to establish one further important "context," namely those "allies" that were arguably closest (and likely influential) to Hardie himself.

---

83. Benn, *Hardie*, 433.

Figure 4.1 "The Socialist Sower," *The Labour Leader*, May 5, 1894.

Chapter 4

THE "FAMILY OF FAITH": HARDIE'S CLOSE ALLIES IN "BIBLICAL" CHRISTIAN SOCIALISM

The significance of the Bible as a text for defending socialism has, we have seen in Chapters 1–2, a celebrated history in the US and UK especially. No longer is this treated as the somewhat amusing and exaggerated idea, or mere crowd-pleasing window-dressing, of socialist rhetoric caught up in the enthusiasm of the moment. Catterall, for example, draws attention to Clement Attlee's interesting observation that: "'There are probably more texts from the Bible enunciated from Socialist platforms than those of all other parties,'" and Catterall comments further that: "It cannot be assumed that this was simply because of the numbers of lay preachers accustomed to building their arguments upon a scriptural passage, active in the Labour movement."[1] Catterall, insightfully, takes note of the fact that there is something of a "hermeneutics" of British socialism in its use of particular passages of the Bible:

> ... The Bible did not ... merely lend itself to such uses. It conjured up images of a providential order blighted by the self-seeking nature of Capitalism ... The spirit of the text, 'He who would be greatest among you let him be servant of all' (Matthew 23.11) was presented as virtually absent from the ethics of the existing economic order ... The language and nature of the Bible furnished ready material for such condemnations. 'What modern Labour man,' asked Keir Hardie in 1912, 'ever used the same strong language towards the rich as Christ did?' [The Bible] ... also provided a stock of familiar precepts such as 'Feed my lambs' that could serve Labour rhetoric, even for atheists like Jack and Bessie Braddock. This was a favourite passage that Rhys Davies, the Congregationalist and Labour MP for Westhoughton, turned to when he wished to remind the Bolton guardians of their responsibilities to dependents of the miners locked out in 1926. So frequently did Bob Smillie resort to this sort of use of scripture during the Royal Commission on the coal industry in 1919 that one of his fellow commissioners, Lord Durham, was moved to ask, 'Is this an ecclesiastical examination?'[2]

---

1. Catterall, *Labour and the Free Churches*, 147.
2. Catterall, *Labour and the Free Churches*, 147–8.

Catterall further suggests that the historical context for which parts of Scripture were preferred may well be attributed to the issues of the day. Nineteenth-century radicals drew on the Old Testament more often, suggests Catterall, because land issues were part of the Chartist activism of England, and the anti-Highland Clearances of the Scottish mid-nineteenth century. But, suggests Catterall, the war years inspired a shift to emphases on peace as well, which interestingly enough brought St. Paul back into use based on the famous "Love" chapter of 1 Corinthians 13. On John 15:12:

> These texts also provided the guiding principles of in which 'Service, Brotherhood, Love (or to call love by its economic equivalent, co-operation), must be the basis of our social system instead of self-interest, individualism and competition.'[3]

In this chapter, we will focus on some of Hardie's clear "allies" to further establish a "hermeneutical context" for Hardie's own comments.

In relation to this, there are a number of reasons why this chapter alludes to Paul's reference to Christian compatriots as the "family" (NRSV, one can read the Greek: "household") of faith (Gal. 6:10). First, although there were many "Christian Socialists" of the late nineteenth century with whom Hardie certainly had sympathies, there are a handful of allies who not only shared Hardie's interest in "Christian Socialism," but were regularly featured in *The Labour Leader*, where Hardie advertised their pamphlets, reported on their speeches, and even more notably, reported (sometimes at length) their (mis)treatment by church authorities (particularly in the case of Dennis Hird, who was himself a clergyman until his exile from the Anglican Church). In the case of young Caroline Martyn, we also have the extended obituary that, even after a century, is still quite moving. It expresses how she had obviously made a lasting impression on large numbers of people who heard her speak. She died before she was thirty years old. In addition to Martyn, we will also briefly consider the Biblical arguments of Dennis Hird and John Morrison Davidson.

Second, however, and more importantly, this chapter will attempt to show that Hardie shared some interesting scriptural arguments with these allies, suggesting that we can identify "key texts" used by these Christian Socialists, especially in Hardie's inner circle, to argue the "biblical basis" for their political views.

Third, however, we will begin with a clarification of an issue that turns up in a few recent historical articles—the relation of Hardie's "theology" to the famous "Labour Church" movement.

Hardie and the Labour Church

There are significant differences in the way that "religious" Socialists made their case in print. It is helpful to cite one important example of these differences by way of briefly

---

3. Catterall, *Labour and the Free Churches*, 148.

discussing a person whose life and witness were certainly appreciated by Hardie—but who was hardly in the same category as the three we are mainly concerned with here, namely the founder of the famous "Labour Church" movement, John Trevor.

The "Labour Church" movement in the late nineteenth century has been the topic of considerable interest and discussion, and Trevor is not only considered the main founder of the movement, but also served as editor of a publication known as "The Labour Prophet." Although Trevor certainly published a number of "what we believe" type articles, a better consideration of his own theological journey is contained in his "spiritual autobiography" entitled: *My Quest for God* (1897). In this highly personal, often "diary-like" work, Trevor tracks his personal journey from a rather strict, Calvinist "free-church" childhood in England, toward Unitarianism (for a time), through to his own quite personal version of his religious faith—a faith which he himself clearly differentiated from either a "Biblical faith" or even "Christianity." Indeed, Trevor often mentioned Christianity as the religion that: "I left," and therefore remained only in his past—finding "God with a closed Bible."[4] But he insisted (and one has little reason to doubt) that he maintained a strong sense of spirituality nonetheless, throughout his years, and his founding of the "Labour Church" (although his own direct participation was short-lived) was based on much more generalized ideals of a lived spirituality.

What is certainly communicated in Trevor's "spiritual autobiography" is a whole-hearted man who struggled inwardly and spiritually, but nonetheless was financially able to sustain a rather significant wanderlust in his life. In long periods between jobs, he made visits to Australia and the United States, and spent long periods of idle residence in the countryside to "commune with nature" and work out his ideas about God and humanity. Trevor's contact with actual working people was, at best, only occasional, even though Trevor himself considers these rare but actual interactions with working people to be important in his thinking through his ideas. Finally, of course, although Trevor was uncertain about how influential he considers the years in the USA to have been, he did, in fact, study Theology formally during two years in the United States (Meadville Theological School) and another year at Manchester College in the UK. Thus, Trevor's life was decidedly middle class and his actual contact with labourers was exceedingly rare, and his theology even more rarified.

What is important to note here is not whether Hardie considered Trevor a friend and colleague, which he certainly did, nor whether Hardie had any interest in the Labour Church, which he also clearly did. Barrow is exaggerating somewhat when he claims that the Labour Church was virtually the ILP at prayer,[5] even though many have noted the "close relationship"[6] with many ILP members. In short,

---

4. John Trevor, *My Quest for God* (London: Labour Prophet Office, 1897), 200.

5. Barrow, "Socialism in Eternity," 43.

6. Mark Bevir, *The Making of British Socialism* (Princeton: Princeton University Press, 2011), 288. Cf. recent monographs: Neal Johnson, *The Labour Church: The Movement & Its Message*, Routledge Studies in Radical History and Politics (London: Routledge, 2018); Jacqueline Turner, *The Labour Church: Religion and Politics in Britain, 1890-1914* (London and New York: I. B. Tauris, 2018).

interesting though it may be, Trevor's theology appears to have had only passing resemblance to, and even less *impact* on, Hardie's own thinking and rhetoric. One can immediately sense the difference between Trevor's speculative approach to a "passage" from a Bible-based faith, and Hardie's Biblical-centered approach, when Trevor writes:

> It never occurred to me to attempt the passage by a new interpretation of the Old Book. I knew now that this Old Book was less than Life, that a Book Religion could never again satisfy my soul, and that this Jewish Literature, on which my life had been built, could never be anything to me again, until I had learned a larger truth and life in God himself.[7]

While Hardie was aware of some scholarly doubts being raised in nineteenth-century academic Biblical Studies, he rarely allows this to reduce his interest in citing the Gospels and the example of Jesus. Contrast this with Trevor's apparent embrace of this issue of historical "authenticity" as defined in his time period:

> We need no longer charge our consciences with accepting as true documents that which wise men tell us are of very doubtful authenticity. We may be able to read weighty reasons for concluding that Jesus never preached the Sermon on the Mount or uttered the Lord's Prayer, without any thought that such conclusions have any relation to our religious life. But though we no longer lie under the heavy responsibility of taking our religion from a book, and of demanding that others shall do likewise, we lie under a burden of obligation still harder to bear, namely, that of making our own lives and consciences so true that they shall be the means of giving us an interpretation of life, not absolutely true, but on the lines of truth, and of progress towards higher knowledge.[8]

This is not to say that there are not significant "moments" of similarity. Trevor's embrace of the condemnation by Jesus of religious authorities is a theme Hardie came back to many times, and Trevor alludes to a similar "passion" in Jesus:

> ... in a world where Sorrow, Oppression and Wrong stalk abroad, absence of passion indicates absence of life, however keen the intellect. Among those who really live, passion of some sort must arise, whether with a blessing on its lips, or a curse; for the wild curse, as Jesus cursed, is infinitely more hopeful than a mere mild message of good will, or the method of following the line of least resistance. At best the Churches still linger with the Jesus in Galilee. They have not begun to understand the Jesus of Jerusalem.[9]

---

7. Trevor, *My Quest for God*, 64.
8. Trevor, *My Quest for God*, 217.
9. Trevor, *My Quest for God*, 138.

In the end, however, Trevor was not interested in a Christianity that was rooted in any way in the interpretation of Biblical texts:

> in place of Systems of Philosophy and Systems of Religion, we shall have Biographies and Autobiographies, which fetter nobody ... No one can stake out the road to God for another. The whole conception of there being Systems and Ways and Masters and Guide-books is a very childish one, and one that man will grow out of – some day.[10]

One could argue that there is a somewhat odd disconnect between Trevor's treasured individuality, and the communal values essential to a discussion of socialist activism. In fact, just as such a radical individualism can clearly have a rather acid-like impact on common efforts toward some level of shared religious understanding, it has classically lent itself to far more "anarchist" political ideals: " ... I wanted a democratic faith, a religion which made me equal with all, though still different from all ...."[11]

Clearly, Hardie is not one to be deeply sympathetic with Trevor's pilgrimage to: " ... find God with a closed Bible,"[12] even if he would wholeheartedly agree with the notion that "otherworldliness is a mistake."[13] After all, Trevor could at times be downright profound, noting such gems as the following: "to the man who lives, his study is not his school but his workshop."[14] Hardie, as was typical for him, was quite open to allies wherever he found them, to the point of often enduring criticism of his lack of dedication to precise "socialist [read: Marxist] doctrine." Hardie's newspaper often expressed sympathy with the Labour Church, and Hardie's editorial policy clearly included closely following events, speakers, and even controversies connected to the handful of Labour Churches judging from the frequent notices in *The Labour Leader*. But Trevor's movement did not provide the allies that are reflected in his own writing. In sum, the Biblical arguments are simply not there. To these we must now turn.

Allies in Hardie's "Proletarian Exegesis"

Caroline Martyn (1867–1896)

The three personalities that I want to highlight in this chapter are (Rev.) Dennis Hird, John Morrison Davidson, and Caroline Martyn. Of the three, far less is known about Caroline Martyn, but we do have the *Life and Letters of Caroline*

---

10. Trevor, *My Quest for God*, 180–1.
11. Trevor, *My Quest for God*, 193.
12. Trevor, *My Quest for God*, 200.
13. Trevor, *My Quest for God*, 263.
14. Trevor, *My Quest for God*, 227.

Martyn published in 1898.[15] This interesting work consists mostly of letters gathered with commentary provided by her cousin, Lena Wallis. In addition, it is notable how closely Caroline Martyn's speaking engagements were followed and noted in *The Labour Leader*, and Hardie was himself in attendance at her funeral, so it is significant to briefly consider her approach.

Martyn was born May 3, 1867, the first child of her parents. By 1874, she had three brothers and a sister, but yellow fever took the girl and one of the boys at a young age. There is little information about Martyn's death, but it seems exhaustion may have played a role—as all descriptions of her note the energy with which she threw herself into her work on behalf of socialist organizing and public speaking. As Wallis commented: "Those who knew her best during the last few years of her life alone knew how earnest and practical she was, and how she was willing to do anything—the merest drudgery—if she believed it would help forward the cause of Socialism."[16]

Sadly, we have few of her own writings, or even extensive notes of her presentation (that I could find, in any case), and we especially have no notes from her (apparently frequent) presentation on the topic: "Jesus and Socialism." Wallis argues frequently in her collection of Martyn's letters that central to Martyn's own life were her convictions about the relationship between her Christian faith and socialism as a practical expression of that faith. This is confirmed by Gerrard's recent commentary on the early supporters of the "Socialist Sunday School" (SSS) movement:

> Indeed, from the 'famously chapel-bred party' came many of the Socialist Sunday School movement's most ardent organizers and supporters, Archie McArthur, Keir Hardie, Lizzie Glazier, Caroline Martyn, and Margaret McMillan were all card-carrying ILP members. For these, and many other ... teachers, their rejection of atheism reflected a fervent belief in the necessity for socialist morality built upon selected Christian principles.[17]

In relation to this conviction about the "necessity" of Christian faith, Wallis writes:

> Caroline knew well how much the Socialist movement lost by its attitude towards Christianity, and she was anxious to reconcile the two in her own life. How well she succeeded those who know her, and loved her most, can tell. No one could possibly meet her, even in private life, without being strongly impressed with a sense of her love and loyalty to Jesus Christ. Nothing pleased her more than to know that her teaching on this subject was understood.[18]

---

15. Lena Wallis, ed., *Life and Letters of Caroline Martyn* (London: Labour Leader Publishing, 1898).

16. Wallis, *Life and Letters*, 34.

17. Jessica Gerrard, *Radical Childhoods: Schooling and the Struggle for Social Change* (Manchester: Manchester University Press, 2014), 68.

18. Wallis, *Life and Letters*, 91–2.

In this same discussion, Wallis comments on the occasion when Martyn happily spoke of a report she was sent after one of the speaking engagements on Socialism and Jesus, where, Martyn noted, the following lines appeared in the report: "I have heard many an expression of admiration for the teaching embodied therein, by many who wholly reject the teaching of Jesus Christ. This I know will give you great pleasure to hear!"[19]

The value of Wallis's collection is that it contains important correspondence wherein Martyn herself refers to the relationship of her faith and her socialist convictions and activities (with very little reference to Scripture, however). Wallis points, for example, to a letter Martyn wrote to her mother (who apparently always worried about her) with the following assurances. After insisting that she does not agree with "Anarchists and Revolutionaries," she explains that:

> All my Socialism I learnt, in the first place, in its broad outlines from the New Testament, and my only motive for endeavouring to propagate my views is that I believe that they are true practical Christianity. As Socialists we come into contact with the scum and off-scouring of the earth in our pursuit of duty, but then we do not consort (for lack of power) with the sinners and harlots whom Jesus came to seek and to save, and among whom He spent His life. We are in the world of coarseness and sin and horror – but not of it. Many of the Socialists are not Christians – they say the two things are incompatible. I am so awfully *ashamed* when they point out the difference between Christianity, in the usual acceptance of the term, and the teaching of Christ. They would rather love man whom they have seen than the God whom they know not – theoretically, I need not remind you of Christ's word on this point. Of course, some are splendid Christians and good Churchmen, a very great many clergymen are found in our ranks …[20]

Notable here is Martyn's careful differentiation between the behavior of churches and the teachings of Jesus, thus confirming Lowe's comment about Martyn, that " … Martyn came to Socialism from the New Testament."[21] This theme of differentiating the church teachings with Jesus Himself, we will see, is a frequent refrain in Hardie's discussions as well. In another exchange with her mother, we learn that Martyn's mother would frequently send articles and publications with highlighted sentences, apparently in efforts to get her daughter to slow down or be more careful about who she was associating with! Among these letters, it seems, were even (somewhat surprisingly) positive references to teachings from other religions when it suited her mother's attempts to get Caroline to slow down! In one interesting example, Caroline's mother had highlighted an insight attributed to the Buddha that "The Impulse to self-sacrifice must not be carried to foolish

---

19. Wallis, *Life and Letters*, 92.
20. Wallis, *Life and Letters*, 34.
21. Lowe, *Keir Hardie*, 105.

extremes." The occasion of her mother's pleading, however, also allows us to take note of Martyn's equally interesting openness to wisdom from other religious traditions even as a devoted Christian. After briefly answering her mother's case with a specifically Christian argument, she then reacts to her mother's apparent dismissal of the Buddhist concepts of Nirvana even in the context of recommending something from Buddhist thought (which we can well imagine she contrasted with Christianity). However, Caroline Martyn's socialist Christianity, it seems, was not so radically exclusive that she could not appreciate insights from beyond its formal writings. Martyn writes to her mother:

> 'The impulse to self-sacrifice must not be carried to foolish extremes' sounds very respectable, and is essentially an axiom of commonsense – but how about a foolish extreme of self-sacrifice that led a certain artisan, whom Christians call our great example, to give up the safe and respectable work of a carpenter in order to perambulate the country with no place to lay His head – who persisted in such self-sacrifice to such a foolish extreme that at last He clashed with the imperial authority and was executed? Again, you have marked a passage, which describes Nirvana as an idle, monotonous existence. I wish people, who denounce other people's religion and ideas, would just take the trouble to study what they are denouncing. Anyone who knows the history and philosophy of Buddha knows that it does not admit of any such final goal. Love as centre, ideal, perfection of existence, is taught as emphatically as in our Gospel, and the 'falling of the dew drop in the ocean' that much sneered at and wilfully misunderstood metaphor, does not preclude an ideal which includes no loss of individuality but the waking of a larger and wider infinite consciousness; the perfection of life and work in the perfection of love. But if this merging into a larger life is not intended, the ultimate result is left no more obscure or indefinite by Buddha than by Christ, who left the description of our ultimate goal as 'Eye hath not seen.' My own spiritual ideals are quite clear and certain, and all my work is done with a view to their attainment by the whole human race, but since I know the law of development, I am aware that those hopes are bounded by the present human limitations, and with growth higher places will develop themselves in the ever-lengthening vistas of Eternal Life.[22]

Among the concerns of her mother, shared apparently by other friends and associates of Martyn, was the common criticism of Socialism that it was necessarily atheist. Wallis wrote how much it "pained her to be termed an atheist," and quoted Martyn to argue that: "I believe the future prosperity of the Church depends on a very great measure upon its attitude towards Socialism."[23] But it is clear that Martyn shared the general Socialist Christian tendency to interpret the Bible, and especially the Gospels, as necessarily involving a very "this world" ethical behavior

---

22. Wallis, *Life and Letters*, 88–9.
23. Wallis, *Life and Letters*, 35.

4. The "Family of Faith": Hardie's Close Allies in "Biblical" Christian Socialism 99

and social philosophy. Wallis gives us a profound insight into Martyn's thinking on this matter in passages when she draws from Martyn's correspondence directly with her:

> I wish I could tell you how I long to be useful; it is not only to please the Father, nor to gratify the Son, but for the sake of alleviating the awful misery which afflicts our brother-men. I do not mean only in regard to material things, though physical development and care are necessary to the complete happiness of the human, neither do I mean only in regard to the mental darkness of ignorance, though reasoning power is also a necessity to full life; I am not even anxious to see all men moral in the conventional sense, for morality does not entail goodness or happiness; I do long to see men enjoy the bliss of the spiritual life ... In this only lately I have seen how perfect freedom is to be attained in the Christian life, but now I do know. If you love Jesus really, you desire what He desires; you have set the right ideal before you, and will not wish to swerve from the path that leads directly to it.[24]

In a passage which quite strikingly associates the Christian "Trinity" with the French Revolutionary "trinity" ("Liberté, Egalité, Fraternité"), Martyn gives a confession of faith:

> I believe there is a Creator who is infinitely good, and a Jesus Christ who is perfect and eternal, life and work, and happiness, and one Spirit that animates humanity, and is above all else. I believe evil to be an illusion which shall be annihilated with the Father of Lies. I believe our work is to aid the work of creation by advancing human development along the lines Christ has revealed—Love—which includes liberty, equality, brotherhood—physical, mental, and spiritual. This necessitates our resistance to all evil, whether it be dirt, disease, or lack of material necessities; whether it be ignorance, immorality, social ills, bad government, or lack of spiritual consciousness. Against every enemy of progress—human, social, individual, in government, life, education, religion—I pray God to make me a weapon. I vow to do my utmost to demolish sin, and ensure the ultimate return to God of every sinner.[25]

Martyn, however, agreed with a central aspect of the socialist Christian critique of their perception of contemporary church life, and spoke of her inability to: " ... square Christian ethics with the Christianity of ordinary profession and the Christianity—not as preached—but as practiced by the Churches ..., " and seemed resigned to the difficulties of being: " ... a Christian Socialist when all your friends are High Church Conservatives!"[26] There were also moments of profound insight

---

24. Wallis, *Life and Letters*, 86–7.
25. Wallis, *Life and Letters*, 87.
26. Wallis, *Life and Letters*, 88.

that Martyn wrote about. In the summer of 1894, she wrote that she: " … had my Pentecost, and so all life is touched with a new meaning …, " and while walking in Newsham Park in Liverpool, among woods and gardens, she wrote that her insights about the "this worldly" aspect of her faith was becoming clearer to her, but continues to affirm the importance of Biblical study for her work:

> The longer I live, and the more I learn, the more real grows the spiritual life. It is only lately that the soul and immortality have ceased to be a mere intellectual belief with me; now they are an ever-present consciousness, for I live in the spiritual life. It makes existence so beautiful and happy that sorrow is impossible … events appear in their true significance, and the eternal soul, which is one and indivisible, is all and in all. I think I have been much helped by coming into contact with so many people, and by the love and brotherhood which I have seen among our comrades; but most of all, of course, by my study of Christ, of Paul, and my attempt to actualize their teaching. As one grows older and wiser the supremacy of Jesus Christ as man, as teacher, as reformer, becomes more and more evident, until one feels and sees that in the spirit which inspired Him is indeed Nirvana, not the loss of individuality, but the growth into fullest consciousness.[27]

There is little doubt that Caroline Martyn made a lasting impression on any who came into contact with her—and the obituaries and reflections on her passing contain a real pathos. Her colleague who shared many of Caroline Martyn's interests in youth education and socialism, Margaret McMillan, wrote in a February 1908 edition of *The Labour Leader* some twelve years after her death:

> Our grand old men were not at all given to sentimentality. I don't think they had shed many tears in the course of their long lives. But I know that the sternest of them wept when Caroline Martyn died. This young girl made a great many people love her – that is certain. She didn't write any book. She didn't go on any public body. She was not in any official position in the party. There was hardly time for all that in her short life. But there was time to win love – and she won it. You would not learn from the papers – no, not from the Labour papers – how dear she was to the Labour people … there are some women who make flowers spring behind them, as Ruskin said, and there is no denying that Caroline Martyn did this. She made a pleasant track through the world. Through the northern cities she went, and her voice, her youth, her gentle ways, her sympathy were like the hands of Spring at the doors of factories, and the fragrance of Spring in the dull committee rooms and lecture halls. How glad she was to find the people, and how glad they were to find her. Her life was not a battle but a joyful meeting with the well-beloved. She stood already in the Vestibule of Home, and she was

---

27. Wallis, *Life and Letters*, 88.

about to enter into the very heart of this wide home of the people's heart … she died young. The aged wept for her, and a thousand said of her, 'She came, but she is gone.' She left them sorrowing, but, for the first time perhaps, expectant.[28]

Writing soon after her death, in an August 1896 edition of *The Labour Leader*, Hardie himself commented that on learning the news of her passing, "For a time, Socialists everywhere had that numbed feeling which follows some great catastrophe," and Hardie commented that he had just recently seen at a meeting in Manchester where: "She reminded me laughingly that it was at my recommendation she had gone north to take up the work of organizing the mill and factory workers, and said if she failed she would put the blame on my shoulders … only those who have lost a near relative can properly understand …." Hardie knew that Martyn had been: " … brought up a rigid Churchwoman and Conservative," and so in her socialist activities, "everything was new and strange to her" but as soon as her friends learned of "the wondrous power of speech of which she was possessed," she was asked increasingly to lecture, and thus: " … she wisely resolved to devote her life to the propagation of the truths of socialism …." Then, interestingly, Hardie continued by addressing comments directly to her grieving parents to say that:

> It may be that they, with their different outlook in life, may consider their daughter a victim to the demands of a movement which worketh only evil. I can to some extent sympathise with their point of view. But history will yet confirm the opinion that Carrie Martyn's life has been given to a cause destined to do more for humanity than Christianity has hitherto been able to accomplish.[29]

To which Hardie added a phrase which surely represents an important perspective of the entire Christian socialist movement when he observed that: "It is not by talking economics alone that the world will be made better …."

There are a number of observations to make about the importance of Caroline Martyn in Hardie's circle of friends and comrades. First, Martyn represented the move of "conservative" Church people toward a sympathy with the conditions of the working class as a direct result of their internalized Christian convictions about the compassion and example of Jesus. At no point does Martyn's criticism of the church extend to a dismissal of either Christian faith itself, or the significance and importance of the Bible. Thus, like the other Christian Socialists we are featuring here—the tendency was not (as it clearly was in a case like John Trevor) a dismissal of Scripture and the importance of Jesus—but rather a refocus on what that means in modern society. While we can only guess at the specific Biblical arguments that she made during her lectures on Jesus, we can take a fairly well-informed guess based on the spirituality of these letters that Lena Wallis has reproduced in her honor. In the cases of Dennis Hird and John Morrison Davidson, however, we

---

28. *Labour Leader*, February 23, 1908.
29. Hardie, *Labour Leader*, August 1, 1896.

are less dependent on second-hand speculation, because we have excellent written sources for a consideration of their specifically Biblical interests.

Dennis Hird (1850–1920)

The case of Dennis Hird is interesting from a number of different perspectives, including not only in his life, but also in his particularly interesting essay, "Jesus the Socialist." Hird was born in 1850, and according to W. W. Craik, his successor as Principal of the Central Labour College in London (which closed in 1929), Hird was born into a "Primitive Methodist Home."[30] He earned a degree in Natural Science at Oxford in 1875 and was appointed a tutor and lecturer to the non-collegiate students at Oxford (that is, students not affiliated with one of the "colleges"). In 1885, he became an Anglican priest and was a Curate at Bournemouth, and then was moved to inner-city London, at Battersea, where it was said that "he preached Socialism inside the church while John Burns preached it outside."[31] He also was appointed Secretary of the England Temperance Society for the Diocese of London, where Craik writes that: " … in this position he did strenuous work for the poor and the outcast—a work that had a powerful influence in directing his theoretical and practical activities in the direction of Labour and Rationalism."[32] In 1893, Hird officially joined the Social Democratic Federation, one of the early British Socialist organizations, and the Bishop of London then confronted him that he must "quit them or us." In 1894 he resigned from his Church responsibilities. Craik notes that: "Mr. Hird was now looked upon from the standpoint of the Church as a 'dangerous' man, and he was destined to encounter many a stormy sea in the course of his subsequent career."[33] He was transferred to an out-of-the-way church—St. John the Baptist Church in Eastnor. It was while he was serving as pastor of this small rural parish that he first delivered his lecture in 1895 on "Jesus the Socialist." Some 70,000 copies of the resulting pamphlet were sold, and it was advertised regularly in *The Labour Leader* for several years. However, when Hird also wrote a satirical novel, *A Christian with Two Wives* (a "Swiftian" challenge to rigid orthodoxies which is still an interesting read), this was apparently too much for the supporting families of the church, and in 1896 he renounced his priesthood.

Craik's obituary speaks of his suffering considerable economic hardship from the refusal of the church to pay an agreed amount of support beyond one year. In 1899, he was invited to become the principal of what was hoped to be a "Labour College" at Oxford named for John Ruskin, thus Ruskin College. He served there for ten years, and Craik wrote that he was considered: " … a pioneer in the work of bringing

---

30. Cf. W. W. Craik, "The Passing of Dennis Hird," *Forward*, July 31, 1920. https://spartacus-educational.com/Dennis_Hird.htm (accessed October 2, 2023).
31. Craik, "The Passing."
32. Craik, "The Passing."
33. Craik, "The Passing."

4. The "Family of Faith": Hardie's Close Allies in "Biblical" Christian Socialism

the Labour movement to appreciate the importance and the need of developing working-class education."[34] When, however, Oxford University (notably in the person of Lord Curzon) tried to interfere in the administration and curriculum of Ruskin College to bring it "into line" with the rest of the University, Hird protested and dozens of the students went on strike to support Hird. Hird was invited to become the principal of the new "Central Labour College" which moved to London in 1911. Central Labour College was an attempt by a federation of unions to create a Labour-based college when it was perceived that Ruskin College had failed to be just that, in their view. Hird accepted, and provided leadership until he became ill in 1915, and he died of health conditions in 1920.

In addition to selling copies of "Jesus the Socialist"[35] (1908, but his original public talk was 1895), many of the controversies surrounding Hird's life were dutifully reported in *The Labour Leader*. While the claims were made by Church officials that it was actually his (presumably satirical!) novel, *The Christian with Two Wives* (1896) that led to his dismissal, it can hardly be supposed that the success of his pamphlet on Jesus was met with enthusiasm by those same officials and wealthy patrons of St. John the Baptist Anglican Church.

What we are interested in considering here, however, is Hird's interesting work on Jesus. Hird states that the object of his writing was to study the teachings of Jesus "directly from the first three Gospels" (i.e., the "synoptic" gospels, though he doesn't use this term). Interestingly, then, he asserts that any attempt to "answer" his arguments with passages from Paul and/or Revelation, therefore, would "miss this point" in this brief work. Note here the favored Socialist emphasis on the Gospels themselves, to the typical (but not universal) neglect of Paul, the Pastorals, or Revelation. Indeed, even the Old Testament would appear more often than appeals to the Apostle Paul. Hird directly addresses his interest in focusing on Jesus, and why:

> There is no greater marvel among men than that any poor man should not love Jesus, and yet how few of the poor find any real help in Him now ... Our inquiry has to do with one aspect of the life of Jesus. If there are other aspects, it is no business of ours now. Was Jesus a Socialist? It is true that he was never called a Socialist; it is also true He was never called a Methodist, or a Baptist, or a Papist, or a Church of England man; thank God, He was called by none of these names.[36]

Furthermore, the pamphlet is not an economic treatise or a discussion of "socialist theory" under the shallow banner of considering Jesus. The focus, clearly, will be a reading of the Bible, and he proceeds to quote Jesus: "Thou shalt love thy neighbour as thyself (Mt. 19:19, and 22:39). I know no definition of Socialism

---

34. Craik, "The Passing."
35. Dennis Hird, *Jesus the Socialist* (London: Clarion Press, 1908).
36. Hird, *Jesus the Socialist*, 2.

to equal this ...."[37] In answer to those who would insist on some "program" or "manifesto" based on the New Testament, Hird clarifies that, in his view, Jesus:

> ... gave us no system of thought, no creed, no cut-and-dried dogmas, no church organizations; He unfolded great principles, and many of those were not new, but were set forth with new vigour and forcible illustrations. We cannot say this too frequently that Jesus gave principles—life-giving principles—and not dead rules.[38]

However, and in this Hird sides with other Christian Socialist exegetes of the New Testament in his time, he insists that these teachings can *nonetheless be the basis of practical, reforming plans for social change*:

> ... above all, we must be clear upon the fact that those principles were to *act in this life* and to regenerate this world. Some think that Jesus came to make a few people ready for heaven. I find no such teaching in His words. It is here, in this struggling world, that there is to be the kingdom of God, or there is no kingdom of God. It is so much easier to worship Christ than to imitate Jesus, that men have taken up the worship, and I think some of them verily believe, when they confess their sins by the aid of a choir, or sing their hymns in fairly good harmony, that God is pleased with the sweet music. Jesus sought men to imitate Him rather than to worship Him. 'If any man will be my disciple, let him take up his cross and follow me.' That is a very different thing from listening to a choral service on a Sunday morning, and giving a small cheque to the curate fund. Jesus seeks imitations, not adulation. A far-away heaven, with a far-away God, enveloped in a far-away glory, is no use to this world, and certainly is no part of the teaching of Jesus.[39]

Note the contrast between a high-Christology and accompanying piety, and Hird's arguments about an imitative response to the teachings of Jesus—to "imitate" rather than "worship," and "imitation" contrasted with "adulation." Note also the reference to Jesus's work to make "a few ready for heaven," clearly an attack on Calvinist Predestination that significantly reminds us of Hardie's Morisonian attacks on extreme Calvinist exclusivity.

It is of particular interest that Hird cites the practical implications of the famous "Lord's Prayer," that God's will be done "on earth," and requests for the very real "daily bread," and the Gospel of Luke, an emphasis on forgiving actual "debts" rather than the use of the saccharine "trespasses" that Church liturgies dutifully draw (to this day, it must be said) from Matthew's less directly "economic" version. We will see that this is a theme that Hird most certainly shares with Hardie. In his

---

37. Hird, *Jesus the Socialist*, 3.
38. Hird, *Jesus the Socialist*, 3.
39. Hird, *Jesus the Socialist*, 3–4.

4. The "Family of Faith": Hardie's Close Allies in "Biblical" Christian Socialism

work, Hird lays out the task of his analysis by suggesting that he will be guided by three central questions:

1. What had Jesus been taught as a Jew?
2. What evils did He chiefly attack?
3. How did He propose to change this world into "the kingdom of God"?

After arguing against a fundamentalist insistence on literal interpretations of Genesis, noting that some of the stories of Genesis even "shock us by coarse language and low morality," he then suggests that by turning to the laws of Moses: " … still we find some striking laws for national welfare." Among the Mosaic values he affirms is the provision of land in the Sabbatical laws of Leviticus 25 (a favorite passage of Socialist readings of the Old Testament) and Numbers 26:52–4 on division of land for tribal members. In his analysis, Hird notes that: "There is no doubt from these passages that the land belonged to the nation, and could never get into the hands of a few hundred land-grabbers." Hird thus argues that the Mosaic law protected a distribution of land by three principles, namely:

(1) by "not moving landmarks" (Deut. 27:17). Hird, noting that this is a passage still being read on Ash Wednesday, writes: "though I do not quite see why, unless it be a fact that this service has prevented the rich churchmen of this country from filching any of the common land of the people." In other words, it doesn't appear to serve much use in contemporary liturgy.
(2) The Jubilee redistribution of land in Leviticus 25, and
(3) The renewal of these land distribution values in Nehemiah 5: 7, 11, and 12.

These values, Hird argues, would be "part of the heritage of every Jewish peasant," and then also takes up the laws against interest and "usury" in Exodus 22:25, 26, 27; Deuteronomy 23:19; Leviticus 25:35, 36, 37. Hird comments that these laws would *appear* to be: " … as wildly untrue as the promises of an election speech. Yet they are a part of Holy Writ, and as such they had helped to mould the character and the ideals of the Carpenter-boy at Nazareth."[40] Hird further believes that the Old Testament attitudes toward the poor are a significant background to a consideration of the teachings of Jesus, and notes particularly Deuteronomy 15:7–9, which reads (in the modern NRSV) as follows:

> [7] If there is among you anyone in need, a member of your community in any of your towns within the land that the LORD your God is giving you, do not

---

40. Hird, *Jesus the Socialist*, 6.

be hard-hearted or tight-fisted toward your needy neighbor.⁸ You should rather open your hand, willingly lending enough to meet the need, whatever it may be.⁹ Be careful that you do not entertain a mean thought, thinking, 'The seventh year, the year of remission, is near,' and therefore view your needy neighbor with hostility and give nothing; your neighbor might cry to the LORD against you, and you would incur guilt.

Hird observes, "From this remarkable passage to the Epistle of St. James there are precepts in favour of the poor which of themselves would stamp the Bible as the most wonderful book of the world."⁴¹ Hird includes the concern of the poor in Wisdom literature by citing Proverbs 19:17: "Whoever is kind to the poor lends to the LORD, and will be repaid in full." Thus, in summarizing his survey of Old Testament passages in answer to his first questions about the Jewish heritage of Jesus, Hird concludes this section by arguing that:

> In forming an estimate of the childhood and growth of the village boy, Jesus, you must collect and examine all these passages, and see how large a part they formed of the religious teaching of the Jewish nation; then you will be ready to come with an enlightened mind to study the gospel story of the Nazarene.⁴²

In the second question, "What Evils did Jesus Attack?," Hird lists "officials" (Mt. 23:13–33, asking sarcastically, "How does that sound as part of a sermon in the Parish Church?"), and contemporary religious teachers in Luke 11:45–54, commenting: "Mark this Perfect Man, the Saviour of the world, with all the reeking wickedness and suffering around Him, turns His full force upon scribes, Pharisees, and lawyers."⁴³ Resisting a temptation to make Jesus's attacks a matter of blatant anti-Semitism and thus an attack on *Jewish* leaders, like many other readers of the New Testament often do (including some socialist writers), Hird makes the association of the opponents of Jesus not with contemporary Jews, but rather with institutional Church leaders in England. Hird defines "Scribes," who came into importance "after Ezra in Babylon" as:

> priests and clergy and preachers of their time. They were leisured, learned, set apart, trained in school and college, ordained, well versed in the law and letter of the law, full of the traditions of the elders, embalmed in a brilliant respectability, keeping the truth from the people, and crucifying the Lord of truth. In a general way they answer to the clerical class of most countries since the crucifixion of our Lord.⁴⁴

---

41. Hird, *Jesus the Socialist*, 6.
42. Hird, *Jesus the Socialist*, 6.
43. Hird, *Jesus the Socialist*, 7.
44. Hird, *Jesus the Socialist*, 7.

Similarly, when he defines "Pharisee" for his pamphlet readers, he refers to them as "puritans" and "ritualists," and states that: "In religion they were as bigoted as Englishmen, and they held that most accursed doctrine, that they only were right …."[45] He criticizes the Pharisaic notion that it was necessary to explain the Mosaic law with an additional "oral law" by equally comparing it to Christian church leaders: "More than one Church claims to have the sole right to that fable."[46]

Noting the passion of Jesus's criticism in Luke 13:31–3, Hird notes that Jesus doesn't appear very "reverent" here: "reverence is not the strong side of his character," and he makes the argument that Jesus did not choose among his followers any scribe, Sanhedrin member, Pharisee, or priest. Why is this important for Hird? Because, for Hird, it seemed to prove: " … that He turned His back on all officials, as the tyrants of the world. In ninety-nine cases out of a hundred, give a man a permanent office with a big salary, and you have ruined that man. He begins to crow, and feed, and fight."[47]

What is significant to note here is that Hardie will also cite especially Matthew 23 as a counter to those who would attack the right to question Church leaders. In other words—to respond to the indignation of those who object to attacking Church leaders in print, Hird (and Hardie) argue that such attacks are themselves an obedience to Jesus's example! Turning from contemporary religious leaders, Hird then asks what Jesus had to say about the rich? On this, Hird states strikingly, that "Here, I confess, that I am astounded at the teaching of the master" noting Jesus's words in Luke 4:18–21, and Jesus's advice to the "rich young ruler" to sell all he has and give to the poor (Lk. 18:18). In response to the ruler, for example, Hird is struck that Jesus does not begin a catechetical lesson about Christian faith:

> There is not a word about sin, not a word about the Atonement, not a word about creeds, worship, sacraments, repentance, conversion, justification, sanctification. All that you call spiritual is left out of sight in his divine answer to the seeker for eternal life. From the Ten Commandments He deliberately chooses those ONLY which have to do with social life …[48]

Hird continues his "astonished" reactions to Jesus's reaction to the ruler, by stating: "It is more difficult to believe that He uttered this than to believe all the miracles at once. It contradicts nearly all Church history; it denies all your pet notions that you are going to heaven because you vaguely believe in Christ and worship Him sometimes. Yet it is written in all the three Gospels."[49] When Hird refers to Jesus's two parables about rich people, he summarizes:

---

45. Hird, *Jesus the Socialist*, 8.
46. Hird, *Jesus the Socialist*, 8.
47. Hird, *Jesus the Socialist*, 9.
48. Hird, *Jesus the Socialist*, 10.
49. Hird, *Jesus the Socialist*, 10.

> ... in one case He makes him a fool (Luke 12:16ff); in the other He places him in hell (Luke 16:19ff), according to the popular notions of His day ... Jesus is constantly dealing with this subject, and always in the same way. There is never a good word for the rich; there is never a censure for the poor. If some curate preached in this way, you would call him a monomaniac, and one Sunday would be the longest time he would be allowed to stay in most parishes.[50]

What does it mean? Hird marveled: " ... that there can be a poor man who does not love Jesus, but I marvel still more than any rich man can endure His teaching." Hird reflects:

> When we have been taking part in a gorgeous function at the dedication of some church, built and endowed by a rich man, it is enough to paralyse the strongest of us, as we walk back through the slums of a large town, and a bowed, pale, ragged man, in the gloaming, says, 'Woe unto you that be rich,' and vanishes in the twilight to the nearest workhouse. And that was Jesus! Great God, which am I to believe? I would like to believe in the lovely luxury of the rich; I am almost compelled to believe in the ragged truth of Jesus. But the wish is vain. They wage an eternal war with each other, and the same world cannot hold both and be at peace.[51]

Hird then turns to a discussion of "constructive" teachings of Jesus: "Now for the test. We have seen the destructive teaching of Jesus; let us see what He has to offer to build up the new kingdom."[52] Again, Hird here proceeds along two general topics, (1) universal precepts in Jesus's own life, and (2) universal precepts in the conduct of the first churches.

His first text on the example of Jesus on the question about taxation is Matthew 22:17, where Hird observes: "The Divine Pauper never had a penny in his pocket ... he had to send a disciple to catch a fish to meet the demand; and on this occasion He had to borrow a penny."[53] Hird notes that the question about taxation was "Is it lawful?" and not "Is it right?" Yet this passage is used to defend taxation and class divisions, and Hird responds that: "If you say that means that, all over the world, the powerful are to grab all they can from the weak, and that the strongest thieves are to form a peerage, and that all Christian people are to support them, I do not agree with you ...."[54]

Hird wants to differentiate particular actions of Jesus against actions that exemplify universal precepts. For example, Hird argues, not all were to "take whips and drive the wicked out of the church." He is not focused on what he called

---

50. Hird, *Jesus the Socialist*, 11.
51. Hird, *Jesus the Socialist*, 12.
52. Hird, *Jesus the Socialist*, 13.
53. Hird, *Jesus the Socialist*, 14.
54. Hird, *Jesus the Socialist*, 14.

4. The "Family of Faith": Hardie's Close Allies in "Biblical" Christian Socialism

"the particular and temporal" teachings of Jesus. Hird claims that the universal precepts are "plain," and takes as his first example the teaching that "the first shall be last," and notes Jesus's critique of the leadership of "Gentile" rulers (in Lk. 25:25–7):

> [25] But he said to them, "The kings of the Gentiles lord it over them; and those in authority over them are called benefactors. [26] But not so with you; rather the greatest among you must become like the youngest, and the leader like one who serves. [27] For who is greater, the one who is at the table or the one who serves? Is it not the one at the table? But I am among you as one who serves."

Hird comments further: "There you catch the keynote of the new kingdom. Its King is the servant of all ... Please, your gracious majesties and you noble lords, come and be servants, or stay outside. What a Democrat is the Son of Man! I dare not have said these things, and many will hate me forever because I have ventured to repeat the words of Jesus."[55] Hird here also praises Jesus's critique of violence, and especially "love of enemies" in Luke 6:35 commenting that such teachings: " ... if put in practice tomorrow, would overturn every nation and nearly every Church on this globe, and give us such a paradise that starving children would think the angels of heaven had come to be their playmates."[56]

Hird argues that Jesus' instruction to sell possessions and give alms in Luke 12:32–3, is a sign that "the New Kingdom is taking shape," and then reflects on the Matthean version of the famed "Golden Rule" (7:12) by stating that the upper classes would certainly not really agree to the famous maxim:

> If YOU like the people to take away all your land, then take away all the land from the poor; if YOU would like to toil from twelve to fourteen hours a day; make your labourers, your bus drivers, your bar-keepers, your waiters toil twelve to fourteen hours a day. Do not defraud them of their hours; for if YOU like slavery, THEY may like slavery too; and besides, you will make bigger dividends, and then you can give something to a missionary society; if you like others to deprive you of your vote, then do not make your servants vote; if you like to stay at home on election day why should not they stay at home! 'ALL THINGS whatsoever he would that men should do to you.'[57]

Hird concludes this striking series of statements with his concluding comment: "Glorious gospel!"

After citing Matthew 19:19 about loving your "neighbour as yourself," Hird continues his sermonizing:

---

55. Hird, *Jesus the Socialist*, 14.
56. Hird, *Jesus the Socialist*, 15.
57. Hird, *Jesus the Socialist*, 15.

> I confess I stand dumbfounded, blinded by the blaze of this brilliant idea of a kingdom of life where there is no murder, and where an equal love has changed cannibals into sons of God. I thank thee, Holy Jesus, for this word of life? And yet I have had clergymen come and talk to me, and say: "You see, my dear fellow, human nature is always the same. It cannot be altered". Well, I am sorry for that, for if human beings cannot be brought into this kingdom of love, Jesus made a mistake, and there is an end of the matter … Now you can see why Jesus objected to the officials and the rich; why He told them to lend without interest, to lay up no treasure on earth, to sell all they had, because they were to come into His kingdom under the shelter of a universal and equal love—that is His Socialism—cooperation of kindness and equality of privilege.[58]

Hird concludes his section of what Jesus taught "by His own life" by observing that:

> If you turn away from Churchianity and Chapelolatry, and watch some man, who has been out of work two months plodding his way from one workhouse to another, you will have the truest picture of the life and social position of Jesus of Nazareth which the world has to show this day.[59]

His last section is to ask about the conduct of the First Churches, and in this, socialist analysis of the New Testament turns to one of its trump cards, the communal life of Acts 2 and 4:

> I suppose you will agree with me that, if the apostles and those around them did not know the meaning of Christ's teaching, that meaning has been lost to the world for ever … That Church was a brotherhood, without the tyranny of paid officials or the oppression of the rich. It was a cooperative institution, bound together by love, where there was not "any among them that lacked" for "they had all things common." There was no private property. If the apostles were wrong in all this, I give up the teaching of Jesus as a riddle which I cannot understand.[60]

Then, towards the end of his pamphlet, Hird turns to address the controversies that had arisen since he delivered the lecture, "Jesus the Socialist" in Eastnor, Herefordshire. Hird observes:

> If these apostles were right, then I am right when I call Jesus a Socialist, and I do not quite see why this highly respectable county of Hereford should feel itself scandalized because I say what the twelve apostles did … If the apostles were right, Jesus was a Socialist, and if Jesus was a Socialist, why should a meeting be called to protest against the title of my lecture? I take it to be little short of blasphemous, to hold the gospel of Christ in their hands, and swear that they

---

58. Hird, *Jesus the Socialist*, 16.
59. Hird, *Jesus the Socialist*, 16.
60. Hird, *Jesus the Socialist*, 16–17.

believe in Him, and with the same breath deny the teaching of Jesus ... The whole evidence is of one piece; the teaching is put into practice, and around the crumbling thrones of kings and among the mouldering tombs of priests a few fishermen of Galilee scattered the seeds of the divine Socialism of Jesus; and even yet those seeds may grow and spring up through the dust of centuries.[61]

In sum, we see in Hird's analysis of Biblical teachings themes that recur in other Christian Socialist expositions of Scripture, but also in Hardie's own writing. One insight from this process is to take note that Hardie's discussions were not so dissimilar from a trained clergyman's argumentation. But before we comment further on this, there remains the longer exposition from the Scottish Christian Socialist, John Morrison Davidson.

John Morrison Davidson (1843–1916)

Like Caroline Martyn, we have mainly the brief journalistic obituaries and reflections about Davidson upon which to base any biographical information. Unlike Hird, we have no attempts to write any kind of a biography of either Martyn or Davidson. But unlike Martyn, we have a considerable number of writings from Davidson, including his important sustained reflection on the Bible, entitled *The Gospel of the Poor: The Christ of the Commune*,[62] which appeared in at least four editions.

The obituary for John Morrison Davidson was written in the December 28, 1916 edition of *The Labour Leader*, by J. Bruce Glasier, the editor who succeeded Hardie in 1904. Glasier identifies Davidson as among the "elders" of the movement, and thus:

> one of the group of outright Radicals who kept the watchfires of democracy burning ere yet the dawn of political Socialism cast its first red flush over the sky. He was one of the few remaining notable men who linked the Socialist movement of our day with the red-Republican movement of forty and fifty years ago.[63]

Davidson was born in 1842 at "Old Deer" (or "Red Deer") in Aberdeenshire. *The Clarion* adds that he was a "frail and sickly child," but overcame his youthful health issues, and married young, eventually having eleven children. He began his academic life by attending college at Aberdeen and also Edinburgh. *The Clarion*'s

---

61. Hird, *Jesus the Socialist*, 18.
62. John Morrison Davidson, *The Gospel of the Poor: The Christ of the Commune* (London: F.R. Henderson, 1903).
63. J. Bruce Glasier, "John Morrison Davidson: Obituary," *Labour Leader*, December 28, 1916.

writer, however, states that Davidson argued with the Professors, and soon decided that he preferred writing. In this same appreciation of Davidson written in *The Clarion* (August 1898), the anonymous writer knew that: "At fourteen he led a debate in which he astounded his elders by maintaining that Milton was a greater poet than Shakespeare because Milton was a Republican." It appears that Davidson tried teaching briefly in Glasgow and was for a short time Headmaster of Circus Place School, Edinburgh. Writing, however, was clearly his passion, and he was published already at sixteen. Equally compelling, however, were his emergent political ideals. In 1863, he was involved with Polish immigrants in working for Polish independence but was not allowed to travel to Poland to join his friends— they wanted a "native" movement exclusively. He qualified for the Scottish bar and was "called" to the Middle Temple in London in 1877, but he never practiced law. *The Clarion* states that he studied for his legal exams for six weeks, eighteen hours a day, but he continued with a career in journalism, which clearly supported his own study. By 1880, he was a correspondent sent to the Western United States to write about mining in Montana and ranching in Nevada and was received by the US President Rutherford Hayes as an important visitor from the British press. In any case, Davidson was certainly interested in a wide variety of issues from his progressive, "anarchist" tinged political perspective. The "anarchist" label seems to derive from his frequent attacks on all political leadership and church leadership (e.g., he served on a committee for the abolition of the House of Lords). Glasier further noted:

> He advocated Republicanism, universal suffrage, Home Rule, the land for the people, disarmament, the brotherhood of nations, and the communal organizations of industry. He threw himself vehemently into the Highland and Irish League agitation, the agitations against the Egyptian War and coercion in Ireland ... He was born with the fire of reform in his heart, with an unquenchable hatred of oppression and a consuming zeal to bring about the 'Parliament of man, the Federation of the world'. The old prophecies clothed his soul as in a radiant garment and the teachings of the ancient philosophers were as green pastures for his thoughts ...[64]

In addition to the picture that illustrates the cover of some of his pamphlets, we also have a charming physical description from 1898 that is worth repeating here:

> Morrison Davidson is a grizzled veteran, with a kindly but shrewd face, and a pair of rather faded but still very keen eyes. In figure he is short and spare, with uncommonly square shoulders. His dress evinces a deep-seated indifference to the terrible Madam Grundy, and his round bowler hat is a joy for ever. He is grave and earnest in manner, but knows a joke when he sees it, and is not afraid

---

64. Glasier, "Davidson: Obituary."

4. The "Family of Faith": Hardie's Close Allies in "Biblical" Christian Socialism 113

of it either. He has the slow, hesitating walk and slight step of the scholar, and the brooding, rather disconnected speech of the thinker; one could own him for a clever man and a 'character' at half a mile; and as for his nationality, the only thing he is uppish and boastful about is the fact that he is a Scotsman. In a very old suit of clothes, with an older hat, I have seen him in all weathers wandering in Fleet Street or Bookseller's Row … he is always hopeful, always ready, always full of kindliness …[65]

Davidson's Christian Socialism drew criticism. Echoing a frequent annoyance with the Christian Socialists generally (that they were not as consumed with Marxist orthodoxies and theoretical clarities as they ought to have been), Glasier thus writes:

He was a Socialist, but would not permit his Socialism any more than his religious beliefs to be fettered by any dogmatic creed … He had more affinity with Tolstoy, Massini, and Henry George than Karl Marx. William Morris's 'News from Nowhere' delighted him. To the end he adhered to his conviction that Christ's teaching represented the highest human ethics and largest hope of deliverance from man's inhumanity to man.[66]

The anonymous obituary for *The Word* further discusses the fact that Davidson was frequently criticized for his insistence on his Christian principles, echoing Glasier and writing that:

It cannot be said that Davidson pursued a logical or a consistent course. He was Liberal and Radical. His outlook was anti-authoritarian and therefore, anarchist. He was not opposed to revolutionary struggle, but he favoured all reformist courses. His view of Jesus as a man and a master agitator, a genius of Freedom, was much opposed to the approach of his agnostic friends. He tolerated what he felt was their ironies and frivolous cynicisms and blasphemies with a shrewd and humorous tolerance. We remember many discussions between him and Ernest Pack, whose forte was ridicule. Pack used to describe Davidson's *The Gospel of the Poor* as 'The Gospel on the Floor.'[67]

Yet, even though Glasier admits that frequent debates in Socialist theory constantly shoved aside any talk other than economic revolution, and thus were frequently impatient with Davidson's emphasis on morality and social values, Glasier nonetheless somewhat graciously concludes his obituary with a cautious appreciation of "the old man":

---

65. Editorial (untitled), *The Clarion*, August 13, 1898.
66. Glasier, "Davidson: Obituary."
67. Editorial/Obituary (unsigned), *The Word* (Glasgow) 1916, 50–1.

We are not now so confident that we can get quit of Capitalism without first creating a real political democracy – if that be possible. It is not so easy, as we now perceive, when we observe the monstrous triumphs of War-lords, secret diplomacy, militarism, and repression of public liberty ... Morrison Davidson was therefore not perhaps so witless as we thought in hammering so persistently and tiresomely in our ears his ethical and political principles. We may even at this stage of our Socialist agitation find much wisdom stored up for us in the quotations from the old prophets, philosophers, poets, and reformers which were a feature of his manifold writings. Anyway, without Morrison Davison, the democratic and Socialist movement would lack much that pertains to the inner glow of its spirit, and the chivalry and pathos of its traditions. Brave old warrior for freedom and humanity – Farewell![68]

We are particularly interested in Davidson, however, for his frequent contributions to *The Labour Leader* under Hardie's editorship, and like Hird's work, the frequent advertisements of his writings for sale, and positive reviews of those same works. For Davidson, however, we give pride of place to his theological "magnum opus."

The Gospel of the Poor: The Christ of the Commune

In the foreword to the fourth edition of *The Gospel of the Poor*, from which I have worked, Davidson begins his work by acknowledging (like Hird) that "Higher Criticism" of the Bible had raised serious questions about "authenticity" of the words of Jesus in the Gospels, precisely who wrote them, and when. However, again like Hird, these late nineteenth-century debates (surrounding New Testament scholars Ernst Renan and similarly William Robertson-Smith in Old Testament issues) did not seem to bother Davidson, nor did he believe that they seriously undermined his approach: " ... the positions taken up in *The Gospel of the Poor*, I find on re-perusal, are not appreciably affected thereby ..., " because he sees in the story and teachings of Jesus a refined picture of what he calls "the Universal religion":

> Christ's religion, therefore, is not *a* Religion, but *the* Religion, because His Gospel corresponds to the inborn capacity of man as revealed in the History of the Race. He is a Master among Masters by the Master ... the Religion of Christ ... can very well survive the complete elimination of the supernatural by Criticism, Higher or Lower ...[69]

It would be an entirely different argument, however, to point out that Davidson's proposed solution (e.g., backing away from claiming that his is a uniquely Jesus-centered argument) would hardly seem necessary in modern New Testament and

---

68. Glasier, "Davidson: Obituary."
69. Davidson, *The Gospel of the Poor*, ii.

4. The "Family of Faith": Hardie's Close Allies in "Biblical" Christian Socialism 115

Christian Ethics, despite over a century of continued text-critical debates. Jesus as a unique Jewish teacher of ethics is not the controversial view it once was.

Although I identified this work as his "opus," Davidson's book consists of an expanded outline rather than a deeply detailed work. The 150-page publication is divided into twenty-seven short sections or chapters (which we will indicate with Roman numerals), followed by appendices that consist of a compendium of eight letters that Davidson has written "to the editor of *The Daily Chronicle*" taking up some of his arguments once again, including a few about Scripture, and specifically Jesus, as well.

In fact, one suspects that what we are actually reading are Davidson's published notes from public presentations, rather than an originally *written* argument. However, for our purposes, it suffices to give us a strong indication of the kind of Biblical arguments that Davidson makes. Therefore, in our analysis, we will only briefly summarize those chapters that do not participate significantly in scriptural analysis and emphasize those that do—and like our consideration of Hird, train our eye on the passages he chooses to focus on, and his accompanying commentary. I will also quote directly from those pages where Davidson's rhetoric is particularly impressive, or even on rare occasion, troubling (on persecution of the Jews, most especially).

The first brief chapter begins with a list of key passages: Jesus reading from Isaiah in Luke 4:17–20; the parable of the King's Supper in Luke 14:16–24; and the brief sentence, "And the common people heard Him gladly" (Mk 12:37). There follows a series of introductory observations about the importance of his subject, and how the issue of *properly reading Jesus* has been blurred by the mistakes of the past:

> The rich have known how to 'exploit' the sublime Communist of Nazareth and his priceless message to mankind as they have exploited all besides. Not merely have they made the Blessed Gospel of none effect by their churchianities, they have actually converted that which was to be 'without money and without price' into a mine of untold 'profit' worked for their own private advantage by competing companies of cunning ecclesiastics 'of all denominations' … in their hands the Gospel of the Poor has become the Gospel of Mammon …[70]

Davidson also notes Hardie's famous speech at Bradford on the socialism of Jesus that created such a stir, where someone argued with Hardie by insisting that "Christ was a friend of the rich," a perspective voiced against Hardie to which Davidson replies, "If I understand Christianity aright [that view] amounts merely to what old Homer would have called 'dog-faced impudence.'"[71]

---

70. Davidson, *The Gospel of the Poor*, 2.
71. Davidson, *The Gospel of the Poor*, 3–4.

Section II continues much the same, featuring continued introductory comments and objections against previous errors of interpretation. Davidson comments, going immediately to the "socialist trump card" in Acts:

> Now we come to the core of the whole momentous business. What was Christ's 'polity'? The answer is, however startling it may appear to some: Anarchist Communism. This I challenge any student of early Christianity to gainsay. Indeed, the Acts of the Apostles is conclusive on that point …[72]

Section III answers the objections to Davidson's arguments which would state that Christianity is not inherently opposed to private property. As this was a common objection against Christian Socialism, Davidson states his amazement that Christianity was ever embraced by a capitalist society like England, which he points out, has far more similarities in social values with the brutalities of Greek and Roman social inequities:

> In truth, how the Gospel of the Poor, which Christ unfolded in such perfect entirety, ever found a lodgment of any kind in a society so diametrically and inveterately opposed to all His distinctive teachings, is to my mind as great a miracle (if not greater) as any to be found in Matthew, Mark, Luke, or John.[73]

Section IV, interestingly, is entitled "Strikes, B.C. 150–170." In this section, Davidson points out the negative presentations of movements of the poor or slaves in Classical history, contrasting Spartacus with Jesus, arguing that:

> The strike-wars of antiquity – the efforts of the Pagan Messiahs to free the workers from their bonds by force of arms – are among the obscurest episodes in the annals of mankind. The reason is not far to seek – *contemporary history was all written by the bitterest foes of the toilers*, and it is very difficult to read between the lines.[74]

He concludes this brief discussion by introducing: "the next great Labour Leader was crucified one hundred years later on Mount Calvary, but from His cross He still directs the grand struggle for human emancipation which will one day be accomplished."[75] Therefore, and similar to Hird, Davidson begins his scriptural analysis with a survey of key texts in the Old Testament. Even though he insists on an "evolutionary view" of the Scripture (that is, that the New Testament will improve on the values of the Old), Davidson believes that it is important to take note of Old Testament "values."

---

72. Davidson, *The Gospel of the Poor*, 9.
73. Davidson, *The Gospel of the Poor*, 17.
74. Davidson, *The Gospel of the Poor*, 19.
75. Davidson, *The Gospel of the Poor*, 19.

4. The "Family of Faith": Hardie's Close Allies in "Biblical" Christian Socialism

There is no reasonable historic doubt that before Troy was sacked or Rome was founded, Moses was the Deliverer and Lawgiver of the unique people to whom the entire human race stands so heavily indebted in all its most precious spiritual and ethical possessions.[76]

Davidson then seeks to summarize "the Social Compact" of Moses in a series of brief observations. First, that God was the "landlord" (Davidson cites Lev. 25 and Num. 26:54). Davidson even takes note of provisions for women to be title holders to land in the famous episode of the "daughters of Zelophehad" in Numbers 27. Again, similar to Hird, Davidson also takes note of provisions against moving land-markers in Deuteronomy 27:17, and how Isaiah 5:8 echoes precisely the Prophet's accusations of land-stealing. His further commentary takes up the stealing of Naboth's Vineyard by Ahab and Jezebel, and Elijah's criticism of this abuse of royal privilege against a common Israelite's "tribal property," and then asks:

> What would Elijah the Tishbite have had to say to a Highland clearance, or such unbridled landlordism as, in the forties, condemned, in the name of rent, a million and a quarter of Irish men, women, and children to death by hunger in the midst of plenty of their own creation? During the famine, Ireland was relatively the greatest food-exporting country in the world![77]

Section VI, still called "The Law and the Prophets," and thus signaling a continued analysis of Old Testament values and history, Davidson takes up a discussion of land use more directly. Estimating the actual land holdings of ancient Israelite peasants as twenty acres, Davidson argues that the sabbatical year suggests that land productivity was such that workers could actually store up enough to take time off for a year! Interestingly, Davidson insists that such "mundane" matters are actually as much issues of revelation as those parts of the Bible otherwise considered more "spiritual." In a creative reading, Davidson believes that God "ordains" craftsmen and farmers every bit as much as God "ordains" prophets (Ex. 31:1–5, and Isa. 28:23–6). Finally, Davidson argues that a central pillar of Mosaic values is the care for the poor, citing Deuteronomy 15:1–2, 4–5, 9–10. Davidson observes:

> Poverty was not treated as we pretended Christians treat it. The poor were not thrust into workhouse bastiles and treated like criminals to the loss of all self-respect and manhood. They were Jehovah's people, and it was the duty of every well-to-do neighbour not merely to minister to their immediate wants, but to encourage them by sympathetic counsel, the only kind of help that is really serviceable in the end – the help that enables the unfortunate, the weak, or the erring to help themselves.[78]

76. Davidson, *The Gospel of the Poor*, 25.
77. Davidson, *The Gospel of the Poor*, 27.
78. Davidson, *The Gospel of the Poor*, 35.

Section VII continues with "The Law and the Prophets." In this section, Davidson takes up the topic of "slavery," and points out that the majority of Old Testament discussions about "slavery" are indentured servitude for the payment of debts, citing Leviticus 25:39-43; Deuteronomy 15:12-18; Leviticus 25:50-2; Deuteronomy 23:15-16 and Deuteronomy 24:7. Davidson recognizes limitations in his "modern" view of Mosaic law, noting that: "They were not perfect, and some of the subsidiary rules laid down seem, in places, to derogate from them. But for the time and circumstances in which they took legislative form they were a marvel of humanitarian achievement."[79] But pointedly, noting the ability to clear debts and start again, Davidson asks:

> What would not our own hopelessly toiling, utterly disinherited 'wage slaves' give for the prospect of such a termination of their ceaseless servitude? What inalienable vine and fig tree can they hope to sit under, in their old age, with none to make them afraid? Their vine is the workhouse, and their fig tree the public asylum with heartless officialdom to embitter existence at its close. While their strength lasts they 'sell' themselves for a 'price' – the price of one-third of their labour's worth; but for them, alas there is neither redemption, seventh year of release, nor year of Jubilee.[80]

Davidson cites unnamed Biblical scholars to have estimated that peasants in Ancient Israel had nearly half a year to themselves in Ancient Israel. In Section VIII, The Law and the Prophets—on usury and charging interest, Davidson claims that: "Moses did not confine his attention to the operations of the humble pawnbroker. He had his eye on the Rothschilds, Vanderbilts, and Jay Goulds" (citing Deut. 23:19; Lev. 25:35-7).[81]

Notable here is an unfortunate discussion with regard to persecution in his time of Jews in Russia. He sounds almost defensive of the persecutions when he tries to argue that Jews were being persecuted not "as Jews," but as "usurers," citing Ezekiel 22:12, 13, 31. This is treacherous territory. Davidson insists that "repentance" from usury will be accepted, and Jews can be welcomed as "fellow workers" but continues to cite the warnings of Nehemiah 5:7, 10, 11-14. Here, one would have hoped for much more awareness of Jewish worker movements in Eastern Europe than Davidson seems to have. To try to blame anti-Semitic violence on usury, for example, is simply to misrepresent the sad history of European anti-Semitic violence and attitudes that persisted for hundreds of years.

Although it does not excuse the odor of anti-Semitism in his arguments, Davidson quickly establishes that Christians are even worse usurers than the "disciples of Moses." In Section IX, Davidson will also criticize Henry George's acceptance of usury, and Davidson bitterly condemns virtually all insurance schemes (always taking in more than is paid out):

79. Davidson, *The Gospel of the Poor*, 38.
80. Davidson, *The Gospel of the Poor*, 38-9.
81. Davidson, *The Gospel of the Poor*, 42.

4. The "Family of Faith": Hardie's Close Allies in "Biblical" Christian Socialism

What chance has the widow or orphan against the Men of Belial, who have set up these high places of Insurance in the land? Truly does 'he require a long spoon who would sup with the devil' of Usury.[82]

Section XI summarizes his discussion of the Mosaic laws:

> It instituted a system of rigorously restricted Individualism. It strove to strangle the rent-fiend by making every Hebrew his own landlord. It prohibited interest or 'usury' and anathematized profit or 'extortion'. It made generous provision for the 'poor,' the 'stranger' and the 'sojourner'. The 'servant' or worker had nearly half the year to himself in Sabbaths, Sabbatical years, Jubilees, etc. The very ox was not to be muzzled while treading out the corn.[83]

Davidson attacks promises of heaven to compensate for servile labour in this world, calling this a "sky-pilot" Church policy, stating that Moses led the people to an actual land rather than promising heaven by and by, thus agreeing with the Chartist poet, Allen Davenport (1775–1846) who spoke of Jesus saying:

> He preached no future worlds of pain or bliss
> To cheat the weak and rob the poor in this.[84]

To this, Davidson adds: "It is not the individual Hebrew, but the Hebrew nation, that was the object of Jehovah's care."[85]

Section XII begins Davidson's turn to the Monarchy and the Prophets. Here, he notes that the democratic, social system envisioned by Moses was betrayed by the choosing of a king in 1 Samuel 8 which constituted a move from a: "Peaceful republic to a warlike monarchy."[86] Anticipating a twenty-first-century series of criticisms of the image of David based on rereading the Historical Books of the Bible, Davidson notes that: "David, it is clear, was both a grossly self-indulgent and negligent ruler, otherwise it is inconceivable that his son Absalom should have been able to head so very formidable a rebellion against him,"[87] and cites many Deuteronomic warnings about limiting the power of the monarchy in Deuteronomy 28:36, 37, 41, 49, 50. Against the monarchy, Davidson contrasts the Prophets (citing Isa. 10:1–2) to say that these prophets who: " … stood up so manfully for the democratic principles of the old Republic were not slow to note the infinite social woes which Hebrew Royalty, according to prediction, brought in its train …."[88]

---

82. Davidson, *The Gospel of the Poor*, 57.
83. Davidson, *The Gospel of the Poor*, 58.
84. Davidson, *The Gospel of the Poor*, 61.
85. Davidson, *The Gospel of the Poor*, 63.
86. Davidson, *The Gospel of the Poor*, 67.
87. Davidson, *The Gospel of the Poor*, 68.
88. Davidson, *The Gospel of the Poor*, 69.

Davidson's own distaste for the British monarchy (and also the "enormous powers" of the American presidency) is clearly evident in his dwelling on the abuses and sins of the monarchy in Ancient Israel. Davidson notes the Highland Clearances in passing, comparing them with warnings about the Israelite monarchy in 1 Samuel 8:13–16, and then Job 20:7–19. Thus, in Section XIII, entitled "Give us a King," Davidson signals where he is going when he notes that Jesus warned against the Gentile's rulers "lording over them," but then notes cynically: " … But being Christians only in name, we care nothing for the Master's plain admonition, and like the Jews of old, we will have Kings to reign over us."[89]

In Section XIV, Davidson turns to his summary of the Prophets, skipping over a discussion of all the other kings of Israel and Judah, which he summarizes by saying that "nine cases out of ten, tyrants and idolaters of the worst type. But there was a vigorous Democratic Opposition in both kingdoms with which we are more concerned."[90] Prophecy, which Davidson suggests started with Samuel, formed a "distinct party in the state," and "their guilds materially influenced national politics and were at the bottom of several radical revolutions."[91]

As part of his discussion of the Prophets, Davidson turns to "Messianic expectation" in Section XV, beginning with a discussion of the "suffering servant" of Second Isaiah. Davidson takes up a long-standing interpretation of the Servant motif, namely that it was originally intended to be a collective interpretation of the (exiled) nation of Israel itself; he still affirms that even if this is true in the first case: " … the kernel of the 'religious kernel of the nation' was undoubtedly the Man of Sorrows, whether the prophet had an absolutely clear conception of His wonderful personality and career or not."[92]

Davidson cites the great Old Testament scholar Robertson-Smith at length, but is especially taken with the view that: "the whole business of scholarly exegesis lies with this human side … to master the full situation and character and feeling of each human interlocutor who has a part in the drama of revelation."[93]

In Section XVI, Davidson engages in a rather standard summary of the events of the exile, and briefly summarizes events through the Hellenistic Period, and in Section XVII also summarizes "Jewish Sects" at the time of Jesus where he not unexpectedly has severe words for the Pharisees as religious leaders of the day. It is finally in Section XVIII that he turns to "The Nazarene," and in a striking opening, he briefly debates with the doubts raised by Renan and Strauss, and states a rather forthright belief in the veracity of the Gospel portrayals of Jesus:

> Suffice it to say that I regard the artless, but vivid narratives of the four Gospels as genuine first century history, as credible as Caesar's Commentaries, and

---

89. Davidson, *The Gospel of the Poor*, 72.
90. Davidson, *The Gospel of the Poor*, 77.
91. Davidson, *The Gospel of the Poor*, 78.
92. Davidson, *The Gospel of the Poor*, 84.
93. Davidson, *The Gospel of the Poor*, 85, citing Robertson-Smith.

entirely inexplicable by the 'myth' theory or any other hypothesis, except that Jesus was what He affirmed Himself to be, the long looked for Messiah. The 'myth' theory will soon be as discredited as the 'sun' theory which preceded it. Twenty Shakespeares rolled into one could not have created Jesus of Nazareth.[94]

Nonetheless, Davidson affirms, these scholars have done a "great service" by emphasizing the human life and setting of Jesus. Notably, then, in his own statements and in also embracing the statement of Burns on Christianity, Davidson's Christology is nothing like Trevor's vague religiosity. Many of the next sections will outline aspects of the message of Jesus.

In Section XIX, Davidson argues that the temptation of Jesus was to be a powerful ruler like those He later warned against:

> The Temptation in the wilderness was therefore no chimera, but perhaps the most decisive turning-point in the whole history of humanity. When Christ deliberately rejected the Jewish conception of an Imperial Messiah, He must have clearly discerned that in rejecting a Throne He was courting a Cross. 'No man (He said) taketh my life from Me, but I lay it down of Myself.' It was in the wilderness of Judea that He laid it down.[95]

In Section XX "The Religion of Christ," Davidson cites the following as a key text (Mt. 22:36–40):

> [36] 'Teacher, which commandment in the law is the greatest?' [37] He said to him, 'You shall love the Lord your God with all your heart, and with all your soul, and with all your mind.' [38] This is the greatest and first commandment. [39] And a second is like it: 'You shall love your neighbor as yourself.' [40] On these two commandments hang all the law and the prophets.

Under which he comments:

> This, the Fatherhood of God and the Brotherhood of Man, is indeed a small programme, but never assuredly was there one propounded for fallible man's adoption more arduous. It is, in truth, a most exacting Credo, and professing Christians in all ages have taken refuge in this baleful theology and in that to escape from its obligations.[96]

In XXI, Davidson outlines his ideas about the people toward which Christ's Kingdom was especially directed, particularly citing the Parable of "the Great Supper" in Luke 14:16–24:

---

94. Davidson, *The Gospel of the Poor*, 97.
95. Davidson, *The Gospel of the Poor*, 105.
96. Davidson, *The Gospel of the Poor*, 109.

First – for guileless children – innocence and simplicity

Second – for the poor – no distinction between 'deserving' and 'undeserving'. Jesus would not have qualified for Charity organizations.

Third –for all manner of social failures, harlots, publicans, prodigal sons, thieves

Fourth – for all manner of heretics – pagans of Tyre and Sidon, Sabbath-breakers, 'persons generally in bad religious odour'. It is the rich, the fashionable, the respectable, the 'unco guid' that are alone excluded from The Kingdom of God, whose foundations He laid on earth.[97]

In contrast, those barred from the supper include the landlord, the capitalist, selfish "family man who systematically set the supposed interests of wife and weans above those of the community at large."[98] Those compelled to come in are from: "the streets and the lanes" which are to be "scoured for the victims of the landlord, the capitalist, and selfish 'family man.' The rural landlord has driven them off what he has been pleased to call his land, and they have been perforce obliged to take refuge in the 'slums' of Jerusalem."[99]

Using a term for the ill-informed poor, namely "Hodge," Davidson states:

It is next poor Hodge's turn. The highways and the hedges of rural Judea must be raided by 'Red Vans' and as Hodge is very ignorant – having been purposely kept in mental darkness for many centuries by those who have iniquitously 'laid field to field and house to house' in collusion with the Priest, the Scribe, and the Levite – to him a little gentle compulsion has to be applied.[100]

Davidson argues that "Dives" was not rich by moral means, citing St. Jerome, "Opulence is always the product of theft committed, if not by the actual possessor, then by his ancestors."[101]

In Section XXII, entitled, "The Kingdom of God and the World," Davidson states that the Sermon on the Mount is the "Magna Carta" of the Kingdom. Even beginning with the Beatitudes, which although often thought "gracious" are in fact: "the sternest declaration of war against this 'world' and all its works."[102] Davidson also notes his sympathy with Christian nonviolence when he calls Matthew 5:38–41 to be among the most distinctive precepts of Christianity:

'Resist not Evil'! I abrogate, nay, flatly reverse the entire Lex Talionis by which the world has hitherto been governed. There are to be no more soldiers, no

---

97. Davidson, *The Gospel of the Poor*, 111.
98. Davidson, *The Gospel of the Poor*, 112.
99. Davidson, *The Gospel of the Poor*, 113.
100. Davidson, *The Gospel of the Poor*, 113.
101. Davidson, *The Gospel of the Poor*, 114.
102. Davidson, *The Gospel of the Poor*, 117.

more policeman, no more lawyers, no more private property'. Such were the astounding announcements from the Mount – more astounding by far in the domain of the ethical than aught set down as 'miracle' or 'sign' in that of the physical.[103]

Davidson also takes up the frequent debates about whether the New Testament ever explicitly condemns slavery. He recognizes that it is often said that the Bible nowhere explicitly condemns it, but states that Christ condemned private property "in toto" and thus "He necessarily proscribed the chattel slavery which was its corner-stone in the ancient world."

> What is a soldier but a murderer hired by the wealthy to defend or acquire for them that which does not rightfully belong to them? What are our dragoons and marines about at Hull at this moment? Coercing Labour in the interest of Capital! Could the 'masses' have a better object-lesson in the true significance of our standing armies and bloated armaments? We were thanking God the other day that we did not, like our American kinsmen, employ 'Pinkertons' in such odious enterprises. But today our rulers are doing worse. They are wantonly terrorizing an industrious and peaceful population by crack national troops recruited from, and paid by, the masses themselves! …
>
> The serious question remains to be considered. Can any man who accepts the Christian faith intelligently become either soldier or lawyer? Frankly, I think not. To the Christian both professions are prohibited. They are the main props of this world and therefore the chief impediments to the advent of the 'Kingdom of God.'[104]

What is notable about Chapter XXIII, on The Lord's Prayer, is not only the fact that prayers were not to be for public show (citing Mt. 6:5–6; 7–8; Lk. 11:10–13) but that Davidson shares Hardie's conviction that the Prayer itself is to be taken as a serious indication of the social mission of Jesus:

> Thy Kingdom Come – This is to say, Abolish, O Just God, the cruel social inequality by which for long ages Thy children have been afflicted. Cast down Mammon in all his polluted sanctuaries of monarchy, hierarchy, aristocracy, and plutocracy, and banish the monster for evermore from the face of Thy fair earth. Exorcise the foul fiend of Competition and replace him by Divine Co-operation, communal and inter-communal, national and inter-national. Erect on the first foundations of absolute social and economic equality a lasting Temple of

---

103. Davidson, *The Gospel of the Poor*, 118.
104. Davidson, *The Gospel of the Poor*, 119–20.

Humanity in which till the end of time the sublime song of triumph shall ascend, 'Glory to God in the highest, on earth peace and goodwill to men'.[105]

He will later in this work state: "In these circumstances, it seems to me a present duty to cast down Mammon by capturing his citadel, Parliament, as speedily as possible, and erecting on its ruins the true City of God. Thy Kingdom Come!"[106] In this midst of his discussion of Jesus, interestingly, Davidson takes up the issue of the liberation of women in Section XXIV, noting that Jesus was called "Son of Mary," and that women were the first to see the Resurrection of Jesus, and that others "marvelled" that Jesus spoke with women (Jn 4:19–24). Davidson calls for the enfranchisement of women arguing that:

> Until women are placed, in all economic and political circumstances, on a perfect footing of equality with men, society remains Pagan rather than Christian. To enfranchise women would be to abolish war with all its burdens and barbarities, with many other hoary iniquity, besides.[107]

It remains to quickly summarize many of Davidson's points in the remaining sections. In Section XXV, "Christ and Labour," Davidson states that "The Messiah's mission was to make the first last and last first; to cast down the 'classes' and exalt the 'masses',"[108] calling the parable of the Sheep and Goats the "decisive victory of labour (Mt. 25:32–40)." When Davidson cites Matthew 20, where Jesus tells the parable about the vineyard owner who pays workers to work in the field, but they complain that all were paid the same even though some worked fewer hours, Davidson makes a number of interesting observations. First, he said that vineyard labour is light and agreeable, "like all labour will be," and second, that the "penny" of the parable was a good wage. Third, however, Davidson states that:

> the upright 'householder' knew that if their deeds were not equal, their needs were. That is to say that in the Kingdom of Heaven, i.e., the Communistic Commonwealth, no man shall suffer for lack of opportunity, intelligence, or physical strength. It will not merely be the duty but the pride and pleasure of the strong to support the weak, doing twice or thrice their own share of the common toil, in order that the least of Christ's brethren may be relieved from burdens to which they are unequal.[109]

---

105. Davidson, *The Gospel of the Poor*, 125.
106. Davidson, *The Gospel of the Poor*, 144.
107. Davidson, *The Gospel of the Poor*, 131.
108. Davidson, *The Gospel of the Poor*, 135.
109. Davidson, *The Gospel of the Poor*, 138.

4. The "Family of Faith": Hardie's Close Allies in "Biblical" Christian Socialism 125

In Section XXVI, while Davidson is critical of the "machines of the state," he seems to direct his interpretation of Jesus against certain kinds of State government: "princes, nobles, scribes, and all,"[110] and argues that:

> Christ did not recognize any necessity for the existence of the State. To Him the State was in its very essence evil ... Personal ambition, warlike enterprise, and commercial competition are the 'civic virtues' which the State applauds and rewards, and the religion of Christ condemns and prohibits in toto.[111]

But what he means, it seems, is a "state" that consists of one class ruling over another:

> Had He come along the streets of Jerusalem in a magnificent State carriage with a superbly-mounted cavalcade of household troops, showering honours and offices on the 'classes' and teaching the 'masses' to keep their distance from his august person, what plaudits would have burst from the throats of landlord, capitalist, and ecclesiastic![112]

Thus, argues Davidson, not only was Christ a lowly king, but also a just and leveling King, "who dissolved the entire 'machine' of State Government." Yet, Davidson does envision a "system" of governance in relation to socialism, and as such, asserts his insistence of "Christian" socialism:

> The Spirit of Jesus is needed to put a soul into materialistic Socialism, without which it can aspire to nothing more than human beaverism. The children of the Kingdom, as in Apostolic days, must not merely have all things in common; they must also be of one heart and one soul; so that not one of them shall say that aught of the things he possesses is his own. And when none shall lack aught, then again will men take knowledge of them that they have been with Jesus, and God will give them favour with the people and multiply converts indefinitely.[113]

In an echo of other Christian Socialists, Davidson shares a dim view of the significance and importance of Paul,[114] but this is only an aside to his final statement triumphantly declaring a "Christian" revolution:

---

110. Davidson, *The Gospel of the Poor*, 142.
111. Davidson, *The Gospel of the Poor*, 141.
112. Davidson, *The Gospel of the Poor*, 141–2.
113. Davidson, *The Gospel of the Poor*, 144.
114. Davidson, *The Gospel of the Poor*, 146.

The Pale Galilean will conquer in the end, and 'make all things new'. The Spirit of Truth shall lead us unto all truth. Hath He not said, 'Lo, I am with you always, Even unto the End of the World!'[115]

Delightful turns of phrase do not detract from his genuine scriptural insights, insights that continue to be debated in contemporary New Testament and Ethics scholarship.

SUMMARY

Hinted at in the memories about Martyn, discussed more briefly in Hird, and more developed in Davidson's extended notes (which hint at the most extensive sets of arguments we are here considering among Hardie's allies), these thoughts all bear striking similarities to a form of radical "Jesus literature" in the twentieth and twenty-first century, beginning with Bouck White's *The Call of the Carpenter* (1911), André Trocmé's classic (Fr. 1961; English in 1973): *Jesus and the Nonviolent Revolution*; John Howard Yoder's 1972 work, *The Politics of Jesus*, and Obery Hendricks Jr., *The Politics of Jesus: Rediscovering the True Revolutionary Nature of Jesus' Teachings and How They Have Been Corrupted* (2007).[116]

The overarching point to be made here is only secondarily that these friends of Hardie often turned to similar Biblical texts in their arguments. The stronger point is their unwavering conviction that Socialism is to be powerfully defended from serious and careful textual analysis *of the Bible* as a primary and dominant source of ethical reflection that buttresses what can otherwise often descend into details of economic analysis with little ethical reflection beyond moralistic generalities that "we all know ... " but rarely defend. Let us now turn our attention directly on Hardie's reading of the Bible.

---

115. Davidson, *The Gospel of the Poor*, 150.

116. André Trocmé's classic (Fr. 1961; English in 1973) *Jesus and the Nonviolent Revolution* (Scottdale: Herald Press, 1973); John Howard Yoder's *The Politics of Jesus* (Grand Rapids: Eerdmans, 1972); and more recently, Obery Hendricks Jr., *The Politics of Jesus: Rediscovering the True Revolutionary Nature of Jesus' Teachings and How They Have Been Corrupted* (New York: Penguin/Random House, 2007). For Bouck White, *The Call of the Carpenter* (New York: Doubleday, 1911), we have David Burns to thank for renewing interest in this American classic that is all but forgotten now, see Burns, *The Life and Death of the Radical Historical Jesus* (Oxford and New York: Oxford University Press, 2013).

Figure 5.1 "When thou doest an alms, let not thy left hand know what thy right hand doeth," *The Labour Leader*, 1891.

Chapter 5

HARDIE AND HIS BIBLE

In previous chapters, we have reviewed important discussions and sources for considering Keir Hardie and his relationship to Christianity more generally, but do not focus on his specific readings of the Bible. In this chapter, however, we turn to the main task at hand—a focused consideration of Hardie's tendencies toward what we are calling a "Proletarian Exegesis"—a way of reading the Bible with a particular assumption about class-interests—and that "assumption" clearly is that Jesus was talking about very similar issues indeed.

The sources

For a serious consideration of Hardie's reading of the Bible there are a few different kinds of writings that we have available to us, with varying degrees of significance. Intriguingly, these overlap with a few of the kinds of suggested "sources" discussed by Michael Gold when he called for "Proletarian literature" (see Chapter 1). In this case, however, all of these are written by Hardie himself.

First, there are simple allusions or references to Jesus apart from any consideration of specific texts, or with minimal allusions to texts. There are dozens of these, of course, and I will here only feature a few in order to illustrate what I mean. Although brief, these are nonetheless interesting because they give us an initial impression of the thoughts of the man, but they are *too* brief to be a serious basis for analyzing Hardie's thought.

Second, there are polemical articles—that is, writings where Hardie is specifically responding to a sermon, letter, or event. Specific Biblical arguments can feature more significantly in these responses, especially when the issue that Hardie is responding to involves someone's use of scriptural texts in the first instance, and so he is effectively engaging in arguing about those texts, and also offering "counter texts."

Third, and finally, there are more than a few important examples of extended articles, some of which turn up as reprinted pamphlets. These are typically the texts of an extended speech, or a series of articles in *The Labour Leader*, or other socialist newspapers or journals, and/or pamphlets addressing specific topics. Not unexpectedly, since Hardie was not an academic theologian or clergyperson, none of these writings are identified by Hardie as a solely "Biblical" debate, but rather feature his use of the Bible *while* he is arguing for wider socialist ideals. What is significant, then, is the extent to which he clearly believed his political goals were *furthered* by expositions of *Biblical* texts without "skipping a beat" and returning, as he often did, to current economic issues. Let us consider each of these three types of evidence.[1]

Brief allusions

Biblical references were common to Hardie's rhetoric, but in some cases these go beyond merely a reference to well-known tropes like referring to someone as "a Good Samaritan," or "beating swords into plowshares" (such as Hardie's acidic reference in the October 1893 edition of *The Labour Leader* to the parable of the "sheep and goats" in reference to MPs who would not vote for provisions for the hungry). Such references are, of course, arguably part of the English language culturally as well as religiously, and have little meaning with regard to how one interprets Scripture, nor the faith commitments of those who would use such well-known references. Perhaps more entertaining, however, are political cartoons which certainly fall into this category, as they are also clearly based on scriptural references.

As we noted previously, Hardie's first regular writing job was as a columnist for the *Ardrossan and Saltcoats Herald*, a Scottish paper that is still in business (North Ayrshire). In the April 15, 1882 edition, there appeared the first announcement of a regular column by "a Practical Miner," where the newspaper announced that the editor:

> ... has much pleasure in announcing to the under-ground workers of this locality that he has made arrangements with a Practical Miner for the commencement of a series of articles entitled: 'The Trapper's Opinion on Things in General' ... these articles will include mining notes from every coal producing district in the world together with remarks on all passing events in any way connected to the trade, whether Parliamentary, Legal, or official. Our correspondent will also be pleased to supply enquirers with information concerning mining laws, such as Mines Regulation Act, General and Special Rules, Employers Liability Act, Track Act, & etc.[2]

Clearly drawn from his own past, Hardie continued under the pseudonym "Trapper," but the column appeared with the normal title: "Black Diamonds: Mining Notes

---

1. I should clarify the notation system used in the references in this chapter. In most cases, the explicit page numbers of the newspaper issues being quoted are no longer legible, especially on digital or microfilm versions. However, dates of the specific issues are provided, and because the editions of *The Labour Leader* are typically under twelve pages, the source is fairly easily located with the dates.
2. Editorial Comment, *Ardrossan and Saltcoats Herald*, April 15, 1882.

Worth Minding." Hardie was recruited to write on mining affairs, and the column regularly featured news and brief analyses of mining affairs with an emphasis on local issues, but which could occasionally include brief observations of events in Europe and the United States. Some years later it was officially acknowledged that "Trapper" was Keir Hardie, but in the early editions it seems that his identity was fairly well concealed. Reading through these columns, it becomes clear that Hardie usually stayed closely within the remit designated in the announcement, but on rare occasions we see a foreshadowing of Hardie's religious interests that would become a more frequent topic of his writing in *The Labour Leader*. For example, Hardie, in an April 1885 issue, inserted a comforting note in the midst of reporting on wage reductions which also clearly foreshadows Hardie's famous "preaching" style:

> To return to the miners, I can only hope that the present reduction may be the means of causing them to draw closer together. Men who are companions in adversity frequently exhibit more faithfulness to a common cause than do those whose circumstances are more favourable, and if this reduction be the means of causing the mean to band together and assist each other, then the future may be much more prosperous and happy than the past has been.[3]

Given the focus on mining issues, it is not surprising that these early written assignments show very little of the religious interests that would regularly occupy Hardie in his own newspaper. However, such interests are not entirely absent. In a February 1884 issue, Hardie gives an early example of his dialogue with sermons he heard, in this case heartily approving:

> In a sermon preached at Leadhills by the Rev. James Symington, the following passage occurs. It is a faithful picture of the feelings of too many employers toward their workmen, and it augurs well for the times when a clergyman has the courage to speak the truth in so plain a manner. 'With a worldly man the question is not how can I best assist my brethren, by giving them what I have. But rather this: How much can I succeed in taking from my brethren? ... The man of the world cares nothing for the crushing of human bones, and the mangling of social happiness, and the irritation of restless souls. He has within the spirit of a beast, that cannot see any farther than the appetites of a beast, and that cares not how he gets his food, provided he gets it. The man of the world has no love for men's highest welfare, it is only themselves they care about.'[4]

A year later, in the March 1885 edition, Hardie wrote at length about a sermon from a Rev. J. S. Robertson of Cumnock, and Hardie's emerging theological concerns are clear from the portions of the sermon that Hardie quoted at length here as well, especially his continued interest in temperance issues:

3. *Ardrossan and Saltcoats Herald*, April 10, 1885.
4. *Ardrossan and Saltcoats Herald*, February 1, 1884.

The address is, on the whole, worthy of a wide circulation, and is fitted to do much good. All through the discourse runs a line of thought clearly recognizing that all men are brethren in the great family of God, and nothing tends more to raise the fallen than this same thought that, no matter how low or degraded a person may have become, God loves such a one with all a father's love, and desires nothing more than the return of such a one to all the rights and privileges of those who are of the household of faith. Here is a sad truth put in small compass: 'A fallen man can never respect himself, and life becomes to him a thing of eating and drinking, toiling and resting, and the man as lost is the animal.' These few words convey only too true a picture of what the existence of only too many of our working people really is. Speaking of the effect of working in the mine has on the mind, he says, 'That there is a tendency in this work to lead men to forget who they are, is evident from the fact that very many of their number are living far below their proper level ... Low down in the bowels of the earth you toil, shut out from God's pure light, in work which is both dirty and dangerous; and it is not perhaps to be wondered at that many of you forget who you are, and so lose your self-respect: 'Only a miner!' Say that, and believe that, and you will become only a miner, and lose all your self-respect. What I wish you to feel now and always is that you are more; in fact, you are not miners at all, and he who says of you 'only a miner' is probably not living his own free self either. You are God's child, you work is mining, but the blackest work to which a man may put his hands can never disguise or blot out the Image of Him in whose likeness he was made and as you pick away at the seam of stone at which you are employed, you can do so in the blessed and soul elevating consciousness that He who curiously places it in the depth of the earth is your Father. Let that idea get possession of your souls and it will redeem your work from insignificance. If it were not beneath God your Father to form that material at first, it cannot be beneath you to bring to light his hidden power, wisdom and love. Your work is honorable if the workman is in right relations with his God; and though I would not choose to work that work, yet when I meet you, blackened almost past recognition, as you return from your labours, do I not know that your work is as honorable as my own, and that you too are God's child? That self-respect which springs from the consciousness of man's true relations to God is not that the sources of true elevation of the working classes? Oh, what a charm your daily work would have for you if done in this spirit.' Speaking of Intemperance, Mr. Robertson says – 'Without sobriety therefore you cannot respect yourself, and without self respect you cannot be brave men; and power is always dangerous in the hands of those who have no consciousness of their own personal dignity – no self-respect.' To this it may be added that so long as the liquor traffic exists in our midst, so long will we have intemperance among the working-classes and therefore it clearly becomes the duty of those who are afraid of the 'new found democracy' to work for the overthrow of the drink shop, and thus rob the people of the dangerous element. Here is another item worth quoting: 'A cessation of this expenditure (on drink) would be equivalent to raising the savings of every poor man's family throughout Great Britain by £10 a year, or 4s a week. It is therefore desirable in the best interest of the working classes that they should realize the terrible obstacle which intemperance presents to their true advancement and progress.' The quotations will help to give an idea of what the whole is like. No man can read the sermon without feeling benefited, and while I am not prepared to say amen to everything contained in it, still I have no hesitation in affirming that the working-men of the district have been placed under a debt of gratitude to Mr. Robertson, and this they can best show by seeking to confirm their lives to the principles which he has laid down for their guidance.[5]

Later, in his work as editor of *The Labour Leader*, Hardie's "religious" writing becomes more explicit and focused on Biblical themes, and especially the person of Jesus. For example, in the first stable year of publishing *The Labour Leader* (1894), there were reports on events of interest around the country, and included in June 1894, was the following report:

At Arkwright Street Wesleyan Chapel the Rev. Mark Guy Pearse said, 'that religious people would be as much amazed to-day if Christ came into the world as the people were in olden times. They would find Christ walking amongst the most disreputable persons. It was Christ's Socialism that perplexed men then; it would be that which would perplex men if He came to-day. He wished they would give up talking about taking souls and talk about the religion of Jesus Christ, who believed that the body was as dear as the soul.' We recommend Mr. Pearse's sermon to the professing Christian politicians.[6]

There are dozens of these affirmations—what one might call "amen" comments—throughout the pages of *The Labour Leader*. We are, however, more interested in Hardie's own arguments.

Christmas editions of his newspaper were—not surprisingly—often occasions for Hardie to cite and discuss Scripture. In the Christmas issue of 1895, Hardie expresses his sympathy and support—first for striking workers in Scotland, and then more generally to all the unemployed. To striking engineers on the Clyde, Hardie writes:

I send the Season's Greetings. They and their dependents are having a bitter experience of what Industrial Christianity means. In days of industrial depression they suffered, without a murmur, reductions in their wages. Now that so-called prosperity has returned to their trade, the good, kind, charitable, benevolent Christian men who employ them refuse to allow them to share in that prosperity. In thousands of homes on the banks of the Clyde and the Lagan Black Care will cast a baleful shadow over the Christmas festivities. 'The labourer is worthy of his hire' said the Christ, by which He explained He meant a full

---

5. *Ardrossan and Saltcoats Herald*, March 6, 1885.
6. *The Labour Leader*, June 23, 1894.

free supply of all the necessaries of life. The shipbuilders interpret the passage to mean the lowest wages man can be starved into accepting. Huge fortunes are piled up by the employers out of the labour of the men who are now idle, whilst all that is left to them is a very niggardly subsistence. 'Quit ye like men, be strong,' friends, 'the Christ is with you in your struggle, not with the masters in their cruel rapacious greed.'

To the Unemployed I send Greetings of Sympathy and promise of service. 'Why stand ye idle in the market-place?' said the Master of the vineyard to the unemployed. 'Because no man hath hired us' they replied, whereupon he hired them. Members of Parliament, town and country councilors, are the modern representatives of the masters of the vineyard. You, the unemployed, still stand wearily idle in the market-place because no man hath hired you, and the modern masters of the vineyard, most of them church-going Christians aforesaid, seeing there, pass you by in the temple. But for ever will it be so, the market-places are becoming over-crowded and you are beginning to overflow into the streets, and the lanes, and roadways. Peace on earth is not meant for you. 'Why say ye peace, peace, when there is no peace' and there must be no peace until Christ's principles are practiced, and industry is based on the Christ-like principle of from each according to his capacity, to each according to his needs ...[7]

Here, Hardie mixed his interpretation of Jesus's instructions to the disciples (Mt. 10:10–11) and the parable in Matthew 20:1–16 with allusions to principles such as "from each according to his capacity ..., " a phrase most consider to be from Marx, but it pre-dated Marx by many centuries, and some suggest its roots are in one of the most favored Biblical passages in Christian Socialist rhetoric, namely Acts 4:34–5:

[34] There was not a needy person among them, for as many as owned lands or houses sold them and brought the proceeds of what was sold. [35] They laid it at the apostles' feet, *and it was distributed to each as any had need* ...

Many of the biographers cite the opening observation of Hardie's later Christmas editorial of 1897, which begins with Hardie's lament, "I am afraid my heart is bitter to-night and so the thoughts and feelings which pertain to the Christmas season are far from me ...." But before this line, Hardie had already stated: "The season's greetings to all who are remembering that Christ came 'not to send peace but a sword' against wrongdoing in all its forms" (the added comment about "against wrongdoing ... " is added by Hardie, of course), and then the editorial comments continued after the "bitter heart" comment:

when I think of the thousands of white-livered poltroons who will take the Christ name in vain, and yet not see His image being crucified afresh in each hungry

---

7. *The Labour Leader*, December 21, 1895.

child, I cannot think of peace. I have known as a child what hunger means, and the scars of those days are with me still and rankle in my heart, and unfit me in many ways for doing the work waiting to be done. A holocaust of every Church building in Christendom to-night would be as an act of sweet savour in the sight of Him whose name is supposed to be worshipped within their walls. If the spiritually proud and pride blinded professors of Christianity could only be made to feel and see that the Christ is here ever present with us, and that they are laying on the stripes and binding the brow afresh with thorns, and making shed tears of blood in a million homes, surely the world could be made more meet for the establishment of His Kingdom. We have no right to a merry Christmas which so many of our fellows cannot share.[8]

Hardie here reflects on Jesus as having endured what working people also endure. Jesus becomes *symbol* as well as hero to the poor, but his anger against institutional Christianity is equally clear. This passage is somewhat unusual in its somber tone, as there are many examples of his enjoying his rhetoric with more relish.

In November of 1900, Hardie noted with obvious glee, the formation of a registered "Limited Liability Company" entitled the "Baptist Industrial Mission" which was said to be formed as a money-making proposition for supporting evangelical mission work. Hardie commented, in a column entitled, "Evangelization Limited":

Evidently the early Apostles were ignorant men and went the wrong way about their work, and 'They didn't know everything down in Juda.' They ought to have formed a Limited Liability Company. When next the Scriptures come to be revised we may expect a certain text to read: 'Go ye unto all the world, beginning at the Stock Exchange.'[9]

That Hardie would continue to make numerous satirical comments like this throughout his life is evident late in his career as editor, as can be seen in the following observation made in the June 26, 1902 issue. He reports on travels into London, arriving at 4 a.m. in Oxford Circus station:

In a few hours these silent streets will be thronged with crowds of well-dressed, well-fed, comfortably-circumstanced people going to worship Jesus the Christ. And yet this Christ was in his day a homeless wanderer and the special friend and champion of just such women as are now trudging weary and footsore to some wretched place of concealment where they may hide themselves until night has again sent these good Christian people within doors. Presumably were

---

8. *The Labour Leader*, December 25, 1897.
9. *The Labour Leader*, November 25, 1900.

Christ living in London now, he would have to keep out of the way of these good folks lest his poverty offend their sense of propriety.[10]

Again, if these were the only kinds of arguments from which we had to work, we would have as little as we do from many other progressive political figures of Victorian and Edwardian England (although a careful reading of the two volumes of Lord Snowden's autobiography, for example, reveals precious few Biblical allusions!). While all of these presume a certain way of reading the New Testament, they are not *direct* citations and discussions. For this, we move to more substantial discussions.

Polemical responses

The following examples further illustrate Hardie, once again, in the role of polemicist, but in these cases, the issues deal with religious and Biblical defenses of (or arguments against) Socialism in Britain. These arguments are a bit more detailed than the previous category.

For example, in May 1889, Hardie responds to the comments of a Rev. Harry Edwards, referring to him as "probably a young man" (in order, it seems, to somewhat excuse the comments which Hardie finds objectionable). But it was precisely Edwards's invocation of Scripture to defend his observations on society that drew Hardie's response. Hardie began with those arguments with which he could agree with Edwards—but clarifying that his agreement depended on where Edwards then goes with his point. Here, Hardie once again invokes the difference that he sees between the Mosaic expectations of sharing and prevention of "usury" (interest) in social practices, but then argues that this was overcome by the Monarchy:

> When, however, he undertakes to make God and the Christian religion responsible for poverty he makes a rather heavy demand on our credulity … Starting with the Mosaic laws, for which he claims divine origin, he points out how the people departed from their tenets, which resulted in the kingdom become 'rotten ripe for destruction' and 'culminating in its overthrow': the question arises here: Did God make a mistake, or were the people responsible? We Socialists hold the latter view. So long as the land could not be sold, and all debts were wiped out every seven years, the nation prospered. When, however, the rulers embarked on great commercial enterprises – claimed the land as their own, added 'field to field' until the land was 'full of silver and gold' and 'mean man bowed down' then trouble came. Jeremiah threatened that the Lord would bring a nation from afar, before the Jews had departed from His teaching. If Mr. Edwards maintains all this to have been according to the will of God, there's an

---

10. *The Labour Leader*, June 26, 1902.

end of the matter; if, on the other hand, he accepts it as due to the violation of the laws laid down for the guidance of the people, then his place is in the ranks of the Socialists who are endeavouring to rid this nation of the those evils which made Israel 'rotten ripe for destruction' and culminated 'in its overthrow.'[11]

To emphasize the level of sophisticated argument here, it may be significant to point out the array of texts to which Hardie is clearly alluding:

(A) Mosaic laws about usury (Ex. 22:25; Lev. 25:36–7; Deut. 23:19);
(B) Explanations for the Babylonian Exile (Jer. 7 among many others; Dan. 9; Ezra 9; Neh. 9);
(C) The Sabbatical Years and forgiveness of debts every seven years (Lev. 25);
(D) Monarchical accumulation of Land condemned by Isaiah (2:9; 5:8; Jer. 5:15);
(E) "Nation from afar," Jeremiah 5:15; Jeremiah 24 about "ripe figs," etc.

After this array of citations, Hardie proceeds to argue that Rev. Edwards suggested that there was punishment of Ancient Israel for their misdeeds, and that such misdeeds led to the Babylonian conquests (a common argument, particularly important in Jeremiah). Hardie, however, believes that Edwards did not proceed to the obvious next steps: What would economic justice—that is to say, correcting their mistakes—actually *look* like? Here, Hardie returns to two of his favorite Biblical themes, namely the social interpretation of the Lord's Prayer, and the communal sharing of Acts 2 and 4:

> 'Thy Kingdom come, thy will be done on earth as it is in heaven.' What do those words mean? Surely that whatever obtains in heaven should also prevail on earth. Will there be private property in land and capital in heaven? Will one set of angels own everything, and be able to make all the other angels toil early and late to make them rich? Will there be millionaires and paupers in heaven? ... If not, if none of those things are there, neither should they be here. Mr. Edwards has much to say about the motive which led the early Christians to adopt Communism as the practical expression of their faith. Their motive was fellowship, fraternity, brotherhood, which can only be secured by community of interest, and for that reason is still the motive of the Socialist movement. Covetousness is the leading principle of the present system: Socialism, on the other hand, is, like Christianity, altruistic. Each for self is the motto of commercialism, each for all that of socialism.[12]

Hardie then takes exception to Edwards's arguments that Socialism is itself "covetous" because it would seek to expand the communal sharing that is described

---

11. *The Labour Leader*, May 14, 1889.
12. *The Labour Leader*, May 14, 1889.

in Acts as only "among Christians" with a more expansive idea of sharing with everyone in the state. Hardie cites Edwards directly to say:

> The early church, he says, confined the distribution of its means within its own circle ... Socialism as such doesn't appear to draw the line anywhere except between itself and capitalism, Agnosticism is no barrier. If the vast fields of capital were secured on Socialistic lines, Hottentot, Agnostic, Jews, and Christian would have an equal share in the booty ... [13]

Hardie replies by marshaling other examples from the ministry of Jesus to establish just such a universalism that Edward accuses him of supporting:

> Appalling thought! God, of course, is not the Father of the Hottentot, the Jew, and the Agnostic, therefore they can with safety be left to starve. I demand the proof for the opening sentence quoted above. I probably know as much about the communism of the early Church as Mr. Edwards, and I know of no authority for such a statement. Did Christ when He fed the five thousand carefully weed out the Jew and the Hottentots? Does God withhold sunshine from Agnostics, Jews, and Hottentots? What about the parable of the Good Samaritan? How would Mr. Edwards interpret his duty towards Jews, Hottentots, and Agnostics in the light of that parable? Socialists believe in the Brotherhood of Man. What brotherhood does Mr. Edwards – minister of the gospel of Christ – believe in?[14]

Warming to the argument, Hardie continues his attacks on Edwards's further arguments in defense of wealthy Church folk who are able to support the church from their riches. Hardie writes:

> It has been my lot to read not a few defenses of private ownership of wealth, but for sheer audacity, verging on blasphemy, Mr. Edwards easily carries off first honours in this: 'How useful Nicodemus and Joseph proved at the Crucifixion, the one with his embalming ointment and the other with his linen and empty tomb. What a shabby burial would the Man of Sorrows have had but for that timely assistance. And this seems to say that rich men, with a right spirit, are helpful under the Christian economy to come to the rescue of a good cause when contingencies arise, as they often do.'

> It is really difficult to write of this without indulging in strong language. If the proper way to come to the rescue of a good cause is to bury a man after he is dead, then no more need be said. Christ, who was born among the poor, brought up in a cottage home, worked with His hands, and proclaimed His mission to be the poor, and was at length murdered by the rich for His steadfast adherence

---

13. *The Labour Leader*, May 14, 1889.
14. *The Labour Leader*, May 14, 1889.

to the cause of the poor, had no need of a rich man's tomb in His death. To help the living is surely better than to bury the dead, and I fear the rich will not thank Mr. Edwards for this line of defence. That it is true I don't dispute, but it is scarcely complimentary to them.[15]

Hardie then continues by pointing out that Edwards advised socialists to preach to capitalists to give up their wealth. But Hardie points out that a wealthy few turning to Socialism (and he notes that there are indeed Socialist landlords and manufacturers) does not actually change the entire system. Wealth would simply transfer to those less principled. But in the end, Hardie issues a challenge to debate the points, *precisely by debating Scripture*, and once again demonstrating his hermeneutical approach—discussing what came in the Bible before Jesus, Jesus Himself, and those (in the Bible and beyond) that followed Jesus:

> Meanwhile, I take leave of him with this offer. If he is agreeable I will discuss with him, either on the platform or through the press, this proposition: That 'the aims of modern Socialists are identical with the aim of Christianity as revealed in the four Gospels.' To be going on with I assert that the Old and New Testament alike condemn the possession of riches as an evil; that Christ expressly taught that rich men could only enter heaven with difficulty, if at all; that for the first four hundred years of Christian faith the fathers taught Socialism and Communism as an integral part of Christianity, and denounced rent and interest as robbery. Mr. Edwards may remember how Jeremiah wailed out from the depths of his sorely stricken heart: 'A wonderful and horrible thing is committed in the land; the prophets prophesy falsely, and the priests bear rule by their means, and my people love to have it so. And what will ye do in the end thereof? [Jer. 5:30–1].' Let Mr. Edwards beware that he is not making the same mistake.[16]

A central observation to be made here, other than taking careful note of the textual content of his polemics, is that Hardie considered it his "socialist duty" to challenge an opponent to *a debate on the Bible*, and decidedly not setting aside all matters of "religion" as merely beside the point.

Another good example from early in Hardie's editorial responsibilities at *The Labour Leader* is from early February 1895. Here, Hardie replies to the comments of a Rev. J. W. Shannon, pastor of The Wilton United Presbyterian Church (Hawick) who had attempted to refute Hardie's arguments about religion and socialism. Hardie begins his reply:

> Mr. Shannon, as becometh a Christian minister, sets out by misrepresenting what I said. But Mr. Shannon did a more grievous thing than that. He perverts – in

---

15. *The Labour Leader*, May 14, 1889.
16. *The Labour Leader*, May 14, 1889.

ignorance, let us charitably suppose – not only the teachings but the very words of Jesus.[17]

The first part of Hardie's response was to cite Jesus's criticisms of religious leaders of His day, contrary to Shannon's defense of "dignitaries and authorities." Yet, Hardie argues:

> Jesus in his day denounced the classes who robbed the poor, and for pretence make long prayers, in language which I have never dared to use. He poured out a healthy virile scorn on the priests who, like Mr. Shannon, made a burlesque of the words of holy writ, and missed the spirit of the teaching. When Mr. Shannon says that Jesus 'did not rail against dignitaries and authorities, blaming one or two classes for existing evils, nor did He strive against the powers that were ordained of God,' he lays himself open to a harsh criticism. What about 'Scribes and Pharisees – hypocrites' [Mt. 23:13, 14, 15, 23, 25, 27, 29; Lk. 11:44] or 'blind leaders of the blind' [Lk. 6:39, but likely referring also to references to the blind in the same chapter of Matthew, e.g., Mt. 23:16, 17, 19, 23, 26] or 'vipers' [Mt. 3:7; 12:34; 23:33; Lk. 3:7] who merit eternal damnation, and a score of other epithets which might be chosen? Jesus was always tender and sympathetic towards the poor, but proud in His scorn of the rich, and the so-called learned classes who did as Mr. Shannon is doing today, made themselves the apologists for the grinding oppressions of the age. If Mr. Shannon means to infer, as he seems to do, that Liberalism and Toryism and Landlordism, and Capitalism are "ordained of God" then his God is a god of hypocrisy and a monster with whom no man, much less any woman, would care to be associated.[18]

Hardie then turns, once again, to the Lord's Prayer as a social manifesto:

> Let Mr. Shannon, as a beginning of the study of Christianity as differentiated from Calvinism, read the Lord's Prayer, and then try whether Socialism or commercialism presents the true picture of God's Will being 'done on earth as it is in heaven'. When he has finished this elementary lesson in Christianity I will set him another easy one.[19]

In the Christmas, 1894 issue of *The Labour Leader*, Hardie refers to "A Preacher on the Poor," which was a critique of comments made by Rev. Stopford Brooke. Brooke was commenting on the homeless poor in London, and the significant point here is that Hardie's debate was focused on an interpretation of Jesus's famous statement, "The poor ye have with you always." Brooke had claimed that this verse was being taken out of the context: " ... in which it was said and in which it had

---

17. *The Labour Leader*, February 2, 1895.
18. *The Labour Leader*, February 2, 1895.
19. *The Labour Leader*, February 2, 1895.

a particular and personal meaning" and was being misused to inform a call to *end* poverty. Hardie claims that the "comfortable classes" of society have claimed the authority of Christ for their own maxim, and have made him say, "The poor ye shall have with you …," as if suggesting that there is nothing to be done about it. But when Hardie refers to providing shelter, he invokes not Jesus directly, but rather the Prophet Isaiah. To provide shelter, states Hardie, would be to:

> fulfil in this small fashion that ancient cry of Isaiah which ought to be written over the lords of the London County Council: 'Wash you; make you clean; put away the evils of your doings; cease to do evil; learn to do well … Seek justice, relieve the oppressed.' [Isa. 1:16–17][20]

Once again, the tactic is "counter texts" rather than dismissing Biblical arguments *tout court*.

A brief notice in March 1898 has Hardie once again turning to the Sermon on the Mount. Referring to an article he had read in the *North British Daily Mail*, the writer:

> … is evidently of [the] opinion that the Sermon on the Mount is a discourse on mysteries to be unfolded in the world to come. He has no theory in support as to this meaning. He considers the sermon 'a sketch of a perfect life never to be realized in this world', which every true believer in Jesus has it in his heart to attain to. We are afraid that *The Mail* theologian doesn't understand that portion of the sermon called 'The Lord's Prayer' which tells us to pray: 'Thy kingdom come, Thy will be done in earth, as it is done in heaven.' If this be not a distinct assertion that Christ's kingdom be established, not in heaven alone, but *on earth*, words have no meaning.[21]

The Lord's Prayer, and especially the beloved "on earth … " phrase is once again used by Hardie.

Against Rev. Andrew Douglas, Arbroath

In another December issue, Hardie turned on another clergyman who had been defending industrialists. He is introduced by Hardie as "a professional Christian. That is to say, he is maintained by the State to expound the principles of Christianity to the citizens of Arbroath." Hardie turns once again to the Gospel of Matthew in his reply:

> If by any chance Andrew should possess a copy of the New Testament (Authorized Version) he might read from the twenty-fifth chapter of Matthew's

---

20. *The Labour Leader*, December 19, 1894.
21. *The Labour Leader*, March 18, 1898.

gospel, but the thirty-first verse to the end of the chapter. It is a picture of the last day of judgment drawn by Jesus. It tells how the King divided the people into two sets – one bound for glory, the other to the outer darkness where there shall be 'weeping and wailing and gnashing of teeth'. Those on the right hand were evidently the Socialists who had done good deeds – fed the hungry, clothed the naked, etc. Those on the left hand were the Andrew Douglases and others who for a pretence made long prayers whilst shielding those who devoured widows' houses or kept back the labourers' wages by fraud. In all sincerity I ask Mr. Douglas for his interpretation of this parable. If it means what it says, what becomes of his denunciations of those who would save mankind by providing them with 'material comforts'? Are not food and drink and raiment 'material comforts'? And it was for providing these that the people getting into heaven. It is worthy of note that the Rev. gentleman had no words too strong in which to denounce the working class – the class to which Christ belonged – whilst from first to last, so far as the printed report goes, he had no word to say of the masters. The inference is plain. Only working men can do wrong. Had Andrew Douglas been among the crowd to whom Pilate gave choice of a prisoner, his voice would have swelled the cry of 'Not that man, but Barabbas.' The young Socialist Agitator of Nazareth need have expected no mercy from Andrew Douglas. And then he has the hypocrisy to pray that working men's faith in God be kept inviolate. How can working men believe in the same God as this man? His God is the friend of the rich, the foe of the poor. Keir.[22]

The "White Slaves" Series: The Lord Overtoun Affair

Probably the most celebrated case of Hardie's journalistic fire is the "muck-raking" series Hardie published in 1899 about the industrial working conditions of the factories owned by Scottish industrialist, Lord Overtoun, who owned chrome-plating works in Shawfield. In her biography, Benn comments:

> Few who have written about Hardie have failed to mention the fact that part of his passion against Overtoun must have been fuelled by a chance to expose a man so very like the one who had fired him from the bakery all those years ago. Overtoun too was a self-satisfied entrepreneur who made much of his Christian philanthropy. Hardie looked behind this model citizen and found that he compelled the workforce in his chemical works to work a twelve-hour day, seven days a week, and gave no meal breaks.[23]

Lord Overtoun was famously celebrated as a Christian philanthropist who was involved in a variety of religious-based charities—involvements on which Hardie would shine a blinding light, in order to reveal a profoundly disturbing hypocrisy.

---

22. *The Labour Leader*, December 11, 1897.
23. Benn, *Hardie*, 137.

The series was so controversial and had become a rather significant *cause célèbre* that the articles were also published as a separate pamphlet. The extent of this debate suggests that it might be better included in the category below featuring longer essays, but this series certainly is the most famous of Hardie's "response" articles as opposed to initiating an essay on a topic, which is the main concern of the final section below.

In the first of the series, Hardie begins with a quotation of the "Golden Rule": "Therefore, all things whatsoever ye would that men should do to you, do you even so to them; for this is the law and the prophets." Hardie then warms to the task. He comments that he likes the word "all" in the quotation, because:

> it seems to leave no loophole of escape. The Christian man will, in 'all things': treat others exactly as he himself would expect others to treat him were he in their place and they in his. Christ was the speaker, and in matters of this kind He never left His hearers in any doubt as to His meaning.[24]

Hardie lays the blame for the industrial conditions he proceeds to delineate squarely at the feet of Lord Overtoun and his immediate family, because there is no limited liability company where a "sinner may shield himself behind the shareholders." Even if a few others are involved, "on him must rest the chief responsibility for the conduct of the works." Hardie insists that his information is not based on hearsay but rather on direct interviews with workers: "every statement concerning the men has been taken down from their own lips." The response to Hardie's attacks were equally emotional. *The Evening Times* had referred to Lord Overtoun as a "Kind-hearted Christian Gentleman," but Hardie replied:

> No man who ruins his competitors, pays his workmen 3d. or 4d. an hour, works them 12 hours a day and seven days a week, fines them if they go to church on Sundays, keeps them working in conditions which destroy their flesh, and does not provide even lavatory accommodations, and who allows his men no meal hours, is either Christian or gentleman.[25]

When a Christian publication known as *The Puritan* ran articles praising Lord Overtoun, holding him in "highest esteem because of his generous support of religion and philanthropic work, and his personal interest in the spread of national righteousness …, " Hardie comments that this article represents "the official reply of official 'churchianity' to our exposures of Lord Overtoun's treatment of his workpeople" and then continues:

> This refined, humane, hospitable, Christian leader can regard with equanimity the destruction, body and mind, of those whom he employs, condemn them

---

24. *The Labour Leader*, April 1, 1899.
25. *The Labour Leader*, April 1, 1899.

to conditions of toil which revolt every sense of humanity, pay them a wage which means perpetual poverty, refuse to make even the most elementary provisions for the men's comfort and convenience, and withal be lauded to the seventh heaven as a very paragon of virtue – the embodiment of all the Christian attributes – but a journal issued professedly in the interests of Christianity![26]

The conditions were seriously abusive. The toxic fumes that the workers breathed caused skin burns, and especially deteriorated the cartilage of workers' noses. Benn notes that workers came to Hardie to talk about rashes, lung problems, and water pollution. There was no provision for medical care, and Hardie notes that a worker's wife had to tear curtains to treat her husband's burns. There were not even washing facilities for the workers to try to rinse out their eyes. With bitter irony, Hardie notes that some of the men must be treated at the Glasgow hospital where Lord Overton serves in executive leadership. The workers must work twelve-hour workdays, with no meal breaks, having to eat in the midst of toxic chemicals. Furthermore, there were no Sundays off—yet another irony given Lord Overtoun's service on committees for the observance of Sabbath. Hardie angrily wrote:

> Whilst Lord Overtoun conducts family worship at Overtoun House, or bends in lowly reverence before the altar of God's grace in church, or offers a grace of thankfulness before breakfast, dinner and tea, his white chrome-eaten victims toil and sweat in the malaria hole at Shawfield, adding to the wealth of their sainted master. Whiles they murder their bodies he prays for their souls, as if God was not also the maker of the body ... only when he has done full homage to Mammon does he turn to Jehovah.[27]

The workers were not paid a generous wage. Lord Overtoun was said to distribute £10,000 to charity, yet Hardie wrote: "Think of it! A human being, made in the image of God, working toilsomely in a hellhole for fourpence an hour!"

In the first article of the series, Hardie turns to Scripture to scold Lord Overtoun, stating: "As I am no hand at invective, I will again quote Scripture ... " and Hardie turns to one of his most frequently quoted chapters of the Gospel of Matthew, ch. 23:1–39. However, Hardie notably did not use the entire passage. Here, I will indicate with *italics* those portions that Hardie chose not to reproduce in his editorial in order to observe his selection of passages:

Matthew 23:1–39 [KJV] **Matthew 23:1** Then spake Jesus to the multitude, and to his disciples, [2] Saying, The scribes and the Pharisees sit in Moses' seat: [3] All therefore whatsoever they bid you observe, *that* observe and do; but do not ye after their works: for they say, and do not. [4] For they bind heavy burdens and grievous to

---

26. *The Labour Leader*, April 1, 1899.
27. *The Labour Leader*, April 1, 1899.

be borne, and lay *them* on men's shoulders; but they *themselves* will not move them with one of their fingers. ⁵ But all their works they do for to be seen of men:

Hardie then skips to the use of the "scribes and Pharisees":

¹³ But woe unto you, scribes and Pharisees, hypocrites! for ye shut up the kingdom of heaven against men:

OMITTED:

for ye neither go in yourselves, neither suffer ye them that are entering to go in.

¹⁴ Woe unto you, scribes and Pharisees, hypocrites! for ye devour widows' houses, and for a pretence make long prayer: therefore ye shall receive the greater damnation. ¹⁵ Woe unto you, scribes and Pharisees, hypocrites! for ye compass sea and land to make one proselyte, and when he is made, ye make him twofold more the child of hell than yourselves.

OMITTED:

¹⁶ *Woe unto you, ye blind guides, which say, Whosoever shall swear by the temple, it is nothing; but whosoever shall swear by the gold of the temple, he is a debtor!* ¹⁷ *Ye fools and blind: for whether is greater, the gold, or the temple that sanctifieth the gold?* ¹⁸ *And, Whosoever shall swear by the altar, it is nothing; but whosoever sweareth by the gift that is upon it, he is guilty.* ¹⁹ *Ye fools and blind: for whether is greater, the gift, or the altar that sanctifieth the gift?* ²⁰ *Whoso therefore shall swear by the altar, sweareth by it, and by all things thereon.* ²¹ *And whoso shall swear by the temple, sweareth by it, and by him that dwelleth therein.* ²² *And he that shall swear by heaven, sweareth by the throne of God, and by him that sitteth thereon.*

²³ Woe unto you, scribes and Pharisees, hypocrites! for ye pay tithe of mint and anise and cummin, and have omitted the weightier *matters* of the law, judgment, mercy, and faith:

OMITTED:

these ought ye to have done, and not to leave the other undone. ²⁴ *Ye blind guides, which strain at a gnat, and swallow a camel.*

²⁵ Woe unto you, scribes and Pharisees, hypocrites! for ye make clean the outside of the cup and of the platter, but within they are full of extortion and excess. ²⁶ *Thou* blind Pharisee, cleanse first that *which is* within the cup and platter,

OMITTED:

that the outside of them may be clean also.

> [27] Woe unto you, scribes and Pharisees, hypocrites! for ye are like unto whited sepulchres, which indeed appear beautiful outward, but are within full of dead *men's* bones, and of all uncleanness. [28] Even so ye also outwardly appear righteous unto men, but within ye are full of hypocrisy and iniquity.

OMITTED:

[29] *Woe unto you, scribes and Pharisees, hypocrites! because ye build the tombs of the prophets, and garnish the sepulchres of the righteous,* [30] *And say, If we had been in the days of our fathers, we would not have been partakers with them in the blood of the prophets.* [31] *Wherefore ye be witnesses unto yourselves, that ye are the children of them which killed the prophets.* [32] *Fill ye up then the measure of your fathers.*

> [33] *Ye* serpents, *ye* generation of vipers, how can ye escape the damnation of hell?

OMITTED:

[34] *Wherefore, behold, I send unto you prophets, and wise men, and scribes: and some of them ye shall kill and crucify; and some of them shall ye scourge in your synagogues, and persecute them from city to city:* [35] *That upon you may come all the righteous blood shed upon the earth, from the blood of righteous Abel unto the blood of Zacharias son of Barachias, whom ye slew between the temple and the altar.* [36] *Verily I say unto you, All these things shall come upon this generation.* [37] *O Jerusalem, Jerusalem, thou that killest the prophets, and stonest them which are sent unto thee, how often would I have gathered thy children together, even as a hen gathereth her chickens under her wings, and ye would not!* [38] *Behold, your house is left unto you desolate.* [39] *For I say unto you, Ye shall not see me henceforth, till ye shall say, Blessed is he that cometh in the name of the Lord.*

Whereupon Hardie continues his narrative stating that:

> … some good, pious Christians will be shocked at this 'irreverent' quotation of Scripture. Heard read from the pulpit, and applied to the religious hypocrites of 2000 years ago, they would esteem it most excellent. May I remind these good souls that Christ spoke these words, not of dead hypocrites, but of those by whom He was surrounded – those who took part in foreign missions, and were the religious leaders of the times, but whose lives were driving the people to atheism. I presume Christ would do the same to-day were He with us, and what He would do is surely the right thing for every professed follower to do.

Anticipating the accusation, once again, that Hardie is attacking Christianity itself, Hardie repeats his frequent insistence that he wants to focus on Jesus's words:

> I believe in Christ's gospel of love and brotherhood and service ... I am not attacking religion, but I mean to try whether the conscience of the Christian church cannot be so stirred up on this matter as to insist on men who make so much profession of Christianity as Lord Overtoun makes first of all giving some evidence of the faith that is in them by their treatment of their work people. If they will not treat these humanely then the Church should not accept the bloodstained gifts which have been procured by the destruction of men.[28]

Hardie insisted that "I hold no personal animus – if he corrects the conditions I will leave it at that ... " but also warned: "Until he has done so I will do my best to make it impossible for him to appear on a public platform in Scotland."[29]

Reading that Lord Overtoun, as part of his Christian philanthropy, had paid to distribute Bibles with highlighted portions that Overtoun believed were particularly important for the spiritual well-being of Scots, stating that "The verses marked in this Testament will, under the Holy Spirit's teaching help to make plain God's way of salvation through Christ," Hardie, however, takes issue with Overtoun's selections. Noting, in passing, that Overtoun had his Bible printed at a non-Union shop, Hardie outlines his objections to Overtoun's selections in a manner that helpfully and further clarifies Hardie's hermeneutic:

> The marked passages prove abundantly that the sayings of Jesus are, in the eyes of Lord Overtoun and his committee, but of secondary importance to these of Paul, the first theologian who began the corruption of Christianity in order to make it fit into the Jewish doctrine of sacrifice. No passage which enjoins upon the Christian his duty towards his neighbour receives the least notice. The whole of the Sermon on the Mount, including the beatitudes is passed over in contemptuous silence. The parable of the good Samaritan is treated in like matter. So, too, is Matthew 25 from the 31st verse to the end of the chapter, wherein the conditions are set down under which men may enter heaven, and which I commend specially to Lord Overtoun's notice. Poor St. James might as well never have written. He receives not a solitary mark. On the other hand, every passage in which God can be made to appear as a blood-thirsty monster, refusing to be appeased in his wrath until the blood of His Son has been shed, are duly lined in black and red. 'I will have mercy and not sacrifice' said Christ over and over again. Lord Overtoun finds the sacrifice idea pays better; mercy would mean reform of the conditions at Shawfield, and that Lord Overtoun would regard as sacrilege. It is cheaper to feed men's souls than to maintain their bodies.[30]

---

28. *The Labour Leader*, April 1, 1899.
29. *The Labour Leader*, April 1, 1899.
30. *The Labour Leader*, April 1, 1899.

Hardie was also contemptuous of Glasgow clergy who held Lord Overtoun in his regard:

> The clergy of Glasgow appear willing to condone the white slavery treatment which Lord Overtoun metes out to his unfortunate men. Like the members of the Liberal Club, so long as he shares the spoil with them they are willing to go on shielding and protecting him. They have had their opportunity of putting themselves right with God and man in this affair. Even yet it may not be too late. But should they continue to play the part of the unctuous Pharisee, they will most of them at least, live long enough to rue it.[31]

The controversy blazed on in the summer months of 1899. Hardie called for public protests of Lord Overtoun's factory conditions in the May 1899 edition of *The Labour Leader*:

> The public platform; the meeting at which these despoilers of Christ's kingdom take the chair; there, in the full light of day, is the time and place to enter the protest; to shame the canting phrase mongers pilloried above, and purge the Christian movement of that influence which is numbing every effort and paralysing the right arm of the righteous. Let these men who believe that Christianity is a life and not a profession speak out, and they will find a body of opinion ready to back them which will gratify and perhaps astonish them.[32]

When Hardie spots Overtoun's name on a protest of the issuing of Sunday editions of the *Daily Mail* and *Telegraph*, when these printing offices have nowhere near the dreadful conditions of Shawfield, Hardie states that the printers Overtoun attacks should reply, "Thou hypocrite, first remove the beam from thine own eye, that thou mayest more clearly see to remove the mote from thy neighbors."

The May 27, 1899 edition of *The Labour Leader* featured a blank column on the front cover to indicate that Lord Overtoun had threatened the printer if they published further articles from Hardie attacking his business. Hardie threatened legal action but had to find a different publisher to carry on printing *The Labour Leader*. Interestingly, on June 10 and 17, Samuel Hodson published two articles praising the Quaker chocolate industrialist George Cadbury, whose works at Bourneville, near Birmingham, were considered a model of care for workers against Overtoun's abuses.

We know that Hardie's attacks often found their mark. In the July 15, 1899 edition, Hardie's "Between Ourselves" column took up Overtoun issues again, but this time praising Rev. Robert Lorimer, who returned a fifty pound donation given to him by Overtoun, stating,

---

31. *The Labour Leader*, April 1, 1899.
32. *The Labour Leader*, May 18, 1899.

I will not touch your gold. Your workmen have a prior claim to it, and I trust you will divide among them the enclosed cheque for £50 ... I am perfectly perplexed by the inconsistency between your profession and practice now brought to light, and I grieve that I must withdraw the esteem in which I have held you.[33]

In short, the Overtoun affair shows Hardie "weaponizing" Scripture in the cause of socialism and social justice. The argument can well be made that it was precisely the polemics over Christianity and scripture that most incensed Hardie in this literary series of tirades. Famously, Hardie turned to Jesus to defend his attacks on establishment figures.

Major essays

Obviously, the most valuable sources we have for Hardie's interpretation of Scripture are from those written occasions when Hardie sets out to intentionally make a theological—indeed Biblical—case for his socialist policies and political activism. I have included here his arguably most important essays.

The "Bradford Incident"—1892

In November 1892, Hardie spoke at the Bradford Labour Church where he shared the stage with Robert Blatchford, editor of *The Clarion* (and rather famous atheist who had little patience for any religious rhetoric of any kind). The sequence of events is a bit unclear, but Morgan[34] suggests that Hardie also took the opportunity to meet with Congregational Christians in the same town, who were discussing some of Hardie's comments made previously. Hardie had said, before the meeting with Congregationalists, that he advocated the use of open land by the poor for their own consumption:

> Let the unemployed and the overworked and all who were tired of the industrial strike, have free access to the uncultivated soil as harbours of refuge in time of storm; let them turn their labour there to profitable account, not for the production of goods to sell, but for their own consumption ... [35]

And Hardie then repeated his frequent attacks on Christian practices in his day: "Christianity today lay buried, bound up in the ceremonies of a dead and lifeless theology. It awaited decent burial ... " after which Hardie then takes up his oft-repeated theme that socialism, in his estimation, sought to revive a more Biblically-centered form of Christianity. Here, notably, Hardie does not consider

---

33. *The Labour Leader*, July 15, 1899.
34. Morgan, *Keir Hardie*, 63.
35. *The Labour Prophet*, November 1895, 85.

his strongly "immanent" ("this world focused") understanding of the message of Jesus to cancel the more traditional views of an "afterlife":

> ... the Labour movement had come to resuscitate the Christianity of Christ, to go back to the time when the poor should have the Gospel preached to them, and the Gospel should be good news of joy and happiness in this life, of God's Kingdom on earth as a preparation for that which was to come in the world beyond the grave.

Hardie concluded that speech, as he had on other occasions, with the lines from Lord Tennyson that finish with:

> Ring in the valiant man and free
> The larger heart, the kindlier hand
> Ring out the darkness of the land
> Ring in the Christ that is to be.[36]

The account notes that there was considerable response to Hardie's speech. But responses continued long after the actual event itself. At one of the meetings of the local Congregational Union in Bradford, the Reverend Dr. Charles Leach (of London), is reported in the *Bradford Observer* to have said that "a Member of Parliament" (alluding to Hardie just recently elected to represent West Ham in South London) had said: "Christianity is dead – (cries of Shame) – it is wrapped in its own lifeless forms and only awaits decent burial," and then claimed that Hardie advocated violent revolution because of his allusions to the Paris Commune of some years ago (1870–1). *The Labour Prophet* reporter continued, however, to say that "Happily, Keir Hardie was present and was allowed a hearing." The *Bradford Observer* reports Hardie's response (and takes note of the crowd's responses as well) as follows:

> Allow me to explain what I did say (hear hear). A lying spirit has been abroad somewhere, and it is well that matter should be put right. I said on Sunday that the Christianity of the schools was dead (hear hear) – and the Christianity of Christ was coming to the front. (Applause). And I thank God for that. (hear hear).[37]

Hardie stated that he hoped that the kind of violence in France would not break out in Britain, but that he warned about the consequences of ignoring severe poverty. When he criticized both Parliament and Church for their failures, Hardie clarified strikingly that:

> ... in speaking thus to the people I was following the dictates and the feelings of Him whom I claim as my Lord and Master (Applause). He did not come to

36. *The Labour Prophet*, November 1892.
37. *The Labour Prophet*, November 1892.

preach to the respectable trade unionists and co-operators of His time – the men who can look after their own interests; He came to search for the poor and the lost, and those who had no helpers; and the reason why the Labour party today turns its back upon the Church is because the Church has turned its back upon Christ (dissension) in this matter.

The article then discusses the agitated reactions of the crowds and Hardie's responses:

> At this stage the marked disapproval of the majority of the audience of what Mr. Hardie was saying broke forth in loud cries of 'no.'
>
> 'You get your congregations' proceeded Mr. Hardie, disregarding the cries, 'You preach to please their respectability.'
>
> Again there were shouts of 'no'
>
> 'You do, you do, you do!' cried Mr. Hardie, and he went on vehemently, 'and you forget the writhing and suffering masses of humanity outside … '
>
> Cries of 'no' interrupted the speaker for a third time, but, nothing daunted, he exclaimed 'I know what you do' a remark which caused two or three delegates to yell, 'False, false'.
>
> 'And in the slums of the city,' continued Mr. Hardie, 'Where men and women and children, made in the image of God, are being driven down into hell for time and eternity, you have no word of hope, and no helping hand; and you disgrace, you the Christian ministers of England; setting up to be …'
>
> Hereupon Mr. Hardie's voice was completely drowned in the cries of: 'False,' 'No,' and 'Chair chair' from the body of the chapel, and after attempting in vain to get a further hearing, Mr. Hardie left the platform, merely saying, as he left, 'I thank you for hearing me.'
>
> The Chairman, rising, said, 'Gentlemen, dinner is waiting' (Laughter). 'It is better for us to hear Mr. Keir Hardie speak out his mind, and it is better for us to think of it' (hear hear) … [38]

As an interesting aside, some two years later, the following rather striking comment was included in an editorial appearing in *The Labour Leader*: "Dr. Leach afterwards discovered that he had made a mistake and apologized in the frankest manner" referring to Leach's accusation that Hardie had openly attacked Christianity itself and had called for violent revolution. Hardie then reproduced a portion of Leach's letter to Hardie from August 16, 1894:

> I have come at last to accept your programme as set forth in the penny tract from your pen, and am seriously thinking of joining the Independent Labour Party, if you will have me. Such influence as I possess, and it is considerable in religious

---

38. *The Labour Prophet*, November 1892.

circles all over England, I think I ought to use in the interests of the class from which I spring, and among which I toil.[39]

Hardie, graciously, then recounted some of Leach's story:

> Dr. Leach's history is remarkable. The son of working class parents, he worked at his trade in the Midlands until he got married. Then, following his religious conversion, he determined to study for the ministry which he did with success … bit by bit Dr. Leach has been developing and now has reached the conclusion that the logical outcome of his Master's teaching is Socialism, and that the I.L.P. offers the best and most effective means of realizing it.[40]

Returning to 1892, however, it is interesting that it was in the same issue that had reported the riotous discussions in Bradford, that *The Labour Prophet* also published Hardie's essay: "The Christianity of Christ." He began by referring to the "Bradford Incident" once again:

> Reams of paper and rivulets of ink have been spoilt in refutation of my statements at the Congregational Congress at Bradford. All sorts of arguments have been used to prove that the Church is the friend of the poor.[41]

Hardie noted how many letters he received talking about social outreach projects conducted by churches. Yet Hardie writes that he was not moved, despite clarifying that he deeply respects church workers who volunteer to work among the poor and "betake themselves to the heart-crushing work of rescuing those who have been trampled down in the mad scramble for wealth which characterizes the industrial life of today." Still, Hardie calls for systemic change, something that he believes those same volunteers would themselves begin to understand: " … many of them, probably most of them now, are awakening to the fact that Christianity means prevention rather than cure, and that it is mockery against the Most High to let the Devil loose in the Church and then to build the mission hall to undo some of his handiwork …."[42]

"The Church and the Labour Problem" (March, 1893, much the same article also published in the magazine, Christian Thought*)*

In March 1893, *The Labour Leader* reproduced Hardie's essay "The Church and the Labour Problem," from another publication known as *The Thinker*. This was one of a number of notable lengthier essays where Hardie responded to direct invitations to address himself to explicitly *religious* topics.

39. *The Labour Leader*, August 16, 1894.
40. *The Labour Leader*, August 16, 1894.
41. *The Labour Prophet*, November 1892.
42. *The Labour Prophet*, November 1892.

Hardie began by affirming his belief in the "immutable principle of righteousness in the universe," and then to express his belief that one should not doubt the "ultimate victory" of such a "righteousness," as this would be virtually the same thing as to " ... deny the existence of God." But Hardie rather quickly turns to one of his most frequent theological arguments—the "straight forward" morality of Jesus in the New Testament. Indeed, Hardie argues that when preachers (usually he refers to "the pulpit," or "Churchianity") of the Christian church falsely complicate the teachings of Jesus—or more serious, suggesting that they only apply to an ancient context, then this case " ... is least defensible." He writes:

> Christ's teachings are clear and unmistakable. With Him, life was everything. He refused to interfere in the miserable squabbling of the two brothers over the sharing of their goods; to the rich young man the irreducible minimum of His demand was, "Sell all that thou hast ...." The rich had had their portion here, and were to weep and howl for the misery awaiting them. The early Christians practised this teaching as is shown in the opening chapters of the Acts and St. Paul preached it in the axiom, "he that will not work, neither should he eat." If there is scepticism in the land to-day (and who can deny it?), the half-heartedness of the pulpit is far more responsible for it than all the destructive criticism of the critics of Scripture ever penned. This is, doubtless, a hard saying, but it is true.[43]

Hardie alludes to a rich variety of passages here. The "two brothers" could be a reference to the "Sons of Zebedee" wanting to be among the closest to Jesus in authority [Mt. 20; Mk 10], but could also refer to the two sons in the brief parable of going to the fields to work in Matthew 21:28ff. Even more likely is a reference to Luke 12:13–15:

> Someone in the crowd said to him, 'Teacher, tell my brother to divide the family inheritance with me.' But he said to him, 'Friend, who set me to be a judge or arbitrator over you?' And he said to them, 'Take care! Be on your guard against all kinds of greed; for one's life does not consist in the abundance of possessions.'[44]

The "Rich young Ruler" is originally Mark 10 [Mt. 19 and Lk. 18], and is among the most celebrated passages dealing with wealth in relation to the teachings of Jesus. Hardie then turns to the equally celebrated passages about shared goods among the earliest Christians in Acts 2:44–6 and 4:32–7 (see final chapter below).

The final reference is especially interesting, given Hardie's usual impatience with Paul. Yet again, Hardie refers to 2 Thessalonians 3:10b: " ... Anyone unwilling to work should not eat." Notably, this passage is often taken as a counsel against laziness or idleness—and was often used *against* labour movements by praising

---

43. *The Labour Leader*, March 15, 1893.
44. I am grateful to my anonymous reviewer who pointed out this most likely reference.

a "willingness to work" rather than be "idle." Strikes, agitation, and union organization were typically pilloried as refusal to work—and thus attacked as idleness or laziness of the lower classes. Interestingly, however, Hardie's particular use of the phrase raises interesting questions about reading this in the larger context of the Thessalonians passage, which certainly complicates this common interpretation, but we will take up the contemporary debates about this famous passage in the final chapter.[45]

Suffice it to say here that if Paul is saying that he did not eat other's bread but earned his own keep—the thought seems to be that Paul was refusing to be privileged, rather than lazy! And it is precisely this meaning that Hardie derives from the famous saying—it was not taken by him to be an attack on laziness, but precisely privilege—that is, as a counsel against being fed without doing work because one is wealthy or of higher status (e.g., living off rents and investments). That Hardie's "worker's exegesis" quite frankly has a good deal to commend it, is clear from a reference in Isaiah to the future where there will be no privileged status whereby some live off the work of others:

> **Isaiah 65:21-2** [21] They shall build houses and inhabit them; they shall plant vineyards and eat their fruit. [22] They shall not build and another inhabit; they shall not plant and another eat; for like the days of a tree shall the days of my people be, and my chosen shall long enjoy the work of their hands.

Hardie addresses the frequent refusal of the churches to address "social questions," e.g., socio-economic needs of people in society, by an astonishment that this should even be controversial:

> Why is there even any discussion of 'social questions' and the Church? Do not social questions affect the welfare of the people at every point – certainly not excluding the spiritual? And what can the relation of the Church be but one of antagonism to everything that comes between man and his highest development? But for the apathy of the Church, there would be no social question to discuss.[46]

Instead, the church honors the achievements of the wealthy and successful, which Hardie calls "bowing the knee to Baal," and (alluding, again, to Jas 2:1-4), the church has " … reserved its seats of honour for the successful man …." Always ready to cite cases of what he considered religious hypocrisy, Hardie then cited a case of a wealthy layperson who paid women in his business so little that many of them had turned to prostitution, yet: " … the church ignored this: He died a millionaire in all the odour of sanctity." Hardie returns to his frequent topic of applying the teachings of Jesus to contemporary issues:

---

45. *The Labour Leader*, March 15, 1893.
46. *The Labour Leader*, March 15, 1893.

5. Hardie and his Bible

A late bishop of the Church of England said that Christianity could not be applied to the affairs of Government. So much the worse, say I, for the nation ... If there is no relationship between employer and employed to which the principles of Christ's teachings cannot be applied, there must be something amiss. Is trade greater than the soul, or commerce than the body? ... I know that it is little short of heterodoxy, if anything, to literally apply the words of Jesus to the worldly affairs of today, and it is at this point where the Church and the Labour movement 'each take off their separate way.'[47]

Hardie (alluding to Mt. 6; Lk. 12:28–32) considered such important questions to be: " ... the modern form of Christ's query about meat and raiment," e.g., that God does, in fact, care about the clothing and feeding of God's people. Hardie then returns to the topic of hypocrisy among contemporary Church leaders and noted laypeople by asking whether Christ would have admitted the owners of slum property among His disciples? Clearly, Hardie chose this particularly worded question specifically, because he then discusses Lord Salisbury, who had by then been convicted of owning sub-standard housing (in contemporary parlance, convinced of being "a slum lord"), and Hardie called for the Church of England to expel him.

Notably, Hardie then turns to the opposition by William Garden Blaikie (D.D., Prof. Theology in Free Church College of Edinburgh) who was opposed to the eight-hour bill—Blaikie arguing that workers should be free to work as many hours as they want. The American publication that summarized world news, known as *The Literary Digest*,[48] summarized Blaikie's arguments that the Church is not "competent to comment on wages and strikes," and also noted in this context, his opposition to the eight-hour bill. But Hardie argued about his concern that young, stronger workers were taking away hours from older, less robust workers who nonetheless needed an income as well. Hardie turns again to an interpretation of Scripture:

> Dr. Blaikie's whole argument makes for expediency, forgetting that the Ten Commandments do not admit of such, and that 'Thou shalt not steal' forbids the young strong compositer from robbing his own father, it may be, of the opportunity of earning a living.[49]

Comparing incomes of £45 for workers against £1700 for owners, Hardie argues:

> I lay it down as a broad, unchallengeable Christian principle that any system of production or exchange which sanctions the exploitation of the weak by the strong or the unscrupulous is wrong, and therefore sinful. The Church

---

47. *The Labour Leader*, March 15, 1893.
48. *The Literary Digest*, vol. VI, no. 15, p. 399.
49. *The Labour Leader*, March 15, 1893.

theory concerning great worldly possessions is that they are held in trust to be administered by their possessors for the alleviation of poverty and misery. The parable of the Good Samaritan is the favourite illustration of this connection.[50]

Yet, Hardie asks, the parable of the Good Samaritan (Lk. 10) can hardly be read to condone the robbery of the man in the story:

> What if the Good Samaritan had turned out to be the robber, and had only given ten per cent of the proceeds towards providing the wine and oil, and the hotel accommodation? Would that have been a fulfilling of the law and the Gospel? That is strictly analogous to the case of the employer who today makes money out of his workers, and then gives handsomely to all sorts of charitable schemes. Would it not be more in keeping for the Church to insist that the robber must first stop his depredations before his aid on behalf of his victims be accepted?

Hardie, in this way, further responds to the common argument, apparently also repeated by Dr. Blaikie, that it is the responsibility of the wealthy to give a "lift" by charity to those in poverty, rather than changing the very economic system that made them wealthy in the first place. Yet, Hardie argues:

> The labourer got no 'lift' when Jesus, born of working-class parents, worked for His living. The worker needed no 'lift' in the sense here implied. Strange that Dr. Blaikie does not say what a knockdown the idle rich got when Jesus became a 'member of the labouring class.' That would be to insult the rich, and the rich won't stand being insulted ... the worker none the less is having his revenge. If he cannot voice his resentment, he can enter his dumb protest, and this he does by not attending Church ... Make the applications of Christianity to the present-day life a reality, and none will support it with more zeal than the workers.[51]

Alluding next to both the story of Jesus duplicating the "loaves and fishes" in the first part of John 6, and then relating this directly to the question Jesus asks His immediate disciples in John 6:67 about "going away" (a clever combination that Hardie proposes that is not obvious in the chapter itself, it must be said), Hardie returns to his insistence that the Church must address "social questions," but realizes that this would have an impact on the present attendance of church—but sees the possibilities that workers, recognizing a Church actually concerned about their lives—would themselves flock back:

> It may be that a faithful stand on this question would drive many away. Better that than have their blood on the skirts of the priest's garment [Possibly alluding to Lam. 4:13, but more likely Mt. 27:6, ed.]. 'Will ye also go away?' said Jesus

---

50. *The Labour Leader*, March 15, 1893.
51. *The Labour Leader*, March 15, 1893.

sorrowfully to His disciples, when the multitude on the outlook for loaves and fishes, and not understanding His teaching, took their departure. If the Church emptied at first it would fill again, and its filling would mean the coming of God's kingdom on earth.

While Hardie would declare with many socialists that the evolution toward a socialist future is inevitable ("With or without the aid of the Church the present industrial system must, in the nature of things, come to an end and give way to a better … "), Hardie's theological interests are nonetheless clear when he then declares that "The democratic movement is spiritual," but notably concludes by observing, with a clear eye once again turned toward Prof. Blaikie, the esteemed Professor of Theology at Edinburgh:

> The religion of Jesus Christ is more than sufficient for all this, though it will first require to be purified from ceremonial and meaningless forms and phrases which pass muster for it today, and be freed from the perverted views of life which theology has so long proclaimed in its name.[52]

Notable throughout, once again, the sheer number of Biblical allusions and his creative uses of them. Hardie is the consummate debater, "proof-texting" with the best of them! The point surely is that Hardie's socialism and his Biblicism are in constant and creative dialogue.

Hardie's speech to Glasgow working men (1893)[53]

One year after his first election to Parliament in August 1892, Hardie delivered a speech in Glasgow (1893) to a gathering of working men. In this earlier speech (before *The Labour Leader* was a stable publication), we see evidence of Hardie's rhetorical flourish, especially his fondness for citing the poetry of Lord Tennyson as his speech began. We have here a transcription of portions of the speech, with the traditional notation of applause and response:

> Cursed be the social wants that sin against the strength of youth!
> Cursed be the social lies that warp us from the living truth!
> Cursed be the sickly forms that err from honest nature's rule!
> Cursed be the gold that gilds the straightened forehead of the fool![54]

Hardie seems particularly concerned to speak to the lack of working men's interest in the churches, but suggested that if the churches were true to the message of the founder of Christianity, things may well be different:

---

52. *The Labour Leader*, March 15, 1893.
53. This speech was summarized also in William Eunson, ed., *Miscellaneous Essays: Thought-coin from the Ages* (Edinburgh: Hunter, 1898), 183.
54. *The Labour Leader*, September 1893.

... Churches and mission halls had been multiplied and increased in the land [cf. Jer. 3:16, ed.]. These churches and mission halls contained a very large proportion of the people of the country within their membership. Christianity was essentially the religion of the poor; its founder was a workman – He never aspired to be anything else; He was not wheedled or cajoled or bought or bribed into being anything else (applause) – was crucified because he refused to be anything else (applause) – and today those who perpetuated the system, or what passed for the system, which he founded were content to go sleepily on, while around their churches and chapels there was a mass of misery and degradation which would have aroused the Son of Man to strongest words, yea, the strongest deeds – to anything and everything rather than allowing this thing to continue in their midst (applause).[55]

The editor summarizes Hardie's words as follows:

What was his complaint against the Churches? His complaint was that if all the Churches were filled, as they professed to be filled, with the spirit of Christ – the reforming spirit of Christ – the evils and abuses which existed would not continue to exist for twelve months longer (applause). What he had said might not be orthodox, but it was true, and that was what orthodoxy seldom was (applause). The church of today would require some more potent argument than the time honoured

'Apostolic blows and knocks
To prove its doctrines orthodox'
(Laughter)[56]

Hardie was known to have complained about the work ethic of Parliamentarians, suggesting that they wasted a considerable amount of time. Some of these comments were more widely reported, such as his humorous references to leisure eating: "Go to the terrace of the House of Commons and you would find lords and their ladies – in the season – indulging in strawberries and cream, and in tea and cake." Hardie was quoted to say that he sometimes thought it would not be a bad thing to add to their Labour program the nationalization of strawberries and cream, so that they would all have a chance of taking their friends to participate (laughter and applause).

Go to the smoking room of the House, and they would find members drinking whisky and smoking cigars; go to the library and they would find members reading; go to the House itself and they would find members sleeping (laughter

---

55. *The Labour Leader*, September 1893.
56. *The Labour Leader*, September 1893.

and applause). There was opportunity provided for anything under Heaven being done in the House of Commons except work (laughter and applause). But work was the one thing they were determined should and must be done within the walls of the House of Commons (applause).[57]

Hardie's words become more serious, note his reference to Isaiah 61, part of which was cited by Jesus in His famous reading in Luke 4:18–19, but Hardie uses more of the Isaiah passage:

> With the wail of the hungry child, the shriek of the suicide, the moan of the strong man, and the curse of the out-of-work ringing in their ears, it was a shame and a disgrace and a discredit to the House of Commons that work should not be attempted and should not be done to make these things impossible (Applause). For what then were they working and living? Wasn't it:
>
> To bind up the broken heart
> To proclaim liberty to the captive
> And the opening of the prison to them that are bound
> (Isa. 61:1–2, partially repeated in Lk. 4:18–19)
>
> To comfort all that mourn (Isa. 61:2)
>
> And give beauty for ashes
> The oil of joy for mourning
> The garment of praise for the spirit of heaviness (Isa. 61:3)
>
> To wipe all tears from all eyes (Isa. 25:8)
>
> Surely such a programme might well inspire them to noble living. For it was true today as it ever had been, that sacrifice was the keystone of success. To you, old and middle aged, therefore, he would appeal and say
> Fight, heroes, fight
> Let ignorance and superstition fly
> The scales are falling from each darkened eye,
> let there be light
> (Great applause)[58]

This second-hand report with occasional quotations gives us yet another good example of hearing Hardie's famous speech-making, but also the ease with which he moved from political policy, criticism, and citation of Scripture.

---

57. *The Labour Leader*, September 1893.
58. *The Labour Leader*, September 1893.

"Can a Man Be a Christian on a Pound a Week?" 1901[59]

One of Keir Hardie's most famous essays, however, was written while an MP for Merthyr, South Wales. Morgan refers to it as a "powerful appeal to the national conscience,"[60] and Benn refers to it as a contribution to Hardie's return to "a defence of working class living standards" as a theme in his political action.[61] Although it was a topic he did not choose, he did accept the challenge to respond with this long essay. In this essay, which went through a number of printings, we have an especially good example of Hardie's reading of the Bible. As in many other writings, Hardie was always willing to criticize the churches and their practice, but he countered this not with atheism (Marxist or otherwise), but with an even greater emphasis on "what Christ taught." As he stated in the "Foreword" to the essay: "In what follows I do not in any way seek to assail Christianity or impugn its teachings. But I cannot accept current theology as being other than a travesty of what Christ taught."[62]

Hardie argued further in the Foreword that he will use the Gospels to make his point, arguing that: "The tendency of theology is to magnify the letter of the word, forgetful of the spirit thereof—the very offence for which Jesus denounced the Pharisees so scathingly."[63] Clearly, his aim is not to raise some extra-scriptural religious ideal, or a materialist program, over against the teachings in the Gospels—but rather to focus on the Bible more specifically.

Among the central texts for Hardie was always the Sermon on the Mount, and he concluded his "Foreword" by further illustrating that interest: "The growing feeling that the solution of all modern problems is to be sought in the application of the principles set forth in the Sermon on the Mount is, to me, full of good promise for the future of the Labour movement, and it is in the hope that what follows may help in this direction that I give it to the public in this form."

At the beginning of the heart of the essay, Hardie places two texts from the Sermon:

> Behold the fowls of the air; for they sow not, neither do they reap, nor gather into barns; yet your Heavenly Father feedeth them. Are ye not much better than they? [Mt. 6:26]

> Consider the lilies of the field, how they grow; they toil not, neither do they spin; and yet I say unto you that even Solomon in all his glory was not arrayed like one of these. [Mt. 6:28–9]

---

59. The pamphlet was reprinted often, Morgan, *Keir Hardie*, 122, has it originally printed in 1901.

60. Morgan, *Keir Hardie*, 122.

61. Benn, *Keir Hardie*, 171.

62. Keir Hardie, *Can a Man Be a Christian on a Pound a Week?* (1901, now public domain), Foreword.

63. Hardie, *Pound a Week*, Foreword.

As we shall see, Hardie had an interesting "social and political" reading of these two texts. As opposed to more traditional understandings of this passage, Hardie is interested in what they imply in terms of a working person's financial security, rather than a utopian idea that imagines a heavenly abode where one does not need to work.

In order to make his argument, Hardie sets up the situation of a family of five attempting to live on "a pound a week." He proposes that the working man is Christian, which Hardie defines by further quoting the Sermon: "A Christian is one who, inter alia, takes no thought for the morrow [Mt. 6:34], and who does not lay up for himself treasures upon earth [Mt. 6:19]." In short, this is not a family that seeks to accumulate wealth, but simply to exist (his examples will presume parents and three children). Thus, Hardie proposes that Christianity, in its origins, had an inherent critique of wealth. In the following sentences, it is to be remembered that the Latin for "rich man" is "dives," which passed into later translated traditions as the actual "name" of the wealthy man in the famous story:

> In the early days of Christianity asceticism was held to be a logical outcome of Christian belief. Dives was sent to Hades for apparently no other reason than that he was rich. Lazarus went straight to Abraham's bosom because of his earthly poverty [Lk. 16:20–5]. James the Epistolian called upon the rich to weep and howl for the miseries awaiting them in the world to come [Jas 5: 1–7]. Christ sent out His disciples with empty purses [Mt. 6:8; Lk. 10:4], and Himself had not where to lay His head [Mt. 8:20; Lk. 9:58].[64]

His summary of this selection of passages suggests his guide for choosing them: "The Sermon on the Mount is a consistent and powerful argument against property in every form." The key to these citations is that Hardie interprets Jesus's references to the yield of the earth and supplying human need as a claim on resources common to all humanity:

> God the Father had so ordained that in response to labour the earth would yield freely enough and to spare for the supply of every human need, and if men would but follow the example of the flowers of the field and the birds of the air and hold all nature's gifts in common, drawing from the great storehouse only what each required for the needs of the day, then life would become free, joyous, and beautiful.[65]

This is seen as contrary, therefore, to: "The acquisition of property," which, Hardie argues, the Christian should:

> ... regard as an impediment to the development of the soul, which is alone immortal and worth caring for. With Christ there was no wealth save life,

---

64. Hardie, *Pound a Week*, 3.
65. Hardie, *Pound a Week*, 3.

and material things were only valuable in so far as they contributed to the production of life.[66]

With this as a theological "preamble," or the values that will guide his comments, he then proceeds to discuss what a person can actually live on—including his rough calculations of amounts necessary for basic purchasing of necessities:

> Living under a Christian system the purchasing power which twenty shillings a week represents would be amply sufficient for his every need. But the God we worship is Mammon, not Christ, which makes all the difference. In Church life, in literature, in politics, Mammon sits enthroned. We have, therefore, not to consider whether a man can be a Christian on a pound a week, that is, live a life in accordance with the will of God under Christian conditions, but whether he can do so under present conditions. My answer is No.[67]

Hardie then paints the picture of the working man and his family in Britain drawing on his own experiences and his observations:

> The townsman with a wife and three children and an income of a pound a week dare not 'take no thought for the morrow.' With the morrow will come the landlord demanding the rent, and if the rent be not forthcoming, out he will go into the street … Enveloped in the meshes of a net from which there is no escape. A sense of injustice never leaves him.[68]

After outlining his theoretical family, and the likelihood that they will face ruin and then be considered lost souls of the under classes often blamed for their own failures, Hardie's next comment refers back to the traditions of Lazarus. Hardie proposes that the landlord seeking to collect his rent would likely call himself a Christian "living an idle luxurious life at the expense of the poor toil-worn workman":

> And yet, sodden it may be with drink, foul of speech, and life too unclean for even the dogs to lick his sores [Lk. 16:18], I would sooner risk my chance of getting to heaven with him than with those who, having robbed him and made him what he is, are respectable church-goers and members of good society.[69]

Hardie constantly contrasts the poor against the self-confessed Christians who nonetheless consider themselves better than the poor workers. Rather clearly

---

66. Hardie, *Pound a Week*, 3–4.
67. Hardie, *Pound a Week*, 4.
68. Hardie, *Pound a Week*, 6.
69. Hardie, *Pound a Week*, 6.

alluding to James [2:1-6], Hardie refers to the workers who believe that they are not welcome in the churches: "Not for him the fellowship of the Christian Church. That sacred place is reserved for people who can wear good clothes, pay seat rents, and subscribe to the minister's salary." Continuing with this theme, Hardie then argues about the lack of condemnation in the Gospels for the poor, only the wealthy or the religious establishment:

> Christ had no hard words for the poor erring sons and daughters of men. All his invective was kept for the Scribes and Pharisees, the hypocrites who professed a faith in God which they neither knew nor understood. The outcast, in his lonely broodings and his fits of remorse, will get nearer to the heart of God than will those who observe all the rites of Christianity but are strangers to its spirit.[70]

Hardie then turns to a calculation of excess under the industrial capitalism of his day. To this, he contrasts a kind of socialist ideal that would become a reality so that:

> ... the nation own its land and employ its own labour in supplying the needs of the people, it could more than double the production of real wealth, reduce toil to a mere incident, abolish all poverty, and dethrone the brute god Mammon.[71]

In reprinted editions, Hardie then moves to respond to a number of common criticisms of his arguments here and in previous circumstances.[72] His critics have said:

1. If the article is right, then the Churches generally do not properly understand what the Gospel of Christ is, and their work is, to a large extent, futile (Rev. Mr. Shaw).
2. That the teaching of the article is materialistic and means that if a man has private property he is not a Christian, but that if he owns property in common with others he is (The same).
3. That in early days of Christianity slaves were set free by their Christian masters (The same).
4. That the article is an attack upon temperance and thrift, and a glorification of the idle, happy-go-lucky tramp (Rev. Mr. Hibbert).
5. That Christian employers should pay their workfolks good wages (Anon).[73]

---

70. Hardie, *Pound a Week*, 6-7.
71. Hardie, *Pound a Week*, 8.
72. Including, for example, arguments that Hardie originally made in *The Labour Leader*, July 20, 1901, against the attacks of a Rev. Shaw.
73. Hardie, *Pound a Week*, 9.

Hardie then responds to each of these criticisms. In response to the first, that churches have not properly understood the Gospels, Hardie replies that his goal is to focus more carefully precisely on what he believes the teachings of Jesus to be:

> I can imagine how presumptuous it must appear to the clerical mind to find a mere ordinary layman arraying himself against them in matters of theology, and yet a considerable acquaintance with Church life and a sincere desire to understand what Jesus taught has driven me irresistibly to the conclusion that modern Churchianity is not only un-Christian, but anti-Christian. I can find no points of correspondence between the teachings of Jesus, as contained in the New Testament, and the teachings of the modern pulpit.[74]

Hardie then marshals Jesus's criticism of religious leaders in the Gospels to defend his own attacks on clergy and churches, but then clarifies:

> Christianity to be effective must be a living vital force; not a dead, soulless creed, or a jungle of mere words. The growing despair of the Church at its inability to reach the masses is of itself sufficient proof of my contention. It is also an admission by the Church itself that it is no longer carrying forward the work of its founder, whose mission was to the poor.

The second criticism relates directly to the issue of common holding of property— the accusation is that Hardie advocates common holding, but not individual holding, of property. Not unexpectedly, Hardie goes straight to one of the two most commonly cited passages from the New Testament in defense of socialist ideals, namely Acts 4:32–5 (the other being Acts 2:44–7), after which Hardie observes:

> Here we have it clearly brought out that the direct outcome of the teachings of Jesus upon those who lived nearest to His time, and who became His followers, was to make them Communists. These early Christians, found it impossible to retain possession of private property after they became Christians, since it raised artificial class distinctions in their midst and prevented the free play of that spirit of fraternal brotherhood which Jesus taught as one of the characteristics of the Kingdom of God.[75]

Hardie's "imitation of Jesus" hermeneutic is clear: "And if that was so in the earlier days of Christianity, it would be equally true of its later days if Christianity were still being preached and practiced."

The third discussion—that early Christians released their slaves—does not have direct Biblical foundation (although debate about what Paul implies about Onesimus in the Epistle of Philemon continues, e.g., does Paul challenge the old relationship while not challenging the legal status? This, however, is not cited by

---

74. Hardie, *Pound a Week*, 9–10.
75. Hardie, *Pound a Week*, 11.

Hardie). For this, Hardie rather draws on an interesting interpretation of a variety of sources:

> In the early ages (of the Christian era) thousands of slaves were liberated, not by such acts as that of our Government when it paid lump sums for the emancipation of slaves in our colonies, but by the operation of those principles of righteousness and love which are inherent in Christianity ... The effect of private property in land and capital is in all essential respects the same as was the effect of private property in human beings: In each case slavery is the result, the form may have changed, but the substance remains.[76]

The substance of the fourth criticism is that Hardie is said to be advocating for people to not have to work at all, and thus result in a "glorification of the idle, happy-go-lucky tramp." To this, Hardie returns to his original interpretation of Jesus's words in the Sermon on the Mount about concern for one's necessities, the very passages with which he began the original essay:

> ... in the Kingdom of God there will be no need for this distraction, since, as in the case of the birds and the flowers, there will be abundance for all in the common store, and thus all cause for anxiety concerning food and raiment will be removed.[77]

To clarify further, Hardie understands these passages to be an attack on waste, and an attack on *forced* idleness:

> Waste is at all times sinful. The man who wastes his life that he may save money is the greatest spendthrift of all. Under Socialism, which is the application to industry of the teachings contained in the Sermon on the Mount, the entire nation, every individual that is, will be interested in promoting true economy, and he who wastes any portion of what will be the common store will be accounted an enemy of society.

Again, Hardie understands this to be a class-based criticism on the supposed moral failures of the "lower" classes of persons, and therefore repeats the positive statements that he made in the original essay:

> Concerning the poor despised tramp, I am prepared to stake my own chances of a seat on the banks of the Jordan that a bigger percentage of these will find entrance to the Kingdom than will be found from the anointed ones who look down so unctuously upon him from the superior height of a classical education and an assured income.[78]

76. Hardie, *Pound a Week*, 12.
77. Hardie, *Pound a Week*, 13.
78. Hardie, *Pound a Week*, 13–14.

The fifth and final objection to which Hardie feels compelled to respond is the notion that the social problems of labour ought to be addressed simply by Christian owners of the means of production paying their workers a fair price. But Hardie is doubtful that this is even possible under capitalism because capitalist competition means that the most unscrupulous owners in any industry will force even a self-identified Christian to attempt to lower prices or go out of business, and thus begin to pay workers less. Hardie thus believes that there are only two reasonable alternatives: either industry attempts to work toward a monopoly (collectivization of industry), which then puts the consumer and worker at a total disadvantage, or socialism—the collectivization of the workers and consumers:

> Under Socialism there would still be monopoly, as in the case of the trust, but with this difference: that whereas the trust is privately owned and run exclusively with the object of making profit, under Socialism land and capital would be owned in common by the entire community, and be controlled and operated and cultivated so as to produce the end in view—the supply of the necessaries of life—with the least expenditure of human effort.[79]

The importance of pointing out this foray into a brief discussion of Socialist analysis of economics is that it is precisely here that Hardie then returns to the Bible, and his discussion of a central theme: The Kingdom of God, which typically leads Hardie to his discussion of the Lord's Prayer. As this affords us a centrally important argument about Hardie's reading of the Gospels, we cite this at some length:

> Christ laid down no elaborate system of either economics or theology ... His words are simple and not to be misunderstood when taken to mean what they say. His prayer—Thy Kingdom come, Thy will be done on earth as it is in Heaven—was surely meant to be taken literally. Are our opponents prepared to assert that in Heaven there will be factories working women and children for starvation wages; coal mines, and private property in land, dividing the population of Heaven into two classes, one revelling in riches and luxury, destructive of soul and body, the other grovelling in poverty, also destructive of all that is best in life? If not, how can they consistently support the system which inevitably produces that state of things upon earth?

> A favourite text of the opponents of Socialism is, 'Seek ye first the kingdom of God and His righteousness, and all these things shall be added unto you.' But that, strangely enough, is also a favourite text of mine. Will our opponents descend from the clouds of meaningless words with which they becloud the

---

79. Hardie, *Pound a Week*, 17–18.

sense of this text and tell us what they mean by the 'kingdom of God and His righteousness,' and what those 'things' are which are to be added to those who become members thereof? This nation is being done to death by war-mongers and money-grabbers. A lying spirit is abroad in the land; poverty does not decrease; children are hungered; drunkenness is rampant; gambling is on the increase, and discontent is growing. Are these the fruits of the Spirit, the 'things' of the kingdom of God? Unless the way of life be found, the future is black with the gloom of the pit. What is the kingdom of God? The question is put in no frivolous spirit; it is the one question which must be answered if we, as a nation, are to be saved from destruction. Believe, says the preacher; believe and act, says the Socialist. Shew us thy faith without thy works, and we will shew you our faith by our works. Which of these methods make most for the realization of the kingdom of God?[80]

In the August 1901 edition of his column "Between Ourselves" in *The Labour Leader,* Hardie mentions that he continues to receive letters about the "Pound-a-Week" article. Most of the most substantive responses were also included in later editions of the pamphlet, but there is one helpful summary where Hardie reiterates that:

The point of my argument was, and is, that in the Sermon on the Mount the message underlying the words is that every form of private accumulation of this world's goods is a hindrance to the development of the Man, since the more he accumulates the more are his thoughts diverted from life itself to the things of life, and that in the end the things become more important than the life, and that in the Kingdom of God there will be no need for the distraction, since, as in the case of the birds and flowers, there will be abundance for all in the common store, and thus all cause for anxiety concerning food and raiment will be removed.[81]

"Can a Soldier be a Christian?"

From 1902, and during the Boer War, we have a good example of Hardie arguing his commitment to nonviolence with an equal commitment to citing the Bible. In this essay, Hardie rather emotionally contrasts what he understands to be the teachings of Jesus against a copy of "The Soldier's Pocket Book for Field Service" written by Viscount Wolseley, "the late Commander-in-Chief." Hardie begins his essay with a clear reference to the teachings of Jesus in the Sermon:

This is a question sometimes asked, but generally by foolish people. The professional soldier hires himself to do his country's bidding 'right or wrong.'

---

80. Hardie, *Pound a Week,* 17–18.
81. *The Labour Leader,* August 1901.

How then can a man-killer for wages be a Christian? The point need not be laboured. No one can read the Sermon on the Mount and not see how clearly and completely Christ abrogated the old Mosaic law of revenge, and substituted that of forgiveness and love.[82]

Hardie continues his dialogue with Wolseley's book:

When we were little boys and went to church (there was no Salvation Army in those days) we used to hear sometimes something about loving our enemies and doing good to those who hated us, but what says Lord Wolseley? – 'It is the infantry's fire that kills and wounds,' and the advice is given to 'fire low and fire slow.' In other words, don't miss your man, aim at the body, you might miss his head. Again, the bayonet is to be used in the charge with a 'ringing cheer' as a line, says the late Commander-in-Chief, 'could not charge in silence.' We suppose because the shrieks and groans of the victims would unnerve some.[83]

Hardie is particularly incensed at the advice of burning farmhouses, destroying infrastructure, and chasing after the retreating enemy. Hardie asks: "Judge the feelings of this mass of humanity as they hear the roar of our Christian guns, and the thunder of our pursuing cavalry endeavouring to crush out their last chance of existence."

Hardie reads on:

If the inhabitants of a town are hostile a good way 'to bring it to reason is to cut off the supplies of provisions and water,' but if we remember rightly Christ said, 'If thine enemy hunger, feed him; if he thirst, give him drink.' Also, how does this compare with 'Blessed are the merciful?' 'Farm harrows with the spikes upward, and ploughs can be used with advantage to retard the crossing of a river at a ford. Broken glass bottles are very effective with a bare-footed enemy.' Or how does this compare with 'Blessed are the meek?' ... [84]

Hardie concludes:

Surely if Christianity means following the mighty Christ, the Prince and Saviour of the world, no Christian with such a handbook as Lord Wolseley's before him can enter upon such a vocation without first renouncing his faith.

---

82. *The Labour Leader*, June 21, 1902.
83. *The Labour Leader*, June 21, 1902.
84. *The Labour Leader*, June 21, 1902.

"Socialism and Christianity" (Ch. 4, From Serfdom to Socialism, 1907)

This essay, under ten pages in length, appears as a singularly important chapter in the closest thing to an autobiography that Hardie ever wrote, entitled: *From Serfdom to Socialism* (1907). In chapter 4, Hardie takes up the topic of "Socialism and Christianity." In his introductory comments, Hardie reiterates that: "Socialism, like every other problem of life, is at bottom a question of ethics or morals."[85] His arguments here are, in the main, familiar: "It would, however, be an easy task to show that Communism, the final goal of Socialism, is a form of Social Economy very closely akin to the principles set forth in the Sermon on the Mount."[86]

In this writing, however, Hardie also briefly mentions the "The Mosaic laws," which contains laws for the: "regulation of the holding of land and the treatment of the poor and the unfortunate."[87] This brief discussion of Old Testament themes is particularly interesting, given that most biographers propose that he never, or rarely, discussed the Hebrew Scriptures. Hardie here admits that Mosaic laws are not "properly to be called socialist," but he nonetheless brings historical context into his argument when he proposes, in regard to these Mosaic laws, that it must be remembered that:

> ... they were framed to meet the needs of a people just emerging from the nomadic pastoral state, in which Communism of a crude but effective sort had been practised, and were intended to put a check upon the growing rapacity of those early Individualists who were adding field to field [Isa. 5] and plying the usurer's calling, we see that they were quite as drastic in their way as are many of the Socialist proposals of our day. Usury was prohibited [Ex. 22:25; Deut. 23:19-20], land could neither be sold outright nor held for more than a limited period as security for debt [Lev. 25]; even the debtor was freed from all obligations when the year of jubilee came round [also Lev. 25]. The prophets and preachers of the pre-Christian era were loud in their denunciations of the folly of those who expected happiness from riches. They beheld the tears of the oppressed, and saw that on the side of the oppressors there was wealth and power. They declared that the profit of the earth was for all, and that even the king was dependent upon the field for his daily food. Men were heaping up riches which they could not enjoy and were only thereby adding to their own hurt, labouring for the wind. Social equality and fierce denunciations of the rich form the staple of the writings we are now taught to look upon as having been inspired [Amos, Mic., Isa.].

> As Renan has it: The prophets of Israel are fiery publicists of the description we should now call Socialists or Anarchists. They are fanatical in their demands for social justice, and proclaim aloud that, if the world is not just nor capable

---

85. Citing Hardie, in Callow, *From Serfdom to Socialism*, 80.
86. Citing Hardie, in Callow, *From Serfdom to Socialism*, 81.
87. Citing Hardie, in Callow, *From Serfdom to Socialism*, 82.

of becoming just, it were better it were destroyed. The rich man was an impious extortioner, whilst he who deprived the workman of his wages was stigmatized as a murderer. Clearly the modern system of wealth accumulation, which is rooted and grounded in land monopoly, usury, and the fleecing of the poor, finds no support in such teachings as are contained in the Old Testament Scriptures.[88]

Hardie then turns to the Sermon:

> The Sermon on the Mount, whilst it perhaps lends but small countenance to State Socialism, is full of the spirit of pure Communism. Nay, in its lofty contempt for thrift and forethought, it goes far in advance of anything ever put forward by any Communist, ancient or modern. Christ's denunciations of wealth are only equalled by the fierceness of the diatribes which He levelled against the Pharisees.[89]

Here we encounter one of Hardie's most interesting uses of an aphorism of Paul in combination with the Epistle of James:

> It was St. Paul who enunciated the doctrine that he who would not work neither should he eat [2 Thess. 3:10], whilst St. James in his Epistle rivals the old prophets in his treatment of those who grow rich at the expense of the poor [Jas 5:1–7].[90]

Alluding, no doubt, once again to the famous "primitive communism" passages of Acts 2 and 4, Hardie continues by noting that, contrary to common opinion: " … it is now known that Communism in goods was practised by Christians for at least three hundred years after the death of Christ."[91]

Hardie also appealed to post-Biblical early Christian sources: "Almost without exception, the early Christian Fathers whose teachings have come down to us spoke out fearlessly against usury, which includes interest also, and on the side of Communism … To those who said that the idleness of the poor was the cause of their poverty, St. John Chrysostom replied that the rich too were idlers living on their plunder."[92] Still, one would like to know the source of Hardie's comment that: "For seven hundred years, says one authority, almost all the Fathers of the Church considered Communism the most perfect and most Christian form of Social organization …."[93]

Significantly, in this source, Hardie will continue to appeal to a kind of "people's history" of Radical Christianity, taking note of changes introduced to Christian faith with what is recently also now commonly referred to as "the Constantinian

---

88. Citing Hardie, in Callow, *From Serfdom to Socialism*, 82–3.
89. Citing Hardie, in Callow, *From Serfdom to Socialism*, 83.
90. Citing Hardie, in Callow, *From Serfdom to Socialism*, 83.
91. Citing Hardie, in Callow, *From Serfdom to Socialism*, 83–4.
92. Citing Hardie, in Callow, *From Serfdom to Socialism*, 84.
93. Citing Hardie, in Callow, *From Serfdom to Socialism*, 84.

shift," which Hardie proposes had transformed: " ... Christianity as the religion of the Roman Empire" and thus involved a significant change in the practice of Christianity itself:

> ... it was only after Christianity, from being the despised and persecuted creed of the poor, had become the official religion of the State, that opinion on this point began to undergo a change. Even then it was not until the thirteenth century that the Church came out into the open as a defender of property. All the great semi-religious semi-political movements from the twelfth to the seventeenth century, had a Communistic basis.[94]

Hardie then turns to a series of precedents of radical Christian movements in European history that he believes carried on "socialist" principles of Christian life citing the "Weaving Friars, a semi-religious and strongly Communistic Trade Guild formed in Bruges by the Flemish woollen weavers"; "the Peasant Revolt in England – led by John Ball, 'the Mad Priest of Kent'"; the "Communistic teachings of Wycliffe"; "John Huss the Communist"; "Thomas Munster, the German Communist"; "The world-famous Anabaptist movement which followed was avowedly Communistic"; and John Lilburne's "Leveller" movement. Notably, Hardie notes that they were all persecuted—thus identifying the contemporary travails he faced with historical precedents in the faith. Not surprisingly, Hardie also expressed his sympathy for the radicals in the English Civil War.[95]

In an interesting statement, however, Hardie notes that his point in this recital of various experiments from the past was not intended to defend socialism *per se*, but rather to argue that these various experiments show that *Christianity itself was understood to inspire this kind of radical social experimentation*:

> Christianity in its pristine purity had Communism as its invariable outcome, and that for nearly seventeen centuries the common people and their leaders believed Communism and Christianity to be synonymous terms. Incidentally it shows how little modern churchgoers know of the history of their own religion when they charge Socialism with being anti-Christian.[96]

By now, we see Hardie's hermeneutic (and the similarities to Hird and especially Davidson)—by proposing important ethical considerations before Jesus, from Jesus Himself, and after Jesus. From the time before Jesus he cites Moses and the Prophets, from Jesus Himself he cites mainly the Sermon but also notably the Lord's Prayer, as well as a singular phrase each from Paul and James, and then from those who interpreted Jesus later in Christian tradition. Thus, socialism, argues Hardie:

> ... is in the true line of apostolic succession with the pre-Christian era prophets, with the Divine Founder of Christianity, and with those who for the first seven

---

94. Citing Hardie, in Callow, *From Serfdom to Socialism*, 84–5.
95. Citing Hardie, in Callow, *From Serfdom to Socialism*, 84–5.
96. Citing Hardie, in Callow, *From Serfdom to Socialism*, 87–8.

hundred years of the Christian faith maintained even to the death the unsullied right of their religious faith to be regarded as the Gospel of the poor.[97]

It is important to point out that Hardie's hermeneutic of Biblical interpretation is not necessarily radically *original*—only that it was a carefully considered interpretation of the New Testament rather than merely "political" or rhetorical window-dressing. But we can establish this even more securely with further examples.

"Labour and Christianity," 1910

Hardie wrote a similar essay in 1910 which appeared in the collection: *Labour and Religion* (based on a series of speeches at Browning Hall, London during Labour Week).[98] Similar themes that we will see recurring in Hardie's approach to Biblical polemics are evident here as well, including his own "statement of faith":

> I have said, both in writing and from the platform many times, that the impetus which drove me first of all into the Labour movement, and the inspiration which has carried me on to it, has been derived more from the teachings of Jesus of Nazareth, than from all our sources combined.[99]

Included in his themes were references to the earthly implications of the announcement of the Kingdom of God, which "means the establishment right here upon earth of a condition of things in which human life would be beautiful and would be free to develop along Godlike lines."[100] Here, however, Hardie hits harder on communal possession of goods in the New Testament:

> Christ in His Gospels denounced property in all its forms. He did not merely denounce those who were rich: Christ's Gospel teaches us that life is the only thing of value, and that the possession of property comes between a man and the development of his life. Christianity on its social side can never be realized – if it is to be interpreted in the light of Christ's teaching – until there is full, free Communism, and the very idea of private property has disappeared from men's minds.[101]

---

97. Citing Hardie, in Callow, *From Serfdom to Socialism*, 88.

98. Keir Hardie, *Labour and Religion by Ten Labour Members*, in Anon. ed. (St. Albans: Gibbs and Bamforth, 1910).

99. Hardie, "Labour and Christianity," in *Labour and Religion*, ed. Anon (Browning Hall: Labour Week, 1910), 49.

100. Hardie, "Labour and Christianity," 51.

101. Hardie, "Labour and Christianity," 52–3.

Hardie completes this particular speech with a call to working persons to remain in the church if they can:

> To those of you who are in Christian Churches, I would say, Don't let yourselves be driven out; remain inside and make the Church more worthy of Christ than it has been. Those of you who are outside the Christian Church, try to be Followers of Christ in actuality if not in professional name. Thus, my comrades and friends, by working together, whether inside or outside the organized Christian Church, we shall be serving Him who loved us, and loved us so much that He gave His life for us.[102]

In order to see how unique Hardie was among Labour speakers on religious topics, one may only compare the speech in the same collection offered by Philip Snowden, "The Religion of the Labour Movement,"[103] where he cites "Love neighbour as yourself" (Lev. 19:18, Mt. 19:19). In fact, it is the single reference to the Bible in his entire talk. One gains a clearly strained sense of addressing the issue. There is no personal testimony of faith, and a lone scriptural reference in the entire (and brief) address. There is nothing of the spirit, the sheer bravado, of Hardie's bold embrace of the topic and the detail, and personal commitment, with which he addresses it.

"Christ and the Modern Movement," 1913

We can set the stage for this section by citing Hardie's speech/essay as published in a 1913 collection entitled *Christ and Labour*.[104] Hardie's talk, entitled "Christ and the Modern Movement," takes up one of his favorite topics—contrasting the teaching and work of the modern church with the teachings and example of Jesus:

> sometimes I ask myself the question whether the Theologians have not built such a scaffolding of theological doctrine, dogma, and learning around the Christ as to obscure him from the view of the common people.[105]

Hardie then presents his image of Jesus as Hardie interprets the Gospels. Jesus, Hardie states, was:

> … a child born to working class parents … living under a military despotism. The Roman soldiers were everywhere. A dictatorship supervened the making

---

102. Hardie, "Labour and Christianity," 54–5.
103. Philip Snowden, "The Religion of the Labour Movement," in *Labour and Religion*, ed. Anon. (Browning Hall: Labour Week, 1910), 37–40.
104. Keir Hardie, "Christ and the Modern Movement," in *Christ and Labour*, ed. C. G. Ammon (London: Jarrold & Sons, 1913), 77–91.
105. Hardie, "Christ and the Modern Movement," 78.

and administration of all their laws. Taxation was heavy and burdensome, poverty was rampant. We have that from the parables of the rich and poor. He could not have drawn a parallel from the hiring of the men in the market because no man had employed them unless He had known about the unemployed from actual experience ... He spoke to the common people in the language of the common people. He used illustrations to enforce His meaning that the minds of the common people were familiar with ... [106]

As he often did, Hardie turned directly to the Sermon on the Mount:

He (Jesus) pointed out that if God was the Universal Father, and if all men were brothers, the proper law governing life of the family was not hatred and bickering, strife and enmity. The law of the family was the law of love. [citing love enemies and pray for those who despitefully use you.] ... Jesus was aware of the Roman compulsion to carry one mile – but Christ's advice to go two. Why? Because you are doing it as an act of comradeship and fellowship, and if some one wants to borrow your coat, give him your cloak also ... God's Kingdom, then, was to be founded upon love, service and humility, and there was to be no sectarianism. Christ told the woman at the well that the time would come when the people would neither worship at the temple at Jerusalem nor at the Holy Hill of the Samaritans, but that all who believed in God would worship God in spirit and in truth ... [107]

When Hardie takes up the critique of worshipping "mammon," he comments:

I wonder how many here could define what is meant by Mammon. It is not merely business success. It means worldliness in every one of its forms. Militarism is part of Mammon. Successful business often means worshipping at its shrine. The working man who wants to get on is in its service. All things that constitute modern life for successful and desirable material things are part of the worship of Mammon.[108]

Hardie's next move was to speak of holding "everything in common." However, Hardie is also aware of the theological move to shift the teachings of Jesus to a future era, or perhaps in heaven:

The Kingdom of God has been relegated to a mythical hereafter, the ruling class think it consistent with Christianity to hold the poor down in their poverty and to console them with a heaven that is to come because they have found no means of investing money there. The Kingdom of God, who dares speak of it in the

---

106. Hardie, "Christ and the Modern Movement," 78, 80.
107. Hardie, "Christ and the Modern Movement," 81–3.
108. Hardie, "Christ and the Modern Movement," 84.

city of London? ... We have our churches and our chapels, but we also have our Imperialism. England is doing for the people what Rome did for Christ. We are holding coloured people in subjection in order that we may exploit them as Rome did Judea and Palestine, and this explains why the Church and the people are becoming divorced.[109]

Hardie also reaffirms his nonviolence: "Thou shalt love thy enemies, and they who take the sword shall perish by the sword, and 450 million pounds are being spent by the Christian nations of Europe in building up armaments!"[110] But Hardie is perhaps at his strongest when he calls for revolution based on Christian principles, affirming both inward and outward aspects of the message:

> Let me say to those of you of the working-classes, we must rescue Jesus Christ from the rich. He belongs to us in a special degree. The other side use Him as a mask behind which they go on violating His teaching, and if you were inclined to say that I am speaking of the worldly side of Christ's teaching, let me say that it was to do that that I came here. But you are apt to forget that there is a second side. I have felt the power of conversion to Christ. I know the peace that arises from a sense of sins forgiven ... I ask you, then, my comrades, to believe me when I say that Christianity has its message not only for the past, but also for the present; that up to now that message has not found its embodiment in the modern Christian Church, but rather in the modern socialistic movement ... Let us work for what we know to be right, and if we are working in the spirit of humanity and for the good of humanity, we can claim Christ as the elder brother and the Great Comrade, and He will not forsake us in the hour of our necessity.[111]

In this first example, it is perhaps notable to point out how frequent Hardie's Biblical references are. In a fourteen-page essay, he made no less than seventeen direct Biblical references:

79 – Lk. 2:41–52 – Jesus "sitting with the teachers"
80 – Mt. 20:1–16 – workers "idle in the marketplace" for the vineyard
81 – Mt. 12:50 – whoever does my will – brothers and sisters
81 – Mt. 5:21–6 – Antitheses – don't kill (first one)
81 – Mt. 5:41 – the extra mile
82 – Mt. 26:52 – Telling Peter to put away his sword
82 – Jn 8 – woman in adultery
82 – Jn 4:4–42 – woman at well

---

109. Hardie, "Christ and the Modern Movement," 85-6.
110. Hardie, "Christ and the Modern Movement," 88.
111. Hardie, "Christ and the Modern Movement," 89-91.

83 – Mt. 5; Lk. 6 – Love enemies
83 – Mt. 6 – Take no thought "what eat?"
83 – Mt. 6; Lk. 16:13 – Mammon
85 – Acts 2:44; 4:32 – held in common
87 – Lk. 16 – Lazarus
88 – Mk 9:34 – be a servant; Who is greatest?
88 – Gen. 1:27 – Image of God
89 – Lk. 12 – sermons and parables against greed
89 – Mk 8:36; Lk. 9:25; Mt. 16:26 – Gain the world but lose soul

SUMMARY

There are a number of things that we can observe about Hardie's "Proletarian Exegesis." First, Hardie reads the New Testament with an assumption that the situation of Jesus is not so different from his own, and he can thus interpret economic issues clearly. The poor in Jesus's day may have looked different, but Hardie still believed Jesus understood what poverty meant.

Second, Hardie draws on the oppositional spirit of the New Testament to empower his attacks on authority figures. This is a significant tactic—because Hardie refuses to countenance the criticism that as a non-clergy person, he should be showing deference to the clergy and their formal education. Hardie also picks up on the anti-authoritarian streak in the New Testament itself. He identifies himself and his allies with Jesus facing the authority figures of his day.

Third, Hardie clearly has his favorite texts—Jesus, first and foremost, and usually the Sermon, or Matthew 23, or the Lord's Prayer. But Hardie can draw widely from the Gospels—parables as well as direct teachings.

Fourth, despite some hesitancy about Paul (and he certainly does not use Paul heavily), the famous aphorism of 2 Thessalonians does turn up frequently.

Fifth, although drawing on Old Testament materials occasionally, these writings are not prominent in Hardie's rhetoric. Jesus is at the center—and the earthly life and teacher rather than a doctrine of a second person of the Holy Trinity. Terms like "Redeemer" and "Saviour" do occur, but doctrinal questions are not part of Hardie's political use of the New Testament.

Finally, as we have seen, Hardie is not unaware of certain theological debates, especially when they might impact his social interpretation of the teachings of Jesus. For example, Hardie is very aware of the tactic to interpret the teachings of Jesus as impossible perfectionism, not really intended to be morally obligatory. Hardie is further aware of utopianism—interpreting the teachings of Jesus to be effective "some day in the future." He clearly disdains both perspectives.

In our last chapter, we will take up a number of Hardie's classic texts and how he uses them, and compare this to contemporary debates in Biblical Studies to see where Hardie may "stand" in relation to modern theological/historical-critical work on the same passages. We will see that the Miner's exegesis strongly relates to ongoing debates about these same passages.

Appendix to Chapter 5: "A Commercial Bible" (Labour Leader)

This is not written precisely in Hardie's normally recognizable style, and although it is unsigned, it is *potentially* from Hardie. The satirical style anticipates Hardie's tone in relation to Lord Overtoun, for example, especially when Hardie attacks Overtoun's "highlighted" edition of the Bible where Hardie attacks the passages that Lord Overtoun emphasizes, and those he does not.

However, although I was hesitant to use this article as part of my primary evidence, it is such a priceless gem that I wish the patient reader of this work to have something to thoroughly enjoy. Herewith, then, is the following deliciously ironic essay, which is claimed by the editor afterwards (and at least the final words, likely, are Hardie's) to not be the famous George B. Shaw ... still, there are some interesting family resemblances to the tone of the following:

The Commercial Bible

"Yes," said J. F. Shaw, "I have been thinking much about the matter. This being an age of reform it has for some time appeared to me desirable to make a thorough revision of the Christian religion in order either to bring the Churches into harmony with the Book upon which they are supposed to be founded, or, the Book into harmony with them. Of course, I am not so extravagant as to hope, or fear, for any change in the former direction, but it has occurred to me that an effective revision of the sacred Scriptures would be most useful in making the teaching of the Church truly expressive of the actual practice of Christians. By this means there would be a manifest gain in consistency all round, while, in an age of doubt, there could be the added advantage of confirming the faith of those who must frequently be not a little startled to find a rule of life prescribed in the Scriptures so utterly at variance with the teachings of the pulpit, their own conscience, and the dictates of good society in general.

OUTSPOKEN ST. JAMES

At present, for instance, when a beneficent capitalist or indulgent landlord has been enabled by a reduction of wages, or by raising his rents, to add a tithe of his increased income to the funds of his favourite charity, and has thus earned the well-deserved plaudits of the public and the press, it must, I fear, by no means conduce to a proper frame of religious calm if he opens his Bible at the epistle of St. James, so unhappily violent in its language. In saying this, be it understood, I by no means undervalue the work done by our bishops and leading divines in explaining the unfortunate language of the founders of the faith. I am well aware that by their ability, St. James himself has been so interpreted that, were he alive and wise enough to accept their explanations of his words, it is by no means impossible he might have attained to a living or some more eminent position in the Church – perhaps even to a bishopric – but, I fear, however true this may be, as long as the words themselves remain, there will always be the danger that some may suppose St. James and others meant what they said, not what they are said to have meant. We read of the founder of Christianity, that the "common people heard him gladly" and, though the process of explanation has so improved the personnel of church-goers, that happily no such statement can be made about His modern apostles with any degree of truth; it is always to be feared that this fundamentally democratic teaching may at any time lead to mischief. Is it not high time to remove that most dangerous insecurity, the Biblical Socialism which we have hitherto successfully ignored?

PROPOSES A COMMITTEE

Moved by these and kindred reflections, I submit that the time has arrived when a competent committee of our leading divines of the Established, Roman Catholic, and Nonconformist Churches should be formed, to revise the canonical books of Holy Scripture in order to make them more thoroughly representative of the views held by our nobility, gentry, and property holding classes generally; more especially as I feel certain that a committee could easily be chosen in whom the public might place every confidence, that nothing capable of giving pain to the wealthy would be permitted to remain, or, if permitted, would be so modified as to become an additional strength, rather than a menace, to the dividends of the pious.

SOME OLD AGITATORS

At the risk of appearing presumptuous, I may suggest that a body so appointed might leave the Old Testament books very much as they are. No doubt the language of some of the prophets, and especially Isaiah, Amos, and Ezekiel is itself very objectionable, not only on account of its frequent violence, but its obvious tendency to unsettle the minds of the lower orders. The former's condemnation of the thrifty landlord who is anxious to improve his condition by adding other houses and fields to those which he is already in possession, is very disturbing to the religious calm of the business man. While Amos would appear to have been little better than an uncouth agitator, the method in which he addresses the gentlemanly high-priest Amaziah is really most distressing. Still it seems to me that even these passages might be left with but little modification as long as we had a thoroughly expurgated New Testament. The preacher of the future might then congratulate the wealthy church-goer upon that new and better covenant which gave him so much liberty – to add house to house and make profit by usury and sweating – which the old had denied. And to prove that this would be a perfectly legitimate application of Christian liberty, I have only to point out that this freedom is already acted upon by thousands of the most eminent pillars of the church at the present day.

POETRY AND TRUTH

With regard to the New Testament omissions, judicious alterations are generally to be preferred to positive additions. The poetry and beauty of Scriptural language is justly praised by church-goers, and I fear might be difficult to imitate. This beauty of language, too, is a perfectly legitimate subject of admiration so long as generally at present, no definite meaning whatever is attached to the words; and especially no meaning calculated to call in question the religious nature of property rights. Such a phrase, for instance, as "Ye cannot serve God and Mammon" might be altered to "Ye can serve God and Mammon" with distinct advantage to the cause of modern Christianity. The text is obviously incorrect as it stands, it being plain that the wardens and deacons of our churches do in fact what is here pronounced impossible; their service of Mammon during the week being much more consistent and devout than their service of God on Sundays. It may, perhaps, be well to examine the fifth chapter of St Matthew in a cursory manner, in order to give an idea of the alterations which might be made in it with advantage. I should suggest the world "pure" should be substituted for "poor" in the 3rd verse, as many devout Christians are not by any means humble; but are exceedingly determined in persecution of all improper persons, unless the profits of vice add materially to the rents of their own property. This alteration, also, would be extremely popular with the ladies whose Christian abhorrence of the wickedness of a fallen sister is so beautiful a testimony to their own virtue. Verse 4 might with advantage be deleted, while in verse 5 it would only be needful to substitute "moneylenders" for "meek" to have a sentiment fully in accord with the religious spirit of the age. I fear it would be necessary to omit all verses from the 13th to the 24th inclusive; but the next two might with little alteration be made a valuable argument in the hands of factors and property agents whose trade is but too little supported by quotations from holy writ. All after the 37th verse would of course be dispensed with.

AN ABSURD SUGGESTION

The reader may perhaps consider I might have given more attention to the alternative suggestion given at the commencement of my remarks – viz., that some attempts might be made to bring the practice of the churches into harmony with the New Testament without alteration in the latter. But, however much this idea may commend itself at first sight, I think a moment's reflection will show that it would be attended with insuperable difficulties in practice. It is obvious that the main supporters of Christianity at present are precisely that class of persons whose manner of life is most frequently and severely criticized in the Bible; and, further, it is most undesirable that any alteration should be made in this state of things. True, the churches are supported out of the labour of the poorer classes, but as the fruit of this labour and the legal right to dispense of it by donation or subscription almost invariably rests with the middle and upper classes, I cannot see how teaching necessarily offensive to them, is to be reconciled with the claims of church building committees, the aesthetic rendering of divine service, and the consequent advancement of religion. In the days of the early church, the gospel, though welcomed by the people, was by no means acceptable to the better class, and its ministers, very far from being gladly received into the houses of respectable and wealthy patrons – as is happily so often the case now – often found it extremely difficult to obtain a living, and were hated or despised by everyone whose esteem was at all likely to be profitable in money or position. Now, though it is well known that the clergy of all denominations are themselves entirely indifferent to such worldly matters as social status or income, still it is often very justly pointed out that a bishop, rector, or leading dissenting minister has, in truth, a position to keep up which it is important for the dignity of the Church should be maintained – not, of course, in the eyes of "the world" from which the Church is a thing apart, but in those of good society, and how this is to be done if this suggestion be adopted I can hardly see. It seems to me most probably that the present supporters of the churches would be seized with a just indignation at the conduct of those who had been so largely supported out of their subscriptions, and might, indeed, treat the bishops themselves pretty much as the Apostles were treated for the like teaching. How the ministry could maintain their positions in society, if unhappily left "naked in dens or caves of the earth" I leave advocates of this wild idea to explain, merely remarking that the danger is by no means so chimerical as might be imagined, the difference between an ancient Pharisee and a modern church patron being one chiefly of eighteen hundred years.

THE REVOLUTION

I think also those who advocate the real practice of the teachings of the New Testament by modern church-goers can hardly have realized the very revolutionary nature of their purpose. It, indeed, practically amounts to an entire reversal of the established practice of the Church in all ages, with the exception of a few heterodox sects, such as the early Anabaptists and perhaps a few primitive Quakers; while even in the cases of these sects, it is to be observed that their successors by no means carry out either the Communism or the non-resistance of their early leaders, but, on the contrary are as staunch defenders of property and privilege as anyone. It may, in fact, be truly pointed out that, whereas the precept of Christ was to give to every asker, and to lend "hoping for nothing again" to every borrower, this subversive idea has invariably been neglected in the practice of the Godly semper et ubique et ab omnibus ["always and everywhere, and by all"]. These things being so, I am sure it will be generally felt that the plan I have proposed at least merits serious consideration. The eminent patience which Christians always display under criticism will doubtless prevent even those who may not see eye to eye with me in this matter from taking exception to views honestly held and delivered in a friendly manner. Cant is considered by many one of the leading vices of the day, and – though, of course, religious people have been conspicuously free from this fault – I fear that in the minds of many prejudiced persons they will be hardly be held entirely spotless until their creed is made conformable to their practice, or vice-versa.

At this point Mr. Shaw – no relation to our only Fabian – gave out, whether from lack of breath or of ideas no one knew.

(*Labour Leader*, May 19, 1894).

Figure 6.1 "As ye sow, so shall ye reap," *The Labour Leader*, 1897.

Chapter 6

THE MINER'S BIBLE: HARDIE IN DIALOGUE WITH NEW TESTAMENT DEBATE

Introduction: Hardie's Exegesis and modern Biblical debate

The last chapter was focused on quoting Hardie's use of the Bible. As a contribution to the field of "History of Interpretation" or "Reception History," what I have gathered up here is thus far fairly standard fare in terms for these methods and projects, other than the emphasis that I have followed from the influence of Gold and Gutman—namely my attention to a particular historical and social "class" of the literature I have been reading, and therefore the kinds of sources I have been investigating.

I am very aware, furthermore, that there are some issues that I have certainly not addressed. I have not, for example, compared Hardie's use of the Bible to the use of similar passages, for example, by clergy or theologians contemporary to Hardie himself, with the exception of considering some elements of his early interest in a particular Scottish Protestant movement known as "The Morisonians" (Chapter 2), and noting the similarities between Hardie, Hird, and Davidson (Chapter 4). The reasons for not developing these kinds of questions are obvious—such a larger comparative historical analysis would take this project in a decidedly different direction, namely toward a monograph in Scottish theological history more generally.[1] As we have noted, with the exception of further discussion of some religious contexts, we already *have* a number of studies that consider Hardie in his historical context(s), and that work continues.

In this final chapter, however, I wish to take an admittedly more controversial step. As we noted in Chapter 1, both Gillingham and Boxall, in their contributions to a recent collection on "Reception History," hinted at the possibility that some Reception Studies may result in new light being shed on historical-critical issues, or in Boxall's language, these readings may serve: "as a 'corrective', in order to do

---

1. These are the kinds of questions others have indeed investigated more widely, see W. W. Knox, "Religion and the Scottish Labour Movement c. 1900–39," *Journal of Contemporary History* 23 (1988): 609–30.

historical criticism better: asking how earlier receptions might force us to rethink consensus views about original context and meaning."[2] What would this look like?

In this final chapter, I will draw on a selected number of Hardie's most frequently cited Biblical passages and bring them into dialogue with (a sampling of) modern exegetical analysis of these same passages. Once again, however, I need to clarify the purpose of this exercise. I am not attempting a *full and detailed examination* of modern exegetical analysis of each of these passages. Readers hoping for a *comprehensive* review of contemporary scholarship on these Biblical passages will be disappointed. At the risk of repeating myself—that would be an entirely different project, and one of the problems of these kinds of projects is attempting to remain within firmly set "parameters." It is arguably not necessary, however, to give a full and detailed discussion of recent exegetical literature in order to demonstrate how interesting it is to bring Hardie's use of these Biblical passages into dialogue with a working "sample" of the general directions of modern scholarship on these same passages. It seems to me that this is the only way we can show how Hardie's self-taught readings actually raise provocative questions in relation to the modern debates about selected New Testament passages (and the issues accompanying that analysis).

Finally, the point is not *necessarily* to claim that Hardie said something that modern New Testament scholars have *not* said. Rather, it is also significant to point out that Hardie's "readings" of these texts are not radically "out of bounds" in relation to contemporary academic debates about these passages—and that in itself is, I believe, worthy of comment and even, perhaps, reflection: *Does* the social, historical (or cultural) setting of a reader impact *positively* on their insights while reading their Bible? This is a variation of the famous Liberation Theology motto that I have always found intriguing and challenging, namely: "The Poor understand the Bible better than the rich ...." I aim to discuss whether there might be something to this, from the perspective of historical-critical Biblical Studies.

At this point I should acknowledge that I know that some colleagues would take serious exception to my entire premise in writing this chapter—presuming that I am merely attempting to exercise a hegemonic, Euro-American, cis-gendered, scholarly "authority" to assess the "value" of alternative readings by subjecting them to "acceptable" scholarly oversight for "approval." There is little that I can say in reply to this obvious accusation, other than it is not my intent to exercise any kind of "authority"—authority that I do not believe I possess in the first place, incidentally. Simply "retrieving" and "recovering" alternative readings are enough for many of my colleagues. I honor the sentiment, but I disagree, however, with the frequent results of such a view.

As I have tried to argue, I am hoping to take a further step here. I am hoping to take alternative readings seriously. It seems to me that one clear sign of taking

---

2. Boxall, "Tracing Patmos Through the Centuries," 156. Susan Gillingham similarly hinted at this in her essay in the same volume: "Biblical Studies on Holiday? A Personal View of Reception History."

6. The Miner's Bible: Hardie in Dialogue with New Testament Debate

such readings seriously is not merely passively "accepting" that they exist,[3] but engaging them as worth critical time and effort to consider. I have frequently cited Fernando Segovia's provocative image of Biblical Studies as a "marketplace" of ideas.[4] I have always liked the image and his use of it, but even in a marketplace, there is haggling! And, as we know, such haggling only gets serious when both parties are intent on a transaction.

Furthermore, and this is not insignificant, I believe Keir Hardie would heartily approve! I do not accept that I am reading Mr. Hardie "without permission" or in any way that he would not approve of. An early Quaker writer named Samuel Fisher wrote a work entitled: "Rusticus ad Academicos"—roughly: "the country/rural man confronts the Academic" (a *seventeenth-century example* of very early "Reception History" indeed!). For Hardie, the notion that the "countryman" ("rustic") might take on the Professors would give him no end of pleasure. We are, after all, speaking of the miner who challenged professional clergy such as Dr. Stalker in his defense of Lord Overtoun:

> If Christ was 'the Friend of the miserable, the Champion of the weak,' then Dr. Stalker must have been following him very far off, indeed, when he sets himself up as the special pleader and defender of the Lord of Shawfield, and had no word of sympathy for the poor and the oppressed of that foul seat of oppression.[5]

Or his questioning of Rev. Andrew Douglas, where he satirically asks:

> ... if by any chance Andrew should possess a copy of the New Testament (Authorized Version) he might read from the twenty-fifth chapter of Matthew's gospel, but the thirty-first verse to the end of the chapter ... In all sincerity I ask Mr. Douglas for his interpretation of this parable. If it means what it says, what becomes of his denunciations of those who would save mankind by providing them with 'material comforts?' Are not food and drink and raiment 'material

---

3. Sugirtharajah once referred to "Exegetical Apartheid." He referred, I think, to a rather smug kind of "acknowledgment" of "other readings" by European and European-American scholars, as if to say, "How nice that you folks have *your* readings of the Bible, too"—setting up a hierarchical academic "us" and "them" scenario. What I take to be a true "acknowledgment" is that my reading is impacted, too. I have been concerned that some versions of readings from "marginalized" people's scholarship also seem satisfied with this lack of engagement, seemingly believing that *any* critical discussion is exercising illegitimate power. This is surely not the way forward. I reflect a bit on this in my essay for the Fortress Bible Commentary project: "Reading the Christian Old Testament in the Contemporary World," in *The Pentateuch: Fortress Commentary on the Bible Study Edition*, eds. Gale A. Yee, Hugh R. Page, and Matthew J. M. Coomber (Minneapolis: 1517 Media/Fortress Press, 2014), 43–66.

4. Smith-Christopher, "Reading the Christian Old Testament."

5. Hardie's editorial "Between Ourselves," *The Labour Leader*, July 22, 1899, p. 227.

comforts?' ... Had Andrew Douglas been among the crowd to whom Pilate gave choice of a prisoner, his voice would have swelled the cry of 'Not that man, but Barabbas.' The young Socialist Agitator of Nazareth need have expected no mercy from Andrew Douglas ...[6]

Thus, I write this in honor of Keir Hardie and his legacy, and in defense of a notion of recovering a "Proletarian Exegesis of the Bible," and in hopes of inspiring further writing and exploration of the profoundly interesting writings, especially from the Christian Socialists from the 1860s through the 1950s, writings that have only begun to be mined for their theological riches.

The Miner's Bible: Four test cases

I have chosen to briefly discuss four classic passages from Hardie's Biblical repertoire. The first is entirely expected, namely the use of the classic phrase in the Lord's Prayer, " ... on earth as it is in heaven." Hardie, of course, is by no means the only one to use this phrase as a clarion call to "this worldly" activism and application of the teachings of Jesus (as opposed to waiting for heaven!).

The second passage, equally unsurprising, is the description(s) of "community of goods" in Acts (chs. 2, 4–5). Once again, Hardie's use of this passage is hardly unique to him, but the sheer number of times he points to it means that we need to acknowledge not only his own use of this famed "go to" passage for Christian socialism in history, but also to take note that the exemplary nature of this passage continues to invoke debate among New Testament scholars—particularly those who are writing from an interest in Biblical Theology, and thus assuming that their work is read and studied in the context of church folks conducting Bible Study as corollary to modern faith and practice.

Third, we will take up a (nearly equally) "classic passage" in Christian Socialism, Paul's counsel in 2 Thessalonians 3, with specific attention to the famous saying that those who will "not work" should "not eat." Here the discussion becomes even more interesting than the Acts passage, because it is arguably the case that the modern "use" of this passage in precisely the ways Hardie so strenuously objected to, is absolutely current, while the Acts passages have been so effectively "inoculated against" in much modern Western Christian faith and practice that they rarely raise emotional responses. However, this passage is also important because Hardie's use of this phrase does indeed continue to resonate with modern debate about this same passage—but in ways that he himself would not have anticipated as a self-taught, largely nineteenth-century Christian labour activist.

Fourth, and finally, we will take up the (in)famous tirade of Jesus against the Pharisees in Matthew 23—another "storm center" passage where Hardie's use of the chapter also resonates profoundly with contemporary debates about this fiery

---

6. Hardie, "Between Ourselves," *The Labour Leader*, December 11, 1897, p. 403.

6. The Miner's Bible: Hardie in Dialogue with New Testament Debate   187

speech. Notably, Hardie's rather constant use of Matthew 23 is a bit more unique to Hardie's own approaches—but some may cynically observe that—especially for a firebrand like Hardie—this hardly seems surprising, and it is not an unfair observation.

Finally, I will conclude with some brief observations of what Reception History may well have to offer to modern Historical-Critical analysis of the Bible in the Post-Modern, Postcolonial, and "Interested Readings" contexts.

"On Earth as it is in Heaven ... "

Hardie is by no means the only nineteenth-century Christian Socialist to make frequent use of the classic phrase from Matthew's version of the "Lord's Prayer" calling for God's will to be done "on earth as in heaven" (Mt. 6:10). This was often taken to be among the strongest statements for a *material ("this worldly") understanding* of the teachings and example of Jesus—a practicality that resulted in political activism among those seeking to follow Him. Notably, the point is still very much in contention in modern Biblical analysis.

One of the central debates in contemporary New Testament analysis of the Lord's Prayer is whether the prayer calls for human participation in God's plan now, or a prayer that hopes for something to come in the near (or perhaps even distant) future. Harrington's 1991 commentary on Matthew, for example, is rather forthright in arguing for the *future* orientation of the prayer. In reference especially to the "second petition" (e.g., the coming of the Kingdom), Harrington argues:

> the reference is to the future, eschatological kingdom. When it comes all creatures will 'hallow' God's name and God's will will be done perfectly on earth ... understood in this eschatological sense the petition does not add new content to the second petition.[7]

Others have obviously taken similar lines but are also a bit troubled about the implication of a strongly future ("eschatological") orientation. Thomas Long, for example, is somewhat ambiguous on this point when he argues that the words:

> 'your will be done on earth' recognize that only God can save the world. No revolutions, no reformations, no program for social improvement can fully heal the wounds of a hurting world, only God can do that.[8]

But Long isn't entirely satisfied with the quietist implications of this statement, and adds:

---

7. Daniel Harrington, *The Gospel of Matthew*, Sacra Pagina (Collegeville: Liturgical Press, 1991), 95.

8. Thomas Long, *Matthew*, Westminster Bible Companion (Louisville: Westminster John Knox Press, 1997), 70.

'on earth' brings us to 'where we live.' A cry to the God of salvation leads us in God's name to our neighbor in need; a plea for the heavenly God to save empowers us to be earthly agents of reconciliation.[9]

Long's ambiguity, however, shows us the significant lines of this debate about those arguments that want to imply a future orientation to the petitions of the Lord's Prayer.

This eschatological perspective is strongly resisted in other New Testament work. For example, in his important 2007 commentary on Matthew in the *Hermeneia* Commentary series, Ulrich Luz begins his analysis with literary observations, pointing out that Matthew contains the "long version" of the Lord's Prayer (as opposed to the Gospel of Luke), and that Matthew's version contains "greater symmetry" and "clearer rhythm."[10] Luz, developing the language widely used by New Testament scholars, refers to the three "you" petitions (vv. 9c–10) and the two-part "we" petitions (vv. 11–13);[11] while Evans cites petition for bread, about sins, about being delivered from trials and evil, thus four parts as well.[12] Luz, however, also notes that Matthew places the Lord's Prayer "at the center of the Sermon on the Mount,"[13] emphasizing its central importance for the Matthean presentation of the central body of teachings of Jesus. Indeed, Luz cites Tertullian approvingly, who had stated that the prayer was "a summary of the Gospel" and notably, a "basic ethical text" (cf. Gregory of Nyssa, "a guide to life"[14]). Its continued importance in the Christian tradition is emphasized when it appears that the Lord's Prayer was "the first prayer for the almost baptized ... the first prayer they said after Baptism."[15] Luz writes movingly that " ... countless human beings have been able to find a home in the Lord's Prayer for their own hopes and petitions and to enter into that home."[16] Clearly, the ethical significance of the Prayer is built into the very literary structure which places *very real material* concerns in the same breath as the Kingdom of God "on earth." But is it to be done *now*?

As we have already noted, however, contemporary debate continues to involve the argument about whether the realities that the Prayer speaks of are intended to be in the *present*, or in the *future* (the "eschatological" perspective). Luz also notes

---

9. Long, *Matthew*, 70.

10. Ulrich Luz, *Matthew 1–7: A Commentary*, Hermeneia (Minneapolis: Fortress Press, 2007), 309.

11. Luz, *Matthew*, 309–10.

12. Craig Evans, *Matthew*, New Cambridge Bible Commentary (New York: Cambridge University Press, 2012), 144–5.

13. Luz, *Matthew*, 310; cf. "center point" of the sermon, Jeannine Brown and Kyle Roberts, *Matthew*, Two Horizons New Testament Commentary (Grand Rapids: Eerdmans, 2018), 70.

14. Luz, *Matthew*, 313.

15. Luz, *Matthew*, 312.

16. Luz, *Matthew*, 314.

the language of "hallowing" God's name, and states: " ... it is linguistically just as possible that God is being asked to hallow his name here and now, in history, rather than in the eschaton."[17]

It is also widely noted[18] that the prayer of Jesus has strong similarities to the Kaddish from the Synagogue, traces of which may pre-date 70 CE, including the following:

> Magnified and sanctified may his great name be in the world that he created as he wills, and may his kingdom come in your life and in your day, and in the lives of all the house of Israel, swiftly and soon.[19]

So, is the Kaddish a wistful hope for the future? France notes, after citing the Kaddish, that " ... to pray such a prayer is, of course, to be committed oneself to honor God's name, accept his kingship, and do his will."[20] Luz also notes that this prayer, as well, can be read just as powerfully as a prayer desiring change in the world now, and not some distant future. In fact, Luz argues; " ... only for an exclusively eschatological interpretation of the petition are there no arguments ... we reject the eschatological interpretation that is dominant today."[21] Even more strongly, Luz asks whether the petition's aim is human action, as if to say, "Let your commanded will happen through people," or does it mean "something God does ...."[22] For Luz, also citing Matthew 26:42, the prayer of Jesus clearly calls for events to happen now. Jesus is: " ... asking for the power to associate himself actively with this will of God. Thus, our petition includes something the praying person actively does."[23] Evans appears to concur. Citing Mark 1:15, Jesus has announced the arrival of the Kingdom of God: " ... the kingdom of God made its appearance in the ministry of Jesus but has not yet arrived in its fullness."[24] Brown and Roberts agree with the doubled idea of "already and not yet."[25]

Equally impressive along these lines, however, is Keener's 1999 commentary, where Keener cites a number of Hebrew Biblical references that would have had profoundly *contemporary* implications: " ... Jesus' Jewish hearers would have understood the implications of the prayer for present existence ... " citing Leviticus 22:32; Jeremiah 34:12; and notably in Ezekiel 13:19, 20:9, 14, 22, 27, 39; 22:16; 36:20; 39:7—passages where the "profaning" of the Name of God had clear

---

17. Luz, *Matthew*, 316.
18. Cf. Evans, *Matthew*, 145; Brown and Roberts, *Matthew*, 70.
19. Luz, *Matthew*, 317.
20. France, *Matthew*, 247.
21. Luz, *Matthew*, 318.
22. Luz, *Matthew*, 319
23. Luz, *Matthew*, 319.
24. Evans, *Matthew*, 146–7.
25. Brown and Roberts, *Matthew*, 70–2.

"contemporary" implications (e.g., dealing with events happening at the time).[26] Citing Luke 22:42, a prayer acknowledging God's will be done in terms similar to the Lord's Prayer, Nolland's study of the Greek grammar points out that the closest Gospel and Jewish parallels are "ethical rather than eschatological in orientation."[27] Nolland further states that Matthew 26:42 (similar to Luke 22:42) "reproduces exactly the petition in the Lord's Prayer," but Nolland then summarizes as follows:

> The best suggestion seems to be that the third petition encompasses the scope of the first two, unifying their respective present and future orientations by focusing on the common central thread: that in a comprehensive way people should come to act in conformity to the will of God.[28]

Osborne proposes that eschatological language can nonetheless have contemporary relevance. Osborne suggests that the Prayer: " ... especially asks that God end this present order and bring the Kingdom to fullness."[29] Anna Case-Winters clarifies:

> ... praying the Lord's Prayer is a subversive activity. We are in fact praying for the overturning of the present order and the coming of God's reign on earth in its place. If we pray this way, we must live this way ... [30]

Similarly, France[31] argues that Matthew 3:2 ("Repent, for the kingdom of heaven has come near.") and 4:17 ("From that time Jesus began to proclaim, 'Repent, for the kingdom of heaven has come near.'") push toward a contemporary understanding of the implications of Jesus's Prayer:

> the coming of God's reign is something already announced. Its actual presence is required by the wording of 12:28 ... when God's kingdom is present not everyone recognizes and acknowledges it. The parables of Ch. 13 will repeat this point ... the 'already-not-yet' tension which underlies the Synoptic uses of the term is vividly illustrated by the doxology later added to the end of the prayer, which requires the disciples who have just prayed that God's kingdom may come to declare immediately afterward that it is already a reality.[32]

---

26. Craig S. Keener, *A Commentary on the Gospel of Matthew* (Grand Rapids: Eerdmans, 1999), 219–20.

27. John Nolland, *The Gospel of Matthew—A Commentary on the Greek Text*, NIGTC (Grand Rapids: Eerdmans, 2005), 287.

28. Nolland, *Matthew*, 287.

29. Grant Osborne, *Matthew*, Exegetical Commentary on the New Testament (Grand Rapids: Zondervan, 2010), 228.

30. Anna Case-Winters, *Matthew* (Louisville: Westminster John Knox Press, 2015), 89.

31. R. T. France, *The Gospel of Matthew*, NICNT (Grand Rapids: Eerdmans, 2007).

32. France, *Matthew*, 246–7.

Thus, argues France, the famous Prayer is not asking that something become true that isn't, but that the Kingdom of God be "fully implemented."

While many readers may undoubtedly be skeptical that the blacklisted, self-taught miner would have something substantial to contribute to Biblical scholarship, I would caution against being hasty on this point. Hardie's instinct to read the phrase "on Earth as in Heaven" as having present ethical force, *lines him up with one side of an important—and stubbornly persistent—debate in New Testament scholarship* on the problem of deriving ethics from what are sometimes argued to be "future oriented" ("eschatological") texts of the Bible. Furthermore, and this is quite interesting, Hardie was well aware of this interpretive move:

> The Kingdom of God has been relegated to a mythical hereafter, the ruling class think it consistent with Christianity to hold the poor down in their poverty and to console them with a heaven that is to come because they have found no means of investing money there. The Kingdom of God, who dares speak of it in the city of London?[33]

Furthermore, the issue refuses to be limited to debates on the Lord's Prayer. When one notes the widespread use of "in Days to Come … " combined with visions of radically transformative ethics, such as beating weapons into farming tools (Mic. 4 // Isa. 2) the issue becomes increasingly serious indeed.[34]

The blacklisted miner was an astute reader of texts and listener to sermons, such that he seems well aware of the argument that constantly seeks to "defang" radical Biblical ethics by consigning them safely and perpetually into an idealized and non-threatening future (e.g., Long's conservative rant against "revolution" or "reformation" as an interpretation of the Lord's Prayer).

We can see similar polemics in our other examples.

Hardie and early Christian Socialism in Acts

However widespread the use of the famous phrase from the Lord's Prayer certainly was in Christian Socialist writing, it (almost) goes without saying that the "classic passages" for Christian Socialism in nearly all ages are the descriptions of "community of goods" in Acts 2 and 4–5. We have already seen that Hardie, as well, points to this famous passage with very little further comment, clearly believing that it simply speaks for itself, e.g.,: " … it is now known that Communism in goods was practised by Christians for at least three hundred years after the death

---

33. Hardie, "Christ and the Modern Movement," (1913), 85.

34. I try to take up this issue of rendering a passage "eschatologically irrelevant" in my work on the famous Peace Passage, see Daniel Smith-Christopher, *Micah: A Commentary*, Old Testament Library (Louisville: Westminster/John Knox Press, 2015), 128–31.

of Christ."[35] Is it possible, however, to get a sense of the contemporary debate surrounding these famous passages? The texts are as follows:

> Acts 2:42–47 42 They devoted themselves to the apostles' teaching and fellowship, to the breaking of bread and the prayers. 43 Awe came upon everyone, because many wonders and signs were being done by the apostles. 44 All who believed were together and had all things in common; 45 they would sell their possessions and goods and distribute the proceeds to all, as any had need. 46 Day by day, as they spent much time together in the temple, they broke bread at home and ate their food with glad and generous hearts, 47 praising God and having the goodwill of all the people. And day by day the Lord added to their number those who were being saved.

> Acts 4:32–37 32 Now the whole group of those who believed were of one heart and soul, and no one claimed private ownership of any possessions, but everything they owned was held in common. 33 With great power the apostles gave their testimony to the resurrection of the Lord Jesus, and great grace was upon them all. 34 There was not a needy person among them, for as many as owned lands or houses sold them and brought the proceeds of what was sold. 35 They laid it at the apostles' feet, and it was distributed to each as any had need. 36 There was a Levite, a native of Cyprus, Joseph, to whom the apostles gave the name Barnabas (which means 'son of encouragement'). 37 He sold a field that belonged to him, then brought the money, and laid it at the apostles' feet.

> Acts 5:1-12 1 But a man named Ananias, with the consent of his wife Sapphira, sold a piece of property; 2 with his wife's knowledge, he kept back some of the proceeds, and brought only a part and laid it at the apostles' feet. 3 'Ananias,' Peter asked, 'why has Satan filled your heart to lie to the Holy Spirit and to keep back part of the proceeds of the land? 4 While it remained unsold, did it not remain your own? And after it was sold, were not the proceeds at your disposal? How is it that you have contrived this deed in your heart? You did not lie to us but to God!' 5 Now when Ananias heard these words, he fell down and died. And great fear seized all who heard of it. 6 The young men came and wrapped up his body, then carried him out and buried him. 7 After an interval of about three hours his wife came in, not knowing what had happened. 8 Peter said to her, 'Tell me whether you and your husband sold the land for such and such a price.' And she said, 'Yes, that was the price.' 9 Then Peter said to her, 'How is it that you have agreed together to put the Spirit of the Lord to the test? Look, the feet of those who have buried your husband are at the door, and they will carry you out.' 10 Immediately she fell down at his feet and died. When the young men came in they found her dead, so they carried her out and buried her beside her husband. 11 And great fear seized the whole church and all who heard of these

---

35. Citing Hardie in Callow, *Serfdom to Socialism*, 83–84.

things. 12 Now many signs and wonders were done among the people through the apostles. And they were all together in Solomon's Portico.

We can begin to illustrate the polemics involved in the analysis of these passages by citing Countryman's 1980 study on "The Rich Christian," surely among the most forthrightly "political" analyses—despite his own criticism of reading politics into these passages. In this study, Countryman acknowledges the controversy that doggedly adheres to seemingly all academic analysis of this issue in Biblical Studies of the book of Acts (and indeed, other Early Church historical analysis). These passages, he writes, have:

> called forth a great deal of literature over the last century and a quarter, largely because it has been caught up in the modern collision between capitalism and communism. Apologists for a variety of political tendencies have sought to use the early Christians as champions of their own or as whipping boys for the opponents' point of view.[36]

Yet Countryman seems to indicate that progressive and socialist use of these passages, beginning in earnest in the European revolutionary years of 1848, belong, he claims, to: " … the history of politics rather than that of scholarship,"[37] and that Karl Kautsky's Marxist reading of early Christianity (for example) has: "proved a nightmare for theologians who were trying to maintain a politically moderate position …."[38] Politically "moderate"? For someone who begins by identifying the complicating interests in this debate, Countryman exhibits his own bias rather clearly. It was 1980, after all—the Cold War was still hot, and postmodernism was barely making serious inroads in Biblical Studies—and Stephen Friesen's 2004 article on Paul and Poverty had not disrupted NT studies of Paul, early Christianity, and social class.[39] Countryman thus participates in a line of analysis that continues to see the "community of goods" passages of Acts 2, 4, and 5 as a form of *almsgiving*, and thus he reads this very much in line with later

---

36. L. Wm. Countryman, *The Rich Christian in the Church of the Early Empire: Contradictions and Accommodations*, Texts and Studies in Religion (New York: E. Mellen Press, 1980), 1.

37. Countryman, *The Rich Christian*, 2.

38. Countryman, *The Rich Christian*, 5.

39. See Steven Friesen, "Poverty in Pauline Studies: Beyond the So-Called New Consensus," *Journal for the Study of the New Testament* 26 (2004): 323–61; cf. Steven Friesen and Walter Scheidel, "The Size of the Economy and the Distribution of Income in the Roman Empire," *The Journal of Roman Studies* 99 (2009): 61–91. For recent processing of these issues, see G. Anthony Keddie, Michael Flexsenhar III, and Steven J. Friesen, eds., *The Struggle Over Class: Socioeconomic Analysis of Ancient Christian Texts* (Atlanta: SBL, 2021); and closely related, Robert Myles, ed., *Class Struggle in the New Testament* (Minneapolis: Fortress Academic, 2019).

developments of academic discussions of almsgiving as a major theme in Church Fathers like Clement and Chrysostom.[40] So, Countryman writes with regard to the famous passages in Acts:

> If we had only their story to go on, we should deduce that the primitive church at Jerusalem practiced not communism, but rather an extravagant form of almsgiving which entailed complete abandonment of goods. In the absence of other information about the matter, it is difficult to know which is in fact the case.[41]

He argues that only with "Coenobitic Monasticism" do we actually have an example of "communism" as a rule of life.[42] The problem is, of course, that in a monograph that begins by scolding contemporary scholars for being caught up in contemporary politics and economic issues in their reading of the Bible, Countryman stretches too far, particularly with comments suggesting that Luke: "did not himself have a burning interest in the poor ...."[43] This last comment was surely among his more contestable observations—quite assertively denied by Scheffler who cites a large number of contemporary scholars who agree on referring to Luke as: "The Gospel of the Poor."[44]

However, since the force of Countryman's argument against a "communal lifestyle" in Acts is his conviction that early Christianity was more concerned with almsgiving, his argument continues to suggest that almsgiving therefore "appreciates wealth,"[45] otherwise how could they give it away? Even the condemnation of private property that Countryman acknowledges to be found in some of the early Church Fathers, must be put into this context:

> The controlling factors, then, were not intellectual but social. If the fathers, at one moment, say that private property has no foundation in God's will and, at another, ascribe phenomenal merit to the correct disposition of it, there lies behind these seeming contradictions that necessity of the church's officers to keep the rich under control, and yet to keep them attached to the church.[46]

Citing John D. Crossan, Finger takes issue with this in her more recent comments, noting that "commensality" is quite different from almsgiving, as almsgiving

---

40. Countryman, *The Rich Christian*, 59.
41. Countryman, *The Rich Christian*, 79.
42. Countryman, *The Rich Christian*, 80.
43. Countryman, *The Rich Christian*, 84.
44. Eben Scheffler, "Caring for the Needy in the Acts of the Apostles," *Neotestamentica* 50 (2016): 131–66.
45. Countryman, *The Rich Christian*, 103.
46. Countryman, *The Rich Christian*, 173.

perpetuates inequality and status differences.[47] How does Countryman's analysis compare with more recent analysis? His study, it must be stated, does not engage in the textual analysis that is typical of serious studies of the book of Acts, but even in his citing of early Christian sources, Clement or Chrysostom hardly exhaust the possibilities. The point could even be made, however, that early monasticism was an attempt to embody the radicalism of Acts 2 and 4, rather than start something entirely new. Brown, for example, argues that a great deal of support for the early monks was a support that was precisely interested in their challenge to the current economic systems and social mores:

> ... those who supported the monks did so because they saw their own social dilemmas writ large ... in the persons of the monks. What happened at this time was like what happened in the Middle Ages, when the extremist poverty of Saint Francis and his followers arose as a comment on the boom and bust economy of the Italian cities of the thirteenth century, or when, nowadays, the mission of Mother Theresa in the slums of Calcutta focuses, in dramatic, personal form, the anxieties of privileged nations in the face of the seemingly limitless poverty of much of the rest of the world.[48]

Brown points out that there was a clear socio-economic critique already even in Anthony's early movement, pointing out that it was:

> ... well over a generation before the conversion of Constantine in 312—that Anthony, a young man and a comfortable farmer (the owner of an estate of some two hundred acres)—decided to move out of his village. He had been converted by hearing, in the village church, the crucial passage from the Gospel of Saint Matthew: 'Just then it happened that the Gospel was being read and he heard the Lord saying to the Rich Young Man: If you would be perfect, go, sell what you possess and give to the poor, and you will have treasure in heaven' (Matthew 19:21).[49]

It therefore seems an odd argument to claim, with Countryman, that early Christian "community of goods" wasn't the same as later monasticism—when it is arguably the case that monasticism itself intended to revive *precisely the community of goods* and radical economic practices that they perceived to be articulated in the New Testament!

---

47. Reta H. Finger, *Of Widows and Meals: Communal Meals in the Book of Acts* (Grand Rapids: Eerdmans, 2007), 186.
48. Peter Brown, "Between Syria and Egypt: Alms, Work, and the 'Holy Poor,'" in *Faithful Narratives: Historians, Religion, and the Challenge of Objectivity*, ed. A. Sterk and N. Caputo (New York: Cornell University Press, 2014), 32–46, here 33.
49. Brown, "Between Syria and Egypt," 35.

Recent commentary on Acts continues this interesting discussion. For example, it is widely acknowledged since Martin Dibelius's work beginning in 1923 (Eng. 1956),[50] that Luke is using "summaries" as a narrative tool to pause between specific episodes in the life of the church. Thus, these passages are included among these examples of Luke's unique literary technique:

> ... The summaries in Acts 2 and 4 showcase the early Jesus movement in Jerusalem as a utopian community in which an entire society operates like a band of friends (or an extended family) by eliminating the barriers imposed by the unequal distribution of wealth. Similarities in theme and diction between these passages and Graeco-Roman utopian thought are widely recognized.[51]

Pervo, in his major commentary for Hermeneia, also repeats a frequent theme in the modern analysis of these famous passages—namely his reference to the "utopian" nature of these summary presentations, but also their possible association with Greco-Roman ideals (and, indeed, their own "utopian" descriptions[52]). But Pervo is clear that opinions differ on the validity of making comparisons with wider Greco-Roman values, noting that some authors believe that Luke would "abhor associations with polytheist mythology."[53] Nevertheless, Pervo does seem to agree with scholarly comparisons with pagan ideals such as the Pythagorean ideals articulated between 250–330 CE.[54]

More to the point, however, Pervo also seems keenly aware of the contemporary interest with regard to whether "community of goods" has any *exemplary* role in modern theological Biblical analysis: "To state that the church once realized the social ideals of the ancient world is not quite the same as maintaining that this fulfillment is part of its enduring life."[55] Pervo agrees with authors like Countryman

---

50. M. Dibelius's early essays, beginning with 1923, are included in *Studies in the Acts of the Apostles* (New York: Scribners and Sons, 1956); which was work affirmed by Cadbury in 1927, also collected in *The Book of Acts in History* (London: A & C Black, 1955). See Richard Pervo, *Acts: A Commentary*, Hermeneia (Minneapolis: Fortress Press, 2009), 89.

51. Pervo, *Acts*, 90.

52. Similarly, Luke Timothy Johnson, *The Acts of the Apostles*, Sacra Pagina (Collegeville: Michael Glazier/The Liturgical Press, 1992), 62. The ubiquity of "utopian" in commentaries on Acts chs. 2 and 4 is impressive, but it is hard to imagine that they mean "utopian" *and* "ought to be considered as a viable ethical ideal in their day and perhaps our own."

53. Citing Seccombe, so Pervo, *Acts*, 90.

54. Cf. Iamblicus's *De Vita Pythagorica* [On the Pythagorean Way of Life] as a "useful parallel to Acts for more than linguistic reasons," discussed in Pervo, *Acts*, 91. Luke Timothy Johnson writes of Acts 2:44: "The Greek phrase *panto koine* ('all things in common') is an unmistakable allusion to the Hellenistic topos concerning friendship, that friends hold all things in common," in *The Acts of the Apostles*, 58–9.

55. Pervo, *Acts*, 91.

who argue that "actual community of goods" doesn't occur until later "coenobitic monasticism"—the significance of which is not lost on modern readers when it is understood that these monastic movements are read by moderns (in contrast to Brown's arguments cited above) as the *heroic* ethics of the exemplary *few*, but hardly *exemplary* for the masses and thus lacking urgent ethical concern (e.g., it does not suggest that all Christians should live this way). Pervo further notes that Protestant Reformers later "took issue" with "literal" interpretations of these passages in Acts, both because of their opposition to monasticism, but also their disagreements with the "Radical Reformation" which were movements that did, indeed, take "community of goods" quite seriously.[56]

What, however, was the nature of the lifestyle described in these passages? Many commentators resist the interpretation of Acts 2 and 4–5 as clearly indicating that the earliest Christians did, in fact, hold all property in common. Pervo, for example, argues that "sharing everything" in 2:44–5 is "ambiguous," and likely refers only to those who sold some of their property for the benefit of the Christian community.[57] When considering the similar picture in ch. 4, however, Pervo argues that 4:34 is:

> ... more picturesque than 2:45, shifting from the ideal ("all in common") to the reality: the needy received support from contributions of those with more means, who liquidated their holdings and presented them to the apostles for distribution. This conveyance is not intended to enhance the status of the apostles but to show how early Christians prevented the more wealthy members of the community from acquiring power by making "clients" of others.[58]

Furthermore, Pervo argues, this selling of property was not required for membership, so the similarities with Qumran common life can be misleading.[59] Thus, the striking story of the deaths of Ananias and Sapphira are to be carefully interpreted:

> ... They wished to enjoy the renown of perfect generosity while retaining something for a rainy day. The narrative assumes that the practice would have been acceptable. What is not acceptable was their deceit. Spiritual power is not limited to healing cripples or opening ears. In this instance, the Spirit serves as both financial auditor and executioner.[60]

---

56. Indeed, as a "Radical Reformationist" myself (a Quaker with an Anabaptist seminary training!) I hardly consider this a compelling critique.
57. Pervo, *Acts*, 92.
58. Pervo, *Acts*, 127.
59. Pervo, *Acts*, 128.
60. Pervo, *Acts*, 129.

Pervo comments, dryly, "The couple who falsely claimed that they had deposited all at Peter's feet were presently deposited six feet under."[61] Yet Pervo argues that the issue here was lying, not greed, or at least lying in the service of greed! Monetary sin, he writes, was clearly considered a serious matter, and Pervo suggests that the narrative in Acts 5 even shows little concern with the deaths of the two landowners.[62] Indeed, Pervo makes the interesting observation about modern discomfort with this passage, stating that Western readers are troubled because the incident focuses on the "welfare of the community"—that is, the good of the group, the *community*—and not the correction of the couple.[63]

Keener's commentary concurs with some elements of Pervo's somewhat older work but is willing to hear more of Luke's presumed prophetic (and thus ethical) messaging. Associating the descriptions of the community of goods with the Pentecost experience in ch. 1, Keener provocatively refers to the community ideal as describing a "proleptically eschatological lifestyle of the kingdom."[64] In fact, Keener sees the descriptions of Acts 2 and 4, in Luke's narrative, as a direct fulfillment of the teachings of Jesus:

> Luke 12:33-34 33 Sell your possessions, and give alms. Make purses for yourselves that do not wear out, an unfailing treasure in heaven, where no thief comes near and no moth destroys. 34 For where your treasure is, there your heart will be also …

Keener, therefore, widens the spectrum of ways in which Luke's picture of "community of goods" speaks to a variety of contexts and social assumptions:

> In this summary section, the Jerusalem community of disciples begins to fulfill Jesus's teachings and model in the Gospel on various points: prayer, continuing signs, eating together, and sharing of possessions (cf. Luke 12:33). Both here and in the Gospel, through explicit quotations and implicit allusions, Luke also grounds this lifestyle in Israel's ideals and the example of the prophets (e.g., Deut. 15:7-8; 2 Kings 4:38-44); he also uses Hellenistic language for the ideal community.[65]

Keener is especially provocative when he proposes a chiastic reading of themes in Acts. Although acknowledging that scholars are often (in my view justifiably)

---

61. Pervo, *Acts*, 129.

62. Pervo, *Acts*, 133. Cf. J. Albert Harrill, who compares this "instant punishments" of the deceitful discussed in wider Greco-Roman sources: "Divine Judgment against Ananias and Sapphira (Acts 5:1–11): A Stock Scene of Perjury and Death," *Journal of Biblical Literature* 130 (2011): 351–69.

63. Pervo, *Acts*, 132.

64. Craig Keener, *Acts*, New Cambridge Bible Commentary (Cambridge: Cambridge University Press, 2020), 169.

65. Keener, *Acts*, 170.

anxious about "finding" chiastic structures (everywhere), nonetheless Keener's proposal is compelling:

A—Effective Evangelism (through preaching 2:41)
    B—Shared worship and meals (2:42)
        C—Shared possessions (2:44–45)
    B'—Shared worship and meals (2:46)
A'—Effective Evangelism (through lifestyle 2:47)[66]

Keener concludes that if this structure is valid, then:

> ... the sharing of possessions is a central (perhaps because so distinctive) feature of Luke's vision of the early Christian community formed by the Spirit leading to a wide impact on the society around them (cf. again in the next corporate outpouring of the Spirit in 4:32–35).[67]

Keener is not adverse to the arguments that compare the idealized picture in Acts 2 and 4–5 with pagan ideals (especially Pythagorean communities), but:

> ... unlike full utopias, Luke does not describe abolition of private property (12:12–13; Luke 6:34–35; 14:12–14). Rather, members sold property to help other members as they had need (Acts 2:45). Their resources do not become community property, but are designated for the poor; they were not against property, but valued people altogether more.[68]

What is particularly interesting in Keener's analysis, however, is his refusal to dismiss the ethical implications of Luke's portrayal of the early church as reflecting a "genuine radicalism in the earliest community" that reflects "countercultural values" in early Christianity.[69] Indeed, Keener's invoking of the "Radical Reformation" (specifically "Anabaptists") is, consequently, of an entirely different spirit than Pervo's dismissal, especially when Keener argues that community of goods as practiced by Anabaptists, Moravians, and the Chinese "Jesus Family," all arguably provide: " ... a consistent and desperately needed witness to the rest of the church in this area."[70] With Keener's analysis, clearly, we are moving closer

---

66. Keener, *Acts*, 170.
67. Keener, *Acts*, 170.
68. Keener, *Acts*, 175.
69. Keener, *Acts*, 175–6.
70. Keener, *Acts*, 177, and I am impressed that Keener is aware of the fascinating "Jesus Family" movement in Chinese Christian history, on which there is precious little in English; but see Xian Li, "The Jesus Family," in *Redeemed by Fire: The Rise of Popular Christianity in Modern China* (New Haven: Yale University Press, 2010), 64–84. One can also, of course, include the traditions of communalism in Russian and Ukrainian tradition, especially

to Hardie's interest in the ethical implications of Luke's descriptions of the early Jesus movement, but also, with Keener's invoking of the Anabaptist Christian tradition we move toward these passages as texts that do indeed suggest serious ethical guidance. Scott Bartchy's often cited article is also important in this regard.[71] Bartchy strongly reacted to the tendency to use "Greco-Roman" utopian descriptions to suggest that the book of Acts was equally mythical:

> Luke employs Greek utopian language as part of his description, not of what he wished had happened or of what he fantasized in order to edify his readers but of what he believed actually had taken place among the Jewish Christians in Jerusalem. He had a substantial cultural context for such a conviction.[72]

Thus, in Bartchy's reading, Luke is not "making something up," but rather talks about a phenomenon that he/they believed to have serious ethical significance.

We thus now turn to the 2007 analysis of Reta Finger, who writes on "Communal Meals in the Book of Acts" from an openly acknowledged Anabaptist perspective: "My roots in a more communal lifestyle have led me back to the account in Acts of the earliest social practices of the Jesus movement in Jerusalem."[73] Finger is, not unexpectedly, quite critical of the vehement denial of the ethical force of the Acts passages:

> … I would call attention to the skepticism or even the hostility many interpreters have shown toward the possibility that the early Christians did successfully share a community of goods and daily commensality in their households. I suggest that some of this reaction is due to their own social locations in a different culture, class, and time. I will, of course, approach the text from my own social location as an Anabaptist Mennonite … If it is not in the economic, political, or theological interests of an interpreter or an interpretative community to share material goods (beyond alms-giving), they will find different ways to explain these texts.[74]

---

influenced by Tolstoy, both in Russia and more widely. It is a fascinating literature. William Edgerton, trans. and ed., *Memoirs of Peasant Tolstoyans in Soviet Russia* (Bloomington: Indiana University Press, 1993). Although tending toward the tiresome "those oddities" approach to communal groups, Alexander Etkind is interesting for sources: "Whirling with the Other: Russian Populism and Religious Sects," *The Russian Review* 62 (2003): 565–88. See also Andrew Donskov, *Leo Tolstoy and the Canadian Doukhobors: A Study in Historic Relationships* (Ottawa: University of Ottawa Press, 2019).

71. Scott Bartchy, "Community of Goods in Acts: Idealization or Social Reality?" in *The Future of Early Christianity: Essays in Honor of Helmut Koester*, ed. Birger Pearson (Minneapolis: Fortress Press, 1991), 309–18.

72. Bartchy, "Community of Goods," 312.

73. Finger, *Widows and Meals*, 5.

74. Finger, *Widows and Meals*, 7 and 13.

Finger is furthermore appropriately skeptical of the tendencies for New Testament scholars to choose the most negative examples available in history to associate with the practice in the book of Acts—such as the deadly Munster experiment of the sixteenth century, and the Jim Jones experiment in Guyana in the twentieth century, both involving massacres that are often read as the "logical results" of community of goods.[75] Thus, Finger is surely correct to observe that: "Few commentators, except some from Anabaptist traditions, consider that these texts describe a lifestyle that Christians ought to emulate in some way."[76]

Finger also notes that the communal meals in Acts are now being seriously "read" within the general poverty of the majority of the Christians in the first two centuries of the common era, when "a third of the population lived in habitual want":[77]

> If communal meals were the central rite of the Christian communities from before Paul wrote to the Corinthians about 50 CE to at least through the death of Ignatius in 107 (or 116) CE they would have been a reality Luke was familiar with. Though he may have used language on friendship from Hellenistic philosophy to characterize the Jerusalem community, Luke was nevertheless speaking of an actual practice of communal eating.[78]

And furthermore:

> The communal sharing which Luke describes must have been similar to the generalized reciprocity that went on all the time among an extended family. What was different – and radical – about it was *who* the kin were. No longer were they just one's blood relatives: all who believed in Jesus were now brothers and sisters and together.[79]

If Finger's Anabaptist ethic proposes that the Church should take this ethical ideal seriously (and on this, see Meggitt's argument about "Mutualism,"[80] and Montero's argument about the ethical power of community or goods in Acts[81]) it is an understandable step for Hardie and his Christian Socialist compatriots to propose that if the Bible is to inform politics, then early Christian "socialism" is a serious

---

75. Finger, *Widows and Meals*, 20. The tendency to dwell on unusual sexual practices in a few historical American experiments serves the same dismissive function.
76. Finger, *Widows and Meals*, 45.
77. Finger, *Widows and Meals*, 123.
78. Finger, *Widows and Meals*, 69.
79. Finger, *Widows and Meals*, 144.
80. Justin J. Meggitt, *Paul, Poverty and Survival* (Edinburgh: T&T Clark, 1998), 155–7.
81. Roman A. Montero, *All Things in Common: The Economic Practices of the Early Christians* (Eugene: Cascade, 2017).

ethical challenge—both to the value and importance of sharing *and* challenging a destructive individualism. What is interesting about Hardie's use of these passages, of course, is how he saw these as a direct expression of the ethics of Jesus—echoing especially Keener's arguments cited above.

On working and eating: 2 Thessalonians 3:10

It is important to proceed to a discussion of Paul's famous comment in 2 Thessalonians 3:10 immediately following a discussion of communal life in Acts, precisely because an important move in recent New Testament scholarship suggests that this passage in Paul's letters may have important *connections* to the exemplary community life in Acts. The specific aphorism in question is 2 Thessalonians 3:10b: " … Anyone unwilling to work should not eat," but it is helpful to see it in a larger context:

> 2 Thessalonians 3:6–13 [6] Now we command you, beloved, in the name of our Lord Jesus Christ, to keep away from believers who are living in idleness and not according to the tradition that they received from us. [7] For you yourselves know how you ought to imitate us; we were not idle when we were with you, [8] and we did not eat anyone's bread without paying for it; but with toil and labor we worked night and day, so that we might not burden any of you. [9] This was not because we do not have that right, but in order to give you an example to imitate. [10] For even when we were with you, we gave you this command: Anyone unwilling to work should not eat. [11] For we hear that some of you are living in idleness, mere busybodies, not doing any work. [12] Now such persons we command and exhort in the Lord Jesus Christ to do their work quietly and to earn their own living. [13] Brothers and sisters, do not be weary in doing what is right.

There is a long tradition of using this passage in a socialist context. For example, in his important study, Catterall notes a debate in 1923 on the "shortcomings of Capitalism" which used religious arguments, but: " … the only one to quote the Bible was Walton Newbold when he described St Paul's dictum (2 Thessalonians 3.10) that 'If a man will not work neither shall he eat' as 'the principle of Communism.'"[82]

Hardie's own understanding of this aphorism can be measured by the occasion where he placed it in conversation with the Epistle of James:

> It was St. Paul who enunciated the doctrine that he who would not work neither should he eat [2 Thess. 3:10], whilst St. James in his Epistle rivals the old prophets in his treatment of those who grow rich at the expense of the poor [Jas 5:1–7].[83]

---

82. Catterall, *Labour and the Free Churches*, 147–8.
83. Hardie, in Callow, *From Serfdom to Socialism*, 83.

And, in March 1893, Hardie also combined the same passage with comments about the example of Jesus:

> Christ's teachings are clear and unmistakable. With Him, life was everything. He refused to interfere in the miserable squabble of the two brothers over the sharing of their goods; to the rich young man the irreducible minimum of His demand was, 'Sell all that thou hast. The rich had had their portion here, and were to weep and howl for the misery awaiting them.' The early Christians practised this teaching, as is shown in the opening chapters of the Acts; and St. Paul preached it in the axiom, 'he that will not work neither should he eat.' If there is scepticism in the land today (and who shall deny it?) the half-heartedness of the pulpit is far more responsible for it than all the destructive criticism by the critics of Scripture ever penned.[84]

Although Hardie had occasionally shown some impatience with Paul, this famous passage was frequently cited. As many commentators note in contemporary Biblical scholarship, this precise passage is often taken as a counsel against laziness or idleness—and was therefore often used *against* labour movements. Strikes, agitation, and union organization were thus typically pilloried as a "refusal to work"—and attacked as idleness or the laziness of the lower classes. Hardie's particular understanding (not to mention his many colleagues who read it similarly to Hardie) raises interesting questions about reading this in the larger context of the Thessalonians passage. If Paul is saying that he himself did not eat other's bread but earned his own keep—the thought seems to be that Paul was refusing to be privileged, rather than lazy! And it is precisely this meaning that Hardie derives from the famous saying—it was not taken by Hardie to be an attack on laziness, but precisely *privilege*—that is, as a counsel against being fed without doing work because one is *wealthy or of higher status* (e.g., living off rents and investments). That Hardie's "worker's exegesis" of this passage, quite frankly, has a good deal to commend it, seems clear from interesting directions that have been taken in recent analysis of this passage—and indeed, Paul's context more widely. None of this recent work would have been known to Hardie (or anyone else at his time), yet it effectively confirms Hardie's instincts. It is important, then, to review some aspects of these recent arguments.

Many recent discussions of the famous phrase in Biblical analysis focus on the context of this passage. For example, modern commentary literature debates the meaning of the key Greek term "*ataktos*" in v. 6, which was once rather routinely translated "idle" or even "lazy." However, the growing consensus points out that the term actually means "disorderly" almost to the point of disobedience (even "undisciplined"[85]). Boring, for example, in his 2015 commentary, asserts

---

84. Hardie, "Christian Thought."

85. Mary Ann Beavis, HyeRan Kim-Cragg, and Linda Maloney, *2 Thessalonians*, Wisdom Commentary 52 (Collegeville: Liturgical Press (Michael Glazier), 2016), 166.

that the writer is taking this matter very seriously, and the "tone" suggests "the disorderly."[86] As Sheila E. McGinn and Megan T. Wilson-Reitz point out, however, this has not prevented modern fundamentalist use of this phrase in the service of right-wing political movements:

> ... in service of a political-economic agenda that undercuts social services, especially unemployment compensation, food stamps, and other supports for persons who have 'fallen through the cracks' of our current market economy.[87]

Liz Theoharis illustrates well the common modern use of this phrase in right-wing political polemics that advocate severe cutbacks to services to the poor in American governmental programs:

> 'He who does not work shall not eat.' The first time I heard this text (2 Thessalonians 3:10) was as a welfare rights activist in Philadelphia in the 1990s. In the lead-up to the 1996 welfare reform act, politicians, religious leaders, and others quoted this verse to justify shutting down food programs and kicking mothers and their babies off public assistance.[88]

Finally, Beavis, Kim-Cragg, and Maloney have also noted the hypocrisy of Christian leaders like Jerry Falwell, who cited this passage to legitimate cuts to financial assistance and welfare, despite (as the authors correctly point out) the millions gained by Falwell by donations, and *not* his own work.[89] However, McGinn and Wilson-Reitz (again, among others) also note the rather profound irony in the fact that this same phrase—and versions thereof—have been used in a striking variety of political contexts in the twentieth and twenty-first centuries:

> In the United States, verse 10 has been quoted in support of a surprisingly diverse array of political and economic viewpoints, including the Populist platform of 1892, socialist John Spargo, and laissez-faire capitalist William Graham Sumner. Max Weber argued that this passage is at the heart of the Protestant work ethic, which he saw as a necessary condition for the rise of American capitalism. On the other end of the spectrum, Vladimir Lenin claimed the injunction as an

---

86. Eugene Boring, *1 & 2 Thessalonians: A Commentary*. NTL (Louisville: Westminster/John Knox, 2015), 294.

87. Sheila E. McGinn and Megan T. Wilson-Reitz, "2 Thessalonians vs. the *Ataktoi*: A Pauline Critique of 'White-Collar Welfare,'" in *By Bread Alone: The Bible through the Eyes of the Hungry*, ed. Sheila E. McGinn, Lai Ling Elizabeth Ngan, and Ahida Calderón Pilarski (Minneapolis: 1517 Media/Fortress Press, 2014), 185–208.

88. Liz Theoharis, *We Cry Justice: Reading the Bible with the Poor People's Campaign* (Minneapolis: 1517 Media, Broadleaf Book, 2021), 135–6.

89. Beavis, Kim-Cragg, and Maloney, *2 Thessalonians*, 178–9.

essential socialist principle—so that no one would live off the labor of others. The Soviet Constitutions of 1918 and 1936 both employ the phrase.[90]

Evangelical scholars, especially, often attempt to challenge the common modern readings of this passage as attacking the American welfare system by insisting that this is not the primary meaning of this passage. It is, we are told, an attack on the "patronage system." However, these same scholars persist in using what can only be described as "dog whistle" terms, so referring to those whom Paul criticizes as "able-bodied," a term suggesting people capable of work but too lazy or unwilling to work—a common term since the Presidency of Reagan who regularly attacked "welfare queens" and those who are "living off of … " others. Again, these are stock phrases for attacking welfare recipients; other scholars still persist in referring to: "sponges, sycophants, and hangers on"—do I even need to comment further on such phraseology? Note, for example, Hughes who speaks of lazy Christians who "sponge" off the rest of the community.[91] Thus, Paul's letter is still arguably being read as an attack on what the conservative evangelicals in the pews would clearly recognize as "lazy welfare recipients," despite the claims to the contrary. The scholarship here needs to be cleared up!

So, is 2 Thessalonians 3:10 a warning against laziness? As we have seen, a key change in modern interpretation has been to move away from the translation of "*ataktos*" as "lazy" or "idle" and toward the modern consensus with "disorderly" (or "acting irresponsibly," cf. "unruly," "disorderly"[92]). Fee even speaks of the "travesty" of translating *ataktos* as "idle"[93] and Boring argues that the Greek term "*ataktos*," especially combined with "*peripateo*" suggests "walking in a disorderly way"—in other words—a particular way of life.[94] A further key to this is the modern reading of v. 11, where Boring translates: "not working but concerning oneself with other people's work" as opposed to those who follow Moffatt and translate "busybodies" (which has a decidedly different nuance in modern English and is no longer considered a helpful translation, but arguably another "dog whistle" term!). Indeed, Boring is surely correct to point out that "in no part of 1–2 Thessalonians is the presumed historical context more important than in this text."[95]

---

90. McGinn and Wilson-Reitz, "2 Thessalonians," 186.

91. Frank Witt Hughes, *Early Christian Rhetoric and 2 Thessalonians*, JNST 30 (Sheffield: Sheffield Academic Press, 1989), 65.

92. Victor Furnish, *1 and 2 Thessalonians*, Abingdon NT Commentaries (Nashville: Abingdon Press, 2007), 174, the same in Gene Green, *The Letters to the Thessalonians*, PNTC (Grand Rapids: Eerdmans, 2002), 343.

93. Gordon Fee, *First and Second Letters to the Thessalonians*, NICNT (Grand Rapids: Eerdmans, 2009), 335.

94. Boring, *Thessalonians*, 295.

95. Boring, *Thessalonians*, 296.

In fact, there are a variety of ways that Paul's instructions are now read, and it is interesting to survey four of them. First, there are those who note the eschatological concerns of 1 Thessalonians, which suggest that many Christians expected the "end of times" to be very soon, so soon that perhaps some of the people are not "working" in a conventional manner (that is, earning their own income) because of their belief that Jesus is returning very soon indeed, and normal life is therefore permanently changed under the imminent expectation of an end of the present world. Witherington, for one, doesn't accept this connection because he believes that the eschatological concerns in 1 Thessalonians were clearly separated from concerns about church life, such that the two issues are not to be read as related.[96]

This first "eschatological" reading, however, has been set aside by many modern commentaries. Before leaving this proposal, however, it is important to note that there have been some interesting nuances associated with this argument. Beavis, Kim-Cragg, and Maloney speculate on the possibility that "revolutionary social forces" were unleashed by apocalyptic speculation, which would have had distinct implications, for example, for women and slaves particularly, who had profound hope in society changing dramatically from their abused status.[97]

Second—there is the view that the people Paul is addressing are to be thought of as disreputable people taking advantage of Christians who were gullible, and often the early Christian document, the *Didache*, is cited where it speaks about warnings not to allow visiting preachers/prophets to be supported as guest visitors for long.[98] But the situation with visiting Prophets—who were expected to stay only a few days—does not seem like the normative life addressed by Paul.

Third, some see these discussions as part of a wider debate about the nature of leadership in the Church. Are there to be paid clergy, for example? Is Paul arguing against a certain kind of "priestly" professionalism among Christian leaders at this early stage in the evolution of the Jesus Movement? Boring reports that some scholars have pointed to the possibility that Paul is arguing for attention to Jesus's own call for apostolic ministry without pay in Matthew 10:8–11, where the term for "freely" in Matthew 10:8 recurs in 2 Thessalonians 3:8 and is usually translated: "without paying for it." Boring provocatively notes a possible satirical comment from Paul at this point. He suggests that if the alleged advocates of a paid clergy were thus hoping for an "ordered" church—then Paul's accusations of these same people acting "disorderly" is an effective "sarcasm."[99] But even further, in regard to v. 10, Boring notes that:

---

96. Ben Witherington III, *1 & 2 Thessalonians: A Socio-Rhetorical Commentary* (Grand Rapids: Eerdmans, 2006), 245.

97. Beavis, Kim-Cragg, and Maloney, *2 Thessalonians*, 169.

98. Beavis, Kim-Cragg, and Maloney, *2 Thessalonians*, 169.

99. Boring, *Thessalonians*, 301.

One can more readily picture the saying as a battle motto against what the author sees as an emerging class of clergy, which would mean those 'full time ministers' who do not earn their own living cannot expect to be supported by the church.[100]

Boring is forthright about the fact that this alleged debate about church polity has nothing to do with the way in which the "work/eat" passage has been used in contemporary evangelical right-wing debate. An opposition to a paid clergy does not mean "don't take care" of the genuine needy! Boring argues:

> The specific historical interpretation argued for here means that the text (esp. 3:10, 12) has nothing to say to or about the complex situation of people in later centuries, including our own who are jobless or underemployed due to the shifting pressures of industrial global economics. The text addresses a particular problem in the emerging 'institutional church' and presents no basis for opposing social welfare programs and other supportive structures for those unable to find enough work to support themselves and their families ... [101]

A fourth interesting argument is used by those who make connections between Paul's advice in 2 Thessalonians, and the same communal life presented in Acts, and thus including communal meals associated with the closely living Christian communities. For example, in a fascinating 1993 study, Jewett explicitly rejects what he called the "bourgeois reading" of Paul's teaching as an "individualist" counsel to "get a job" and "take care of one's own family," and Jewett argues instead that the context presumes early Christian communal meals to which everyone was expected to contribute.[102]

Fifth, and finally—it is now widely proposed that Paul is severely critical of Christians who are engaged in a particularly Roman social and economic relationship usually termed "Patronage." As Nicols defines this Roman system—a "patron" was a wealthy and well-known public figure who economically supported a number of "clients." These "clients" were obligated with responsibilities toward the patron, including frequent public praise (even showing up in person regularly to express this praise!), as well as being busy with chores for the benefit of the patron. Notably, there were expectations of benefit to both parties:

> Surely important to the client, though not always manifest in the sources, were the vague promises of protection and the possibility of benefactions. So, too, was

---

100. Boring, *Thessalonians*, 303.
101. Boring, *Thessalonians*, 305.
102. Paul Jewett, "Tenement Churches and Communal Meals in the Early Church: The Implications of a Form-Critical Analysis of 2 Thessalonians 3:10," *Biblical Research* 38 (1993): 23–43. Cf. Fee, *First and Second Letters to the Thessalonians*.

it of some importance to the patron that the client would provide assurances that the patron's generosity would not be forgotten.[103]

Witherington further points out that the responsibilities could include religious actions:

> For example, of the imperial cult or make a sacrifice at one of the longstanding Greco-Roman temples in Thessalonike, this compromising their exclusive allegiance to the biblical God (see 1 Corinthians 8–10).[104]

Rice also summarizes elements of this system in his analysis:

> In summary … patronage, comprised of a single patron and client, was underwritten by a strong sense of reciprocity, existed beyond explicit constructs of legality, and was predicated upon the recognition of social asymmetry. Patrons provided various services for their clients in exchange for loyalty and honor so that each party achieved real benefits. This pattern remained unchanged from the emergence of clientage in the Greek Republic through the period of the Roman.[105]

Clearly, reading Paul's advice in the context of the temptations of the Roman patronage system dramatically changes the meaning. Indeed, Malina and Pilch strikingly argue that the reason that the "communal" property was presented *to the Apostles* in the "community of goods" passages in Acts is precisely to prevent the private "awarding" of property to other members and thus establishing a patronage relationship with others in the community.[106] These kinds of arguments would point to a notion that these "disorderly," in fact, were members of the community who either sought to establish such economic relationships, or perhaps continued prior relationships with *wealthy, likely unbelieving patrons* instead of giving up the income and social status the patron–client relationship could provide. There are further aspects of the patronage relationship that are crucial for understanding the force of Paul's attacks on being "disorderly" if, in fact, what he is attacking are Christians engaged as clients to Christian—or perhaps even non-Christian—patrons (Beavis, Kim-Cragg, and Maloney propose that it was more

---

103. John Nicols, *Civic Patronage in the Roman Empire* (Leiden: Brill, 2014), 13.

104. Witherington, *Thessalonians*, 249, also Winter believes that the criticism is against those who were "too busy" *with a patron's affairs*, cf. Bruce W. Winter, *Seek the Welfare of the City: Christians as Benefactors and Citizens*, First-Century Christians in the Graeco-Roman World (Grand Rapids: Eerdmans, 1994), 46 and 50.

105. Joshua Rice, *Paul and Patronage: The Dynamics of Power in 1 Corinthians* (Eugene: Pickwick, 2013).

106. Bruce J. Malina and John J. Pilch, *Social-Science Commentary on the Book of Acts* (Minneapolis: 1517 Media/Fortress Press, 2008), 46.

likely that these were *non-Christian* patrons of Christian *clients*[107]). Finger also argues that those seeking this kind of relationship with a patron are not the "lazy poor" at all, but:

> Those eating with superiors were seeking social advancement, and those entertaining people below them on the social ladder used this method to gain honor or confirm their own superiority. Rules and taboos constantly dictated who would be invited to a meal, how it would be eaten, who would be served when and where, who would recline or sit where, and the like.[108]

As McGinn and Wilson-Reitz summarize, these clients would *not* be the "poor"—but rather "upwardly mobile social climbers," and thus: " … an ambitious person's career could be made—or broken—depending upon the favor (or favors) of a powerful and well-connected patronus."[109] Indeed, McGinn and Wilson-Reitz also note the importance of Thessalonica itself as a capital of the Roman province of Macedonia, an "important commercial center with a valuable harbor, situated on two busy trade routes … " and boasting "a diverse cosmopolitan population."[110] In short—a city with considerable opportunity for cultivating economic relationships with wealthy patrons so that one would not have to engage in what was widely disdained in "successful" Roman society as manual labour. In other words, "success" would hardly be defined in Paul's manner of "earning your bread." Thus, as McGinn and Wilson-Reitz argue, the author reproaches the "*ataktoi*" ("disorderly") for their "obedience to the cultural norms of their city and the Empire, rather than their disobedience to those cultural norms."[111] Paul is, they note, actually being *counter-cultural* by attacking dependence on a patron, and even more significantly:

> When read with attention to Paul's own 'countercultural' bent, it becomes clear that, far from admonishing the poor for freeloading, 2 Thess. 3:6–15 actually critiques ancient 'yuppies' who were grasping at upward mobility … this passage advocates that all members of the Christian community participate in the economic system at the same (low-status) level, abandoning intra-ecclesial class divisions created by socioeconomic disparities and maintained by the patron-client system.[112]

What is furthermore important in this analysis is that such "clients" would have to be anything but "lazy" or "idle." In fact, they were to be busy with the patron's interests and affairs:

107. Beavis, Kim-Cragg, and Maloney, *2 Thessalonians*, 169.
108. Finger, *Widows and Meals*, 171.
109. McGinn and Wilson-Reitz, "2 Thessalonians," 188.
110. McGinn and Wilson-Reitz, "2 Thessalonians," 190.
111. McGinn and Wilson-Reitz, "2 Thessalonians," 188.
112. McGinn and Wilson-Reitz, "2 Thessalonians," 189.

> The *ataktoi* are criticized for violating apostolic instructions by minding other people's affairs; but taking care of someone else's business is precisely what clients in the Roman patronage system are expected to do ... owing to this heavy commitment of time to the patron, clients were unable to work for their own living or to 'eat their own bread' (2 Thess. 3:8, 11–12).[113]

Working in the manner that Paul advises would be a humiliating "come down" for those aspiring to Roman definitions of wealth, and in this context Malherbe takes note that Paul boasted at having worked for free![114] Notably, it was even suggested in the 1980s that Paul himself may have shared some of the upper-class disdain for manual labour.[115] However, this suggestion seems entirely incongruous not only with Paul's positive references to his own ability to support himself with manual work, but as Still suggests, such an attitude would also be at variance with Hebrew attitudes:

> ... work is consistently affirmed in the Hebrew Scriptures, with which Paul shows himself to be intimately acquainted in his letters (e.g., Gen 2:15; Exod 20:9–10; Prov 6:6–11; 10:4–5; 24:30–4; 31:13–27; cf. Sir 7:15; 38:24–34; 51:30). It does, in fact, seem unlikely that biblical affirmations of and instruction about labor would be wholly lost on or completely disregarded by one who was in his own estimation a Jew through and through (see esp. Phil 3:4a–6; cf. Rom 9:3; 11:1; 2 Cor 11:22; Gal 1:13–14).[116]

However, in arguing against an arrogant upper-class, Still unfortunately seems to revert to the old interpretation of 2 Thessalonians 3:10 as an attack on lazy people: "From all appearances and for whatever reasons, certain persons in the congregation had stopped working and had started sponging off other believers."[117]

As we have seen, however, the increased acceptance of the idea that Paul is actually attacking the patronage system of Roman economic society—a decidedly upper-crust affair—continues to overturn the older traditions (and the modern persistence of this idea) that Paul is attacking poor, "lazy" people. Thus, McGinn and Wilson-Reitz entirely overturn the modern abuse of this passage by pointing

---

113. McGinn and Wilson-Reitz, "2 Thessalonians," 202–3. Cf. A. Johnson, *1 & 2 Thessalonians*, The Two Horizons New Testament Commentary (Grand Rapids: Eerdmans, 2016), 220.

114. Bruce Malherbe, *The Letters to the Thessalonians*, Anchor Bible Commentary (New York: Doubleday, 1964), 451.

115. Ronald F. Hock, *The Social Context of Paul's Ministry: Tentmaking and Apostleship* (Philadelphia: Fortress Press, 1980).

116. Todd D. Still, "Did Paul Loathe Manual Labor? Revisiting the Work of Ronald F. Hock on the Apostle's Tentmaking and Social Class," *Journal of Biblical Literature* 125, no. 4 (2006): 781–95, here 791–2.

117. Still, "Did Paul Loathe," 790.

out that Paul's injunctions would be understood in modern terms as virtually "identifying with the working classes":

> ... the affluent members of the congregation who participate in the patronage system might well balk at this injunction. To give up their patrons and adopt lives of manual labor would require voluntary acceptance of serious downward mobility on their part—similar to what Paul extolls in the kenosis hymn of Phil. 2:6-11. Such a challenging command easily might inspire 'insubordination' against the apostle's authority ...

> ... The author's insistence upon overturning the routine social divisions of the patron-client system effectively challenges the Thessalonian Christians to downward mobility. For a Roman aristocrat, to live as Paul commands would entail a significant loss of power, social status, wealth, and dignity. It would be a humiliating venture.[118]

Witherington, similarly, writes that Paul's great concern was that Christians live exemplary lives, and this does not fit:

> the social nexus of sponges, sycophants, and hangers on and the patrons who support them. If prominent Christians were behaving like such, it would bring no credit to the community which was supposed to be modeled on equity and self-sacrificial behavior.[119]

Despite his unfortunate choice of language (and here again, I think the use of triggering terms in the present political atmosphere is to be avoided, unless, of course, conservative values are indeed being invoked here), I agree with Witherington that Paul also cautions that the patronage system could be "ethically compromising,"[120] and Winter goes further to state bluntly that Paul: "is forbidding the life of a client for members of the Christian community."[121]

As in our other discussions of other Biblical passages, it is unnecessary to comprehensively survey modern commentary on 2 Thessalonians 3:10 in order to observe that the recent emphasis on Paul challenging the Roman patronage system moves much closer to Hardie's use of this phrase as a socialist maxim. Beavus, Kim-Cragg, and Maloney assert that:

> One may paraphrase 2 Thess 3:8 positively as a critique of this kind of economic exploitation system: those in power in the making of the nation ate the food that

---

118. McGinn and Wilson-Reitz, "2 Thessalonians," 205–6.
119. Witherington, *Thessalonians*, 248.
120. Witherington, *Thessalonians*, 249.
121. Winter, *Seek the Welfare*, 51.

was produced by foreign workers without properly paying for it. Here economic class is mediated and substantiated by race and national origin.[122]

Johnson even proposes that some Christians in the congregations addressed by Paul wished to establish some form of patronage system among the Christian communities themselves.[123] In fact, there are frequent attacks against the conservative political (defending "free market capitalism,"[124]) use (and abuse) of this passage. Johnson, in his 2016 commentary, strongly argues against attempts:

> ... to use the explicit language of this passage as some sort of 'timeless word' to ground a particular form of social or economic policy for a twenty-first-century, pluralistic, capitalist society would be to use it for a purpose that is not analogous to its purpose in this letter.[125]

Finally, we have seen that this realization of the potential significance of Roman patronage as a widespread social practice even influences discussions about community life in Acts, and the practice of community sharing at meals. As Finger observed:

> Those eating with superiors were seeking social advancement, and those entertaining people below them on the social ladder used this method to gain honor or confirm their own superiority. Rules and taboos constantly dictated who would be invited to a meal, how it would be eaten, who would be served when and where, who would recline or sit where, and the like.[126]

In sum, Hardie's instinct on reading Paul as an ally in defense of the poor rather than attacking the poor has rather dramatically been confirmed in recent analyses of Paul in Roman context, if one wants to read Paul in the context of widespread food precarity, and the temptations of the Roman patronage system.

Hardie on Jesus and the Pharisees: Matthew 23

On a number of occasions, Hardie cited the strong language of Jesus against the Pharisees as reported in Matthew 23 but was perhaps the most vehement in his use of this Gospel passage in his attacks on Lord Overtoun's industrial practices (Chapter 5 above), where he cited extensively from this very chapter. How does Hardie's use of this passage compare with contemporary debates about this controversial section of the Gospel of Matthew?

---

122. Beavis, Kim-Cragg, and Maloney, *2 Thessalonians*, 174.
123. Johnson, *Thessalonians*, 215.
124. Johnson, *Thessalonians*, 214.
125. Johnson, *Thessalonians*, 217.
126. Finger, *Widows and Meals*, 171.

Hardie's use of Matthew 23 is consistent and clear—it is used as his defense of attacking *Christian* religious leaders of the day. Hardie *never* uses it in a context of attacking Jews as Jews, but always in defense of his "right" (one may say) to challenge religious authorities. It is, in short, Hardie's stock response to offended letters and comments constantly demanding: " … how can you dare use such language about respected church leaders??"

In his time, of course, Hardie would not have known how this chapter would become a storm center of debate after World War II, the Holocaust, and the rise of Christian–Jewish dialogue, as well as the dramatic rise of Jewish participation in contemporary academic Biblical analysis. Nolland, for example, notes in his 2005 commentary on Matthew that: "Criticism of some of the Pharisees some of the time, or even aspects of the Pharisaic movement in general is easily turned into a portrait of all the Pharisees, all the time."[127] In his important 1992 essay, Saldarini summarizes the new significant context of the twentieth century for reading this passage:

> Matthew 23, with its seven woe oracles and its charges of hypocrisy and blindness against the scribes and Pharisees, strikes the liberal Westerner or ecumenically minded Christian as malevolent and offensive. Because of the history of Christian antisemitism and because of our proximity to the Holocaust, accusations of blindness and hypocrisy, corruption and murder, are not the rhetoric of polite and rational religious discourse in the twentieth century.[128]

As a result of the changed context of the twentieth, and now twenty-first centuries, Matthew 23 is enmeshed in debates about anti-Semitism, and particularly the question as to how early one can locate the beginnings of anti-Semitism in the Christian tradition. Therefore, Matthew 23 can often, and certainly has been prominently, cited as a prime example of anti-Semitism in the Gospels themselves by some scholars. On the other hand, there is a strong reaction against this judgment, proposing that Matthew 23 is an example of "Jews criticizing Jews," and thus not yet to be judged on the same level as later non-Jewish Christian leaders (the classic example being the frightful comments of John Chrysostom, 347–409 CE).

As John Kampen clarifies, the different perspectives among New Testament scholars are identified as those who see Matthew 23 as an example of Jewish debates: "intra muros" (lit: "within the walls"—that is, debates *among Jews*, whether Jesus followers or not), and those who see Matthew exhibiting an anti-Semitic viewpoint because it is already "extra muros"—one distinct group attacking another distinct group. This is an important consideration, because many scholars view Jesus's

---

127. Nolland, *Matthew*, 921.

128. Anthony J. Saldarini, "The Gospel of Matthew and Jewish-Christian Conflict," in *Social History of the Matthean Community*, ed. D. Balch (Philadelphia: Fortress Press, 1991), 695.

critique as certainly in line with the strongest and harshest words of the Prophets, directed (of course) at fellow Hebrews/Jews. Those who consider this to represent an "extra muros" attack presume, in the words of Kampen, that: " … the decisive break with Judaism has already occurred, and Matthew is charting a new course for the followers of Jesus while defining its relationship to that which it has left behind."[129] Amy-Jill Levine, however, wonders if we can recognize a clear social break between groups, but still thinks that Matthew exhibits a sense of being apart:

> Determining when a sect ceases to be part of the parent body and becomes its own distinct movement is, especially for antiquity, arbitrary. The gospel appears, at least to me, to be moving outward, and so moving away from Jews, if not from what fits under the rubric of Judaism … Sects require specialized vocabulary to differentiate themselves from the parent body. Hence Matthew speaks of 'their synagogues.' 'Their synagogues' may not imply the opposite, 'our synagogues.' Instead, for Matthew, the opposite is the ἐκκλησία where the followers of Jesus gather.[130]

However, as Boxall observes, the accusations in Matthew 23 consist of:

> … stock polemic used against religious and philosophical opponents in the ancient world. Matthew's polemic against the scribes and Pharisees would have sounded far more conventional to ancient audiences, and indeed, by comparison with other texts, remarkably mild … its primary function would probably have been to legitimate the early Christian readers, and delegitimate their main Pharisaic rivals … [131]

This is not to say, of course, that anti-Semitism was not a serious issue in Hardie's own perception. It most certainly was, but Hardie's use of Matthew 23 represents a fascinating episode mainly because he did not read this chapter as having much to do with Jewish/Christian relations in his time!

For modern scholars, a corollary issue is the relation of Matthew 23 to other presentations of the teachings of Jesus. As many have noted, the curse language of Matthew 23 "sits uneasily" in a Gospel where Jesus had already explicitly warned about calling another person a "fool" (Mt. 5:22), as well as the general tenor

---

129. John Kampen, "The Problem of Christian Anti-Semitism and a Sectarian Reading of the Gospel of Matthew: The Trial of Jesus," in *Matthew within Judaism: Israel and the Nations in the First Gospel*, ed. Anders Runesson and Daniel Gurtner (Atlanta: SBL Press, 2020), 371–97.

130. Amy-Jill Levine, "Concluding Reflections: What's Next in the Study of Matthew?," in *Matthew within Judaism: Israel and the Nations in the First Gospel*, ed. Anders Runesson and Daniel M. Gurtner (Atlanta: SBL, 2020), 449–66, here 452.

131. Ian Boxall, *Matthew Through the Centuries*, Wiley Blackwell Bible Commentaries (Oxford: Blackwell, 2019), 333.

of compassion and love of enemies that is seen as typical of the teachings and example of Jesus.

Ian Boxall's 2019 commentary in the "Wiley Blackwell" series is especially noteworthy because it is a commentary series with a particular interest in mapping certain highlights of "Reception History" as well. Notably, Boxall agrees with many scholars who see Matthew 23 to be a combination of earlier Markan material under Matthean editing—including sayings paralleled in Luke 11:39–52.[132] Again, as others have noted, Boxall also reads the "seven woes" of vv. 13–36 as comparable to Hebrew tradition, noting the "sevenfold judgments" of Genesis 4:24; Leviticus 26:18; Proverbs 6:31; and alluded to in Revelations 8–9, and 16. Therefore, Boxall approvingly cites George Aichele's "Reception History" analysis of Pasolini's famous film *The Gospel of Matthew*, where Aichele writes:

> Pasolini's Jesus is not the anti-Jewish Jew of the written gospel. Despite the movie's inclusion of the explicit 'hypocrites' sayings from Matthew 23, his opponents are not so much specifically Jewish Pharisees and scribes as they are the bureaucrats, owners, and bosses of every age and culture.[133]

Horsley, as another example, argues that the "Pharisees" in Matthew 23 represent, essentially, the Roman-supported "establishment":

> It is increasingly clear that the Pharisees and other learned scribes functioned as intellectual-legal 'retainers' of the Judean rulers, as advisers and representatives of the priestly aristocracy thoroughly trained in the cultural heritage for service in the temple-state.[134]

Furthermore, in Horsley's reading, this very condemnation by Jesus in Matthew 23 would likely have generated considerable *sympathy from the Judean peoples*:

> Generally … scribes and Pharisees served the temple-state and in that role were suspect and evidently were resented by the people … It seems that the scribes and Pharisees, who were based in Jerusalem, had little or no rapport with villagers and ordinary Jerusalemites, despite Josephus's statements that they were (at times) allied with the 'people' of Jerusalem.[135]

Thus, Horsley identifies the words of Jesus in Matthew 23 even more closely to the anger of the Hebrew Prophets centuries before—especially very similar to a Micah or Amos attacking the elite for their wealthy lifestyle at the cost of the poor:

132. Boxall, *Matthew*, 333.
133. George Aichele, "Translation as De-canonization: Matthew's Gospel According to Pasolini: To the Memory of Paul Hessert," *CrossCurrents* 51 (2002): 524–34, here 531.
134. Richard Horsley, *Jesus and the Politics of Roman Palestine* (Columbia: University of South Carolina Press, 2013), 151.
135. Horsley, *Jesus and the Politics*, 152.

Jesus's conflict with the scribes and Pharisees is thus closely linked to his renewal of the Mosaic covenant at the center of his renewal of Israel against the rulers of Israel. The 'flip side' of his renewal of the Mosaic covenant in village communities was his condemnation of the Pharisees and scribes for enabling the expropriation of resources needed by families and village communities to support their subsistence living. Ironically, the learned scribes and Pharisees who served as the established guardians of the laws of the Judeans that were supposedly rooted in Mosaic covenantal torah were facilitating the rulers' exploitation of the people whose life was guided by that same Mosaic covenantal torah in its popular version.[136]

Saldarini, on the other hand, sees the intensity of Jesus's attack as a clear attempt to "delegitimize" the authority of the Jewish leaders. Again, however, the emphasis appears to be on their authority, rather than their cultural identities:

> Matthew's polemics, even his famous attack on scribes and Pharisees as hypocritical (ch. 23), and his underlying view of Judaism are nuanced. Matthew attacks the Jewish leadership (scribes, Pharisees, and Jerusalem leaders) and their interpretation of how the Jewish community should live in order to replace their understanding of Torah and Jewish life with the community's reformed program. He is dealing with real time, concrete history, and living people.[137]

There has also been a line of analysis that attempts to determine the "redactional history" of the passage, believing it to be composed of a variety of sources. In Newport's 1995 analysis, for example, he agrees that some of the material may originate with Jesus himself,[138] but that a considerable amount of the material likely drew upon an early "Jewish Christian polemical tract" which had a different context than the use put to it by the editor of Matthew (and this may explain the stronger language in this passage than the language we find from Jesus elsewhere in the Matthew tradition). Nonetheless, Newport appears to agree that the criticism is unacceptable, if "understandable":

> Matthew's harsh castigation of the Jewish nation is surely indefensible, though it is somewhat understandable. Despite the apparent contradiction, Matthew was, it seems, both a Jew and anti-Jewish. Religious polemics often bring forth tirades of abuse and arouse the bitterest of feelings.[139]

---

136. Horsley, *Jesus and the Politics*, 153.
137. Saldarini, "Gospel of Matthew," 44.
138. Kenneth G. Newport, *The Sources and Sitz Im Leben of Matthew 23*, JSNTSupp 117 (Sheffield: Sheffield Academic Press, Bloomsbury Publishing, 1995), 11–12.
139. Newport, *The Sources*, 65.

Still, one wonders what Newport believes is the proper way to assess the implications of this passage, when he writes toward the end of his study:

> Matthew 23 is a scathing attack on the perceived opposition, and Christian commentators who seek to wriggle out of the embarrassing implications of this chapter by viewing it as a paradigm cannot really be said to have taken the level of animosity found in the passage seriously.[140]

France's observations are also notable here. First, he acknowledges that the severity of the attacks in the famous chapter are not to be lightly dismissed, stating it is:

> … clear that historically Jesus did find himself in sharp disagreement with the Jewish leadership, especially in Jerusalem, and there is no reason to suppose that this antagonism was kept within the confines of gentlemanly debate, on Jesus' side any more than on theirs.[141]

However, France is interested in seeing the wider implication of Matthew's portrayal of Jesus's attack, including the possibility that it would be seen to be a criticism of Christianity's own failings as well:

> The attitude attacked in this chapter is a religion of externals, a matter of ever more detailed attention to rules and regulations, while failing to discern God's priorities … the attack on this group of 'hypocrites' is probably intended by Matthew to apply also to people in his own church context who have similarly missed the point, and in v. 8–12, this secondary target becomes visible. The failings here ascribed to scribal/Pharisaic religion have their parallels in most religious traditions when the form comes to matter more than the substance.[142]

Garland also represents the "intra muros" perspective in his 2001 commentary. Garland concurs with commentators who read this as an attack on the authority of those who bore the brunt of Jesus's attack, which was:

> … designed to defrock recognized authorities and is the outgrowth of a family row—frequently the most vitriolic. It is also no more anti-Semitic or anti-Judaism than the scorching denunciations found in the prophets and other Jewish literature that announce God's wrath on those who are judged to be false stewards … one should look within one's own life and one's own religious circle to see where these denunciations apply.[143]

---

140. Newport, *The Sources*, 185.
141. France, *Matthew*, 854.
142. France, *Matthew*, 855.
143. David Garland, *Reading Matthew: A Literary and Theological Commentary* (Macon: Smyth & Helwys, 2001), 231–2.

Similarly, Turner's 2015 study places Matthew 23 within the wider context of the Hebrew Biblical polemics that bitterly condemn the mistreatment of prophets in Israelite history.

> Matthew's narrative presents Jesus as the ultimate rejected prophet and Jesus' disciples as a remnant community of persecuted prophets. This understanding places the severe polemical language of Matthew 23 into an intramural Jewish context where different voices contend for the mantle of authentic Biblical religion during turbulent times. If this is the case, the dominant supersessionist understanding of Matthew 23 in the history of Christian exegesis is blatantly mistaken.[144]

Turner thus reads Matthew 23 (among other texts) in the same mindset as other Jewish polemical texts such as 2 Chronicles 36:15–17 and 2 Maccabees 6:12–17.[145]

Hauerwas's theological commentary on Matthew is a notable place to end our brief survey of contemporary commentary. Hauerwas is, of course, well aware of the accusations of anti-Semitism directed against this passage. However, his analysis includes a critique of the arguments that Matthew 23 is somehow incompatible with the nonviolent Jesus. Hauerwas objects:

> Some commentators are so taken aback by the vehemence of his attack on the scribes and Pharisees that they wonder if Jesus could have actually pronounced these judgments against the scribes and Pharisees. It is often assumed that Jesus' judgmental tone and his unforgiving judgments are incompatible with the great commandment, but even more at odds with his admonition that we should love our enemies (Matt. 5:38–48). Yet … the love that Jesus preaches is not incompatible with judgment and, in particular, judgment on hypocrisy. Faithful love, if it is faithful, is judgment.[146]

In an observation virtually identical in spirit to Hardie's use of the passage, Hauerwas trenchantly observes that the problem is not that Christians criticized the kind of religiosity that was condemned in Matthew 23, but rather the problem is that:

> … we have failed to apply those judgments to ourselves. We cannot forget that Jesus condemns the scribes and Pharisees from a position of weakness. He has no power to act against those he condemns. Christians betray Jesus when they make judgements—like those that Jesus makes against the scribes and Pharisees—from positions of power that transform those judgments into violent and murderous actions rather than attempts to call ourselves and our brothers and sisters to a better life.[147]

---

144. David Turner, *Israel's Last Prophet: Jesus and the Jewish Leaders in Matthew 23* (Minneapolis: 1517 Media/Fortress Press, 2015), 11.

145. Turner, *Israel's Last Prophet*, 371.

146. Stanley Hauerwas, *Matthew* (Grand Rapids: Brazos Press, 2006), 195.

147. Hauerwas, *Matthew*, 197.

I believe it is clear from even a brief survey of contemporary literature on Matthew 23 that Hardie's comments about, and his use of, Matthew 23 are very much in the spirit of critical attitudes toward abusive authority and power that Christians are too often reticent to criticize amongst themselves, and particularly those authorities and powers in government. Hardie's use of Matthew 23 charts a more radical path, and it is hardly surprising that a prophetic modern scholar like Hauerwas clearly echoes the same sentiment. For those who are skeptical that this passage can be used in a manner that is not inherently "anti-Semitic," Hardie presents a good case study.

SUMMARY—*What now is to be done?*

The significance of the Bible as a text for defending socialism has, we have seen in Chapters 1–2, a celebrated history in the US and UK especially. No longer is this treated as the somewhat amusing and exaggerated ideas, or mere crowd-pleasing window-dressing, for socialist rhetoric caught up in the enthusiasm of the moment. The Christian Socialists were socialists, and they were Christians—Christians who took the Bible seriously. Catterall takes note of Clement Attlee's interesting observation on the occasion when Attlee stated that: " … 'There are probably more texts from the Bible enunciated from Socialist platforms than those of all other parties,'" and Catterall comments further that: "It cannot be assumed that this was simply because of the numbers of lay preachers accustomed to building their arguments upon a scriptural passage, active in the Labour movement."[148] Catterall, with typical insight, takes note of the fact that there is something of a "hermeneutics" of British socialism in their use of particular passages of the Bible:

> … The Bible did not … merely lend itself to such uses. It conjured up images of a providential order blighted by the self-seeking nature of Capitalism … The spirit of the text, 'He who would be greatest among you let him be servant of all' (Matthew 23:11) was presented as virtually absent from the ethics of the existing economic order.[149]

The legacy of Hardie, Hird, Martyn, Davidson, and others clearly carried on the tradition, as Catterall notes, that:

> The language and nature of the Bible furnished ready material for such condemnations. 'What modern Labour man,' asked Keir Hardie in 1912, 'ever used the same strong language towards the rich as Christ did?' [The Bible] … also provided a stock of familiar precepts such as 'Feed my lambs' that could serve Labour rhetoric, even for atheists like Jack and Bessie Braddock. This was a favourite passage that Rhys Davies, the Congregationalist and Labour MP

---

148. Catterall, *Labour and the Free Churches*, 147.
149. Catterall, *Labour and the Free Churches*, 147.

for Westhoughton, turned to when he wished to remind the Bolton guardians of their responsibilities to dependants of the miners locked out in 1926. So frequently did Bob Smillie resort to this sort of use of scripture during the Royal Commission on the coal industry in 1919 that one of his fellow commissioners, Lord Durham, was moved to ask, 'Is this an ecclesiastical examination?'[150]

Catterall further suggests that the historical context for which parts of Scripture were preferred may well be attributed to the issues of the day. Nineteenth-century radicals drew on the Old Testament more often, suggests Catterall, because land issues were part of the Chartist activism of England, and the anti-Highland Clearances of the Scottish mid-nineteenth century. But, suggests Catterall, the war years inspired a shift to emphases on peace as well, which interestingly enough brought St. Paul back into use based on the famous "Love" chapter of 1 Corinthians 13. On John 15:12:

> These texts also provided the guiding principles in which 'Service, Brotherhood, Love (or to call love by its economic equivalent, co-operation), must be the basis of our social system instead of self-interest, individualism and competition.'[151]

Catterall notes that even though both sides of a debate in 1923 on the "shortcomings of Capitalism" used religious arguments: " ... the only one to quote the Bible was Walton Newbold when he described St. Paul's dictum (2 Thessalonians 3.10)" that "If a man will not work neither shall he eat" as "the principle of Communism."[152]

Naming this section of Chapter 6 as I have is, of course, in the socialist tradition of writing essays and pamphlets entitled: "What Must be Done?" or "What is to be Done?" a step which thus attempts to propose concrete steps forward in progressive social change, in order to try to argue that there is, in fact, a method to this language. In this case, I propose that what is to be done, is to take the miner's reading of the Bible seriously and consider his thoughts in the context of contemporary Biblical debate. Furthermore, I hope that this inspires many other students and scholars to hit the archives!

Once again, I want to be clear what I am arguing for here—and what I am *not* arguing for. I am *not* intending to suggest that Hardie is somehow "right" in his readings of the Bible based solely on my political sympathies with his life work and social location. He is not *accidentally* "right" in his readings of the Bible solely because of his class identity. He is not "right" because I am trying to "one up" historical-critical Biblical scholarship in favor of the miner, as entertaining as Hardie's writing certainly is in those terms.

What I *am* arguing for is that the careful investigation of many of the texts of Christian Socialism—and in this case Keir Hardie—reveal interesting

---

150. Catterall, *Labour and the Free Churches*, 147.
151. Catterall, *Labour and the Free Churches*, 148.
152. Catterall, *Labour and the Free Churches*, 148.

traditions of reading the Bible. Furthermore, among these interesting traditions are observations about Scripture that can be, and ought to be, part of the wider contemporary academic discussion of these Biblical passages. I believe that Hardie's class-based, "justice assuming" reading of the New Testament allowed him to interpret with insight. In sum—these readings should be attended to as important voices whose views are not to be easily dismissed as of no critical significance. *Sometimes*, these voices simply add to opinions already expressed by other scholars—but occasionally these "working-class readers of the Bible" present challenging notions.

Furthermore, instead of presuming that academics can know what people in difficult social and political circumstances "would," "could," or "should" think about the Bible—we can read what they *did* think (sing, and pray). This is not, I submit, an insignificant point. Earlier, I compared this discussion to Liberation theologians, like Ernesto Cardenal, who talk about "peasant exegesis" and (rightly, in my view) demand that it be taken seriously. Already in the brief introduction to his (now famous) series, *The Gospel in Solentiname* (1976, 1984), Cardenal observed about the "peasant readings" he was recording:

> The commentaries of the *campesinos* are usually of greater profundity than that of many theologians, but of a simplicity like that of the Gospel itself. This is not surprising: The Gospel, or 'Good News' (to the poor), was written for them, and by people like them.[153]

In short, like Ernesto Cardenal, so were Michael Gold and Herbert Gutman "on to something," but wouldn't they both be somewhat bemused to know that *Biblical* scholars are among those willing to take each of them seriously. Hardie, of course, would be delighted (and then likely ask, "So where were *YOU* during the last meeting, then?").

An important observation, it seems to me, is this: Biblical scholars, especially those who are intrigued with post-modern informed assumptions that interpretation is heavily influenced by presuppositions and any (and all) reader's own social context, often draw on social sciences to lend some kind of further credibility to their proposed readings. It is as if the references to social studies, sociological surveys, or anthropological literature are thought to lend a kind of "real world authenticity" or at least "real world suggestiveness" to the exegetical arguments about Biblical passages especially when one argues for similar social contexts. It is important to ask, "Do people—any people—actually behave in the manner I am proposing? How and in what circumstances?"

I am describing my own work here, too. Indeed, I have routinely drawn on social science literature for ideas and suggestions about, for example, refugee behavior, or the impact of trauma, or cross-cultural contact in violent circumstances—all in order to try to make further sense of Biblical passages that clearly allude to violent

---

153. Cardenal, *The Gospel in Solantiname*, vii.

experiences, exile, and forced migration.[154] I have not experienced these kinds of realities myself—I must try to learn them second hand. Similarly, then, how can we make arguments about the "relevance" of a passage to those from, for example, working classes who are struggling for social justice? One way, of course, is to listen as they themselves talk about Scripture, on those wonderful occasions where such discussions are available to us. As we have seen, at least in the case of Keir Hardie, it most certainly is available to us.

Therefore, among the recommendations in a section entitled "What is to be Done?" I propose that academic Biblical Studies take up Gold's and Gutman's challenge to continue to find the "proletarian" voices (as well as the "indigenous voices," the "gendered voices," the "African-American voices") of reading the Bible and listen carefully enough, and treat them seriously enough, to actually assess whether we may find some of these suggestions worthy of critical consideration—worthy of following up—worthy of actually changing how we read the Bible—as part (but certainly not the whole) of our analysis of Scripture. I know that many will object that I propose to "assess" at all! But I would respond that actually listening with appreciation means critical engagement—not passive acknowledgment. That has been the proposed purpose of this final chapter, which must be called—with the book as a whole—experimental.

---

154. Daniel Smith-Christopher, *A Biblical Theology of Exile*, Overtures to Biblical Theology (Minneapolis: Fortress Press, 2002), also idem, *The Religion of the Landless: The Social Context of the Babylonian Exile* (Eugene: Wipf & Stock, 2015). Although the second title bears a later date, it is a reprint of my 1989 book based on my 1986 dissertation at Oxford, which was significantly reworked for the 2002 volume in the Overtures series.

BIBLIOGRAPHY

Adamson, William. *The Life Of The Rev. James Morison, D. D., Principal Of The Evangelical Union Theological Hall, Glasgow*. London: Hodder and Stoughton, 1898.
Aichele, George. "Translation as De-canonization: Matthew's Gospel According to Pasolini: To the Memory of Paul Hessert." *CrossCurrents* 51 (2002): 524–34.
Aitken, James K., Jeremy M. S. Clines, and Christl N. Maier, eds. *Interested Readers: Essays on the Hebrew Bible in Honor of David J.A. Clines*. Atlanta: Society of Biblical Literature, 2013.
Backstrom, Philip. *Christian Socialism and Cooperation in Victorian England*. London: Croom Helm, 1974.
Baker, Kelly. *Gospel According to the Klan: The KKK's Appeal to Protestant America, 1915-1930*. CultureAmerica. Lawrence: University of Kansas Press, 2017.
Baptist, Edward. *Half has Never Been Told: Slavery and the Making of American Capitalism*. New York: Basic Books, 2014.
Barrett, James R. "The Blessed Virgin Made Me a Socialist: An Experiment in Catholic Autobiography and the Historical Understanding of Race and Class." In *Faith and the Historian: Catholic Perspectives*, edited by Nick Salvatore, 117–47. Chicago: University of Illinois Press, 2007.
Barrow, Logie. "Socialism in Eternity: The Ideology of Plebeian Spiritualists, 1853-1913." *History Workshop* 9 (1980): 37–69.
Bartchy, S. Scott. "Community of Goods in Acts: Idealization or Social Reality?" In *The Future of Early Christianity: Essays in Honor of Helmut Koester*, edited by Birger Pearson, 309–18. Minneapolis: Fortress Press, 1991.
Beavis, Mary Ann, HyeRan Kim-Cragg, and Linda Maloney. *2 Thessalonians*. Wisdom Commentary 52. Collegeville: Liturgical Press (Michael Glazier), 2016.
Belfrage, Cedric. *Let My People Go*. London: Victor Gollancz, 1940.
Benko, Ralph. "Bernie Sanders and the Resurgence of Socialist Sentiment in America." *Forbes*, December 14, 2017.
Benn, Caroline. *Keir Hardie*. London: Richard Cohen Books, 1997.
Bevir, Mark. "Labour Churches and Ethical Socialism." *History Today* 47 (1997): 50–5.
Bevir, Mark. *The Making of British Socialism*. Princeton: Princeton University Press, 2011.
Bissett, Jim. *Agrarian Socialism in American: Marx, Jefferson, and Jesus in Oklahoma Countryside, 1904-1920*. Norman: University of Oklahoma Press, 1999.
Boer, Roland. *Marxist Criticism of the Bible*. 2nd edn. London: Bloomsbury/T&T Clark, 2015.
Boring, Eugene. *1 & 2 Thessalonians: A Commentary*. NTL. Louisville: Westminster/John Knox, 2015.
Boxall, Ian. *Matthew Through the Centuries*. Wiley Blackwell Bible Commentaries. Oxford: Blackwell, 2019.
Boxall, Ian. "Tracing Patmos Through the Centuries." In *Reception History and Biblical Studies Theory and Practice*, edited by E. England and W. Lyons, 155–68. Edinburgh: T&T Clark, 2015.

Boxall, Ian, and Christopher Rowland. "Reception History." In *The Oxford Encyclopedia of Biblical Interpretation*, edited by Steven McKenzie, 206–15. Oxford and New York: Oxford University Press, 2013.

Braude, Ann. *Radical Spirits: Spiritualism and Women's Rights in Nineteenth-Century America*. 2nd edn. Bloomington: Indiana University Press, 1989/2001.

Brown, Jeannine, and Kyle Roberts. *Matthew*. Two Horizons New Testament Commentary. Grand Rapids: Eerdmans, 2018.

Brown, Peter. "Between Syria and Egypt: Alms, Work, and the 'Holy Poor.'" In *Faithful Narratives: Historians, Religion, and the Challenge of Objectivity*, edited by A. Sterk and N. Caputo, 32–46. New York: Cornell University Press, 2014.

Bryan, Pauline, ed. *Keir Hardie & the 21st Century Socialist Revival*. Edinburgh: Luath Press, 2019.

Bryan, Pauline, ed. *What Would Keir Hardie Say?* Edinburgh: Luath Press, 2015.

Burnett, John, ed., *Useful Toil: Autobiographies of Working People from the 1820s to the 1920s*. London: Allen Lane, 1974.

Burns, David. *The Life and Death of the Radical Historical Jesus*. Oxford and New York: Oxford University Press, 2013.

Cadbury, Henry Joel. *The Book of Acts in History*. London: A & C Black, 1955.

Callahan, Richard J. *Work and Faith in the Kentucky Coal Fields: Subject to Dust*. Bloomington: Indiana University Press, 2009.

Callow, John., ed. *Keir Hardie, From Serfdom to Socialism*. London: Lawrence & Wishart, 2015.

Cantwell, Christopher, Heath W. Carter, and Janine Giordano Drake, eds. *The Pew and the Picket Line: Christianity and the American Working Class*. Working Class in American History. Chicago: University of Illinois Press, 2016.

Cardenal, Ernesto. *The Gospel in Solentiname* (4 vols). Maryknoll: Orbis Books, 1976.

Carter, Heath. *Union Made: Working People and the Rise of Social Christianity in Chicago*. Oxford & New York: Oxford University Press, 2015.

Case-Winters, Anna. *Matthew*. Louisville: Westminster John Knox Press, 2015.

Casey, Janet Galligani. "Reviving the Thirties: The Case for Teaching Proletarian Fiction in the Undergraduate American Literature Classroom." *College English* 70 (2008): 233–48.

Catterall, Peter, *Labour and the Free Churches, 1918–1939: Radicalism, Righteousness and Religion*. London: Bloomsbury Academic, 2016.

Chalamet, Christophe. *Revivalism and Social Christianity: The Prophetic Faith of Henri Nick and André Trocmé*. Cambridge: Lutterworth Press, 2017.

Chura, Patrick. *Michael Gold: The People's Writer*. Albany: SUNY Press, 2020.

Clark, Emily Suzanne. *A Luminous Brotherhood: Afro-Creole Spiritualism in Nineteenth-Century New Orleans*. Chapel Hill: University of North Carolina Press, 2016.

Cockburn, John. *The Hungry Heart: A Romantic Biography of James Keir Hardie*. London: Jarrolds, 1956.

Cole, G. D. H. *The Life of Robert Owen*. Routledge Library Editions: The Labour Movement. London: Routledge, 2018.

Conner, J. McArthur. *Jas. Keir Hardie's Life Story: From Pit Trapper to Parliament*. Toronto: Banner Press, 1917.

Countryman, L. Wm. *The Rich Christian in the Church of the Early Empire: Contradictions and Accommodations*. Texts and Studies in Religion. New York and Toronto: Edwin Mellen Press, 1980.

Craik, W. W. "The Passing of Dennis Hird." *Forward*, July 31, 1920. https://spartacus-educational.com/Dennis_Hird.htm.

Daggett, Melissa. *Spiritualism in Nineteenth-Century New Orleans: The Life and Times of Henry Louis Rey*. Jackson: University Press of Mississippi, 2017.

Davidson, John Morrison. *The Gospel of the Poor: The Christ of the Commune*. London: F.R. Henderson, 1903.

Davis, David Brion. *Inhuman Bondage: The Rise and Fall of Slavery in the New World*. Oxford: Oxford University Press, 2008.

Dibelius, Martin. *Studies in the Acts of the Apostles*. New York: Scribners and Sons, 1956.

Dochuk, Darren. *From Bible Belt to Sunbelt: Plain-Folk Religion, Grassroots Politics, and the Rise of Evangelical Conservatism*. New York: W.W. Norton & Co., 2012.

Dombrowski, James. *The Early Days of Christian Socialism in America*. New York: Octagon Books, 1966.

Donskov, Andrew. *Leo Tolstoy and the Canadian Doukhobors: A Study in Historic Relationships*. Ottawa: University of Ottawa Press, 2019.

Dorien, Gary. *American Democratic Socialism: History, Politics, Religion, and Theory*. New Haven: Yale University Press, 2021.

Duke, David N. *In the Trenches with Jesus and Marx: Harry F. Ward and the Struggle for Social Justice*. Tuscaloosa and London: University of Alabama, 2003.

Edgerton, William, trans. and ed. *Memoirs of Peasant Tolstoyans in Soviet Russia*. Bloomington: Indiana University Press, 1993.

England, Emma, and William John Lyons, eds. *Reception History and Biblical Studies Theory and Practice*. Edinburgh: T&T Clark, 2015.

Etkind, Alexander. "Whirling with the Other: Russian Populism and Religious Sects." *The Russian Review* 62 (2003): 565–88.

Eunson, William, ed. *Miscellaneous Essays: Thought-coin from the Ages*. Edinburgh: Hunter, 1898.

Evans, Craig. *Matthew*. New Cambridge Bible Commentary. New York: Cambridge University Press, 2012.

Fahey, David. *Temperance and Racism: John Bull, Johnny Reb, and the Good Templars*. Lexington: University Press of Kentucky, 1996.

Fahey, David M. "Temperance and the Liberal Party – Lord Peel's Report, 1899." *Journal of British Studies* 10 (1971): 132–59.

Fee, Gordon. *First and Second Letters to the Thessalonians*. NICNT. Grand Rapids: Eerdmans, 2009.

Ferguson, Robert Hunt. *Remaking the Rural South: Interracialism, Christian Socialism, and Cooperative Farming in Jim Crow Mississippi*. Athens: University of Georgia Press, 2018.

Finger, Reta H. *Of Widows and Meals: Communal Meals in the Book of Acts*. Grand Rapids: Eerdmans, 2007.

Fink, Leon, and Nick Salvatore (reply). "Herbert Gutman's Narrative of the American Working Class: A Reevaluation" [with Response], *International Journal of Politics, Culture, and Society* 12, no. 4 (1999): 662–70.

Fivecoate, Jesse A., Kristina Downs, and Meredith McGriff. "The Politics of Trivialization." In *Advancing Folkloristics*, edited by Jesse Fivecoate, Kristina Downs, and Meredith McGriff, 59–76. Bloomington: Indiana University Press, 2021.

Foley, Barbara. *Radical Representations: Politics and Form in U.S. Proletarian Fiction, 1929–1941*. Durham and London: Duke University Press, 1993.

Foner, Philip S., ed. *The Black Socialist Preacher: The Teachings of Reverend George Washington Woodbey and His Disciple, Reverend G.W. Slater, Jr*. San Francisco: Synthesis Press, 1983.

Fones-Wolf, Ken. *Trade Union Gospel: Christianity and Labor in Industrial Philadelphia, 1865–1915*. American Civilization. Philadelphia: Temple University Press, 1986.

France, R. T. *The Gospel of Matthew*. NICNT. Grand Rapids: Eerdmans, 2007.

Fraser, Hamish W. "Keir Hardie: Radical, Socialist, Feminist." *Études écossaises* 10 (2005): 103–15.

Friesen, Steven. "Poverty in Pauline Studies: Beyond the So-Called New Consensus." *Journal for the Study of the New Testament* 26 (2004): 323–61.

Friesen, Steven, and Walter Scheidel. "The Size of the Economy and the Distribution of Income in the Roman Empire." *The Journal of Roman Studies* 99 (2009): 61–91.

Furnish, Victor P. *1 and 2 Thessalonians*. Abingdon NT Commentaries. Nashville: Abingdon Press, 2007.

Fyfe, Hamilton. *Keir Hardie*. "Great Lives" Series. London: Duckworth Press, 1935.

Garland, David E. *Reading Matthew: A Literary and Theological Commentary*. Macon: Smyth & Helwys, 2001.

Geoghegan, Vincent. "Socialism and Christianity in Edwardian Britain: A Utopian Perspective." *Utopian Studies* 10 (1999): 40–69.

Gerrard, Jessica. *Radical Childhoods: Schooling and the Struggle for Social Change*. Manchester: Manchester University Press, 2014.

Gillingham, Susan. "Biblical Studies on Holiday? A Personal View of Reception History." In *Reception History and Biblical Studies Theory and Practice*, edited by E. England and W. Lyons, 17–30. Edinburgh: T&T Clark, 2015.

Glasier, J. Bruce. "John Morrison Davidson: Obituary." *Labour Leader*. December 28, 1916.

Gold, Michael. *Jews Without Money*. New York: Public Affairs, 2009.

Gorman, John. *Banner Bright: An Illustrated History of the Banners of the British Trade Union Movement*. London: Allen Lane, 1973.

Green, Gene. *The Letters to the Thessalonians*. PNTC. Grand Rapids: Eerdmans, 2002.

Gutman, Herbert. "Protestantism and the American Labor Movement: The Christian Spirit in the Gilded Age." *The American Historical Review* 72 (1966): 74–101.

Halker, Clark D. *For Democracy, Workers, and God: Labor Song-Poems and Labor Protest, 1865–95*. Urbana and Chicago: University of Illinois, 1991.

Hanley, Lawrence, "'Smashing Cantatas' and 'Looking Class Pitchers': The Impossible Location of Proletarian Literature." In *The Novel and the American Left: Critical Essays on Depression Era Fiction*, edited by Janet Galligani Casey, 132–50. Iowa City: University of Iowa Press, 2004.

Hardie, K. *Androssan and Saltcoat Herald*. March 6, 1885.

Hardie, Keir. *Can a Man Be a Christian on a Pound a Week*. 1901, now public domain.

Hardie, K. "Christ and the Modern Movement." In *Christ and Labour*, edited by C. G. Ammon, 77–91. London: Jarrold and Sons, 1913.

Hardie, K. "Labour and Christianity." In *Labour and Religion*, edited by Anon., 48–55. Browning Hall: Labour Week, 1910.

Hardie, K. Various articles. *The Labour Leader*.

Harrill, J. Albert. "Divine Judgment against Ananias and Sapphira (Acts 5:1–11): A Stock Scene of Perjury and Death." *Journal of Biblical Literature* 130 (2011): 351–69.

Harrington, Daniel. *The Gospel of Matthew*. Sacra Pagina. Collegeville: Liturgical Press, 1991.

Hauerwas, Stanley. *Matthew*. Grand Rapids: Brazos Press, 2006.

Hendricks, Obery. *The Politics of Jesus: Rediscovering the True Revolutionary Nature of Jesus' Teachings and How They Have Been Corrupted*. New York: Penguin/Random House, 2007.

Hird, Dennis. *Jesus the Socialist*. London: Clarion Press, 1908.
Hirschfield, Claire. "The British Left and the 'Jewish Conspiracy': A Case Study of Modern Antisemitism." *Jewish Social Studies* 43 (1981): 95–112.
Hock, Ronald F. *The Social Context of Paul's Ministry: Tentmaking and Apostleship*. Philadelphia: Fortress Press, 1980.
Holman, Bob. "Christianity: Christian and Socialist." In *What Would Keir Hardie Say?*, edited by Pauline Bryan, 35–48. Edinburgh: Luoth Press, 2015.
Holman, Bob. *Keir Hardie: Labour's Greatest Hero?* London: Lion Hudson, 2010.
Homberger, Eric. "Proletarian Literature and the John Reed Clubs 1929-1935." *Journal of American Studies* 13, no. 2 (1979): 221–44.
Horn, Gerd-Rainer. *The Spirit of Vatican II: Western European Progressive Catholicism in the Long Sixties*. Oxford: University of Oxford University Press, 2015.
Horn, Gerd-Rainer. *Western European Liberation Theology (1924-1959): The First Wave*. Oxford: Oxford University Press, 2015.
Horn, Gerd-Rainer, and E. Gerard, eds. *Left Catholicism, 1943-1955: Catholics and Society in Western Europe at the Point of Liberation*. Leuven: University of Leuven Press, 2001.
Horsley, Richard A. *Jesus and the Politics of Roman Palestine*. Columbia: University of South Carolina Press, 2013.
Hostetler, John A. *Hutterite Society*. 2nd edn. Baltimore: Johns Hopkins University Press, 1997.
Hughes, Emrys. *Keir Hardie: A Pictorial Biography*. London: George Allen & Unwin, 1956.
Hughes, Frank Witt. *Early Christian Rhetoric and 2 Thessalonians*. JNST 30. Sheffield: Sheffield Academic Press, 1989.
Hunter, James, ed. *For the People's Cause: From the Writings of John Murdoch, Highland and Irish Land Reformer (1818-1903)*. Edinburgh: Crofter Press, 1986.
Hyslop, Jonathan. "The World Voyage of James Keir Hardie: Indian Nationalism, Zulu Insurgency and the British Labour Diaspora 1907–1908." *Journal of Global History* 1 (2006): 343–62.
Jenkins, Philip. "Review: James Murphy, The Proletarian Movement." *Comparative Literature Studies* 31 (1994): 195–8.
Jewett, Paul. "Tenement Churches and Communal Meals in the Early Church: The Implications of a Form-Critical Analysis of 2 Thessalonians 3:10." *Biblical Research* 38 (1993): 23–43.
Johnson, A. *1 & 2 Thessalonians*. The Two Horizons New Testament Commentary. Grand Rapids: Eerdmans, 2016.
Johnson, Luke Timothy. *The Acts of the Apostles*. Sacra Pagina. Collegeville: Michael Glazier/The Liturgical Press, 1992.
Johnson, Neal. *The Labour Church: The Movement & Its Message*. Routledge Studies in Radical History and Politics. London: Routledge, 2018.
Jones, Peter d'A. *The Christian Socialist Revival 1877-1914*. Princeton: Princeton University Press, 1968.
Kampen, John. "The Problem of Christian Anti-Semitism and a Sectarian Reading of the Gospel of Matthew: The Trial of Jesus." In *Matthew within Judaism: Israel and the Nations in the First Gospel*, edited by Anders Runesson and Daniel Gurtner, 371–97. Atlanta: SBL Press, 2020.
Keddie, G. Anthony, Michael Flexsenhar III, and Steven J. Friesen, eds. *The Struggle Over Class: Socioeconomic Analysis of Ancient Christian Texts*. Atlanta: SBL, 2021.
Keener, Craig S. *A Commentary on the Gospel of Matthew*. Grand Rapids: Eerdmans, 1999.

Keener, Craig S. *Acts*. New Cambridge Bible Commentary. Cambridge: Cambridge University Press, 2020.

K'Meyer, Tracy. *The Story of Koinonia Farm: Interracialism and Christian Community in the Postwar South*. Charlottesville: University of Virginia Press, 1997.

Knox, W. W. "Religion and the Scottish Labour Movement c. 1900–39." *Journal of Contemporary History* 23 (1988): 609–30.

Levine, Amy-Jill. "Concluding Reflections: What's Next in the Study of Matthew?" In *Matthew within Judaism: Israel and the Nations in the First Gospel*, edited by Anders Runesson and Daniel M. Gurtner, 449–66. Atlanta: SBL, 2020.

Li, Xian. "The Jesus Family." In *Redeemed by Fire: The Rise of Popular Christianity in Modern China*, 64–84. New Haven: Yale University Press, 2010.

Long, Thomas. *Matthew*. Westminster Bible Companion. Louisville: Westminster John Knox Press, 1997.

Lowe, David. *From Pit to Parliament: The Story of the Early Life of James Keir Hardie*. London: The Labour Publishing Company, 1923.

Luz, Ulrich. *Matthew 1–7: A Commentary*. Hermeneia. Minneapolis: Fortress Press, 2007.

Lyon, Eileen Groth. *Politicians in the Pulpit: Christian Radicalism in Britain from the Fall of the Bastille to the Disintegration of Chartism*. Aldershot: Ashgate, 1999.

MacColl, Allan. *Land, Faith and the Crofting Community: Christianity and Social Criticism in the Highlands of Scotland, 1843–1893*. Edinburgh: University of Edinburgh Press, 2006.

Malherbe, Bruce. *The Letters to the Thessalonians*. Anchor Bible Commentary. New York: Doubleday, 1964.

Malina, Bruce J., and John J. Pilch. *Social-Science Commentary on the Book of Acts*. Minneapolis: 1517 Media/Fortress Press, 2008.

McGinn, Sheila E., and Megan T. Wilson-Reitz. "2 Thessalonians vs. the *Ataktoi*: A Pauline Critique of 'White-Collar Welfare.'" In *By Bread Alone: The Bible through the Eyes of the Hungry*, edited by Sheila E. McGinn, Lai Ling Elizabeth Ngan, and Ahida Calderón Pilarski, 185–208. Minneapolis: 1517 Media/Fortress Press, 2014.

McGreal, Chris. "'The S-word': How Young Americans Fell in Love with Socialism." *The Guardian*, September 2, 2017.

McGregor, Jonathan. *Communion of Radicals: The Literary Christian Left in Twentieth Century America*. Baton Rouge: Louisiana State University Press, 2021.

McLean, Iain. *Keir Hardie*. London: St. Martin's Press, 1975.

Mead, Julia. "Why Millennials Aren't Afraid of Socialism." *The Nation*, January 10, 2017.

Meggitt, Justin J. *Paul, Poverty and Survival*. Edinburgh: T&T Clark, 1998.

Mesters, Carlos. *Defenseless Flower: A New Reading of the Bible*. Maryknoll: Orbis Books, 1989.

Montero, Roman A. *All Things in Common: The Economic Practices of the Early Christians*. Eugene: Cascade, 2017.

Morgan, Kenneth O. *Keir Hardie: Radical and Socialist*. London: Phoenix, 1997 (reprint from 1975).

Murphy, James. *The Proletarian Moment: The Controversy over Leftism in Literature*. Urbana: University of Illinois Press, 1991.

Mussey, Mabel H. B. *Social Hymns of Brotherhood and Aspiration*. Boston: Universalist Publishing House, 1914.

Mutch, Deborah. "Intemperate Narratives: Tory Tipplers, Liberal Abstainers, and Victorian British Socialist Fiction." *Victorian Literature and Culture* 36 (2008): 471–87.

Mutch, Deborah. *Women, Periodicals and Print Culture in Britain, 1830s–1900s: The Victorian Period*. Edinburgh: Edinburgh University Press, 2019.
Myles, Robert, ed. *Class Struggle in the New Testament*. Minneapolis: Fortress Academic, 2019.
Newport, Kenneth G. *The Sources and Sitz Im Leben of Matthew 23*. JSNTSupp 117. Sheffield: Sheffield Academic Press, Bloomsbury Publishing, 1995.
Nicols, John. *Civic Patronage in the Roman Empire*. Leiden: Brill, 2014.
Nolland, John. *The Gospel of Matthew – A Commentary on the Greek Text*. NIGTC. Grand Rapids: Eerdmans, 2005.
Noyes, John Humphrey. *The History of American Socialisms*. Philadelphia: J.B. Kippincott, 1870.
O'Neill, Morna. "Pandora's Box: Walter Crane, 'Our Sphinx-Riddle,' and the Politics of Decoration." *Victorian Literature and Culture* 35 (2007): 309–26.
Orens, John R. *Stewart Headlam's Radical Anglicanism: The Mass, the Masses, and the Music Hall*. Urbana: University of Illinois Press, 2003.
Osborne, Grant. *Matthew*. Exegetical Commentary on the New Testament. Grand Rapids: Zondervan, 2010.
Peel, Mark. *The Last Wesleyan: A Life of Donald Soper*. Lancaster: Scotford, 2008.
Pehl, Matthew. *The Making of Working-Class Religion*. Urbana: University of Illinois Press, 2016.
Pervo, Richard. *Acts: A Commentary*. Hermeneia. Minneapolis: Fortress Press, 2009.
Ravenhill-Johnson, Annie. *The Art and Ideology of the Trade Union Emblem, 1850–1925*. London and New York: Anthem Press, 2013.
Reid, Fred. *Keir Hardie: The Making of a Socialist*. London: Croom Helm, 1978.
Rice, Joshua. *Paul and Patronage: The Dynamics of Power in 1 Corinthians*. Eugene: Pickwick, 2013.
Roberts, Jonathan. "Introduction." In *The Oxford Handbook of the Reception History of the Bible*, edited by Emma Mason, Michael Lied, and Jonathan Roberts, 1–9. Oxford and New York: Oxford University Press, 2011.
Robertson, Michael. *The Last Utopians: Four Late Nineteenth-Century Visionaries and Their Legacy*. Princeton and Oxford: Princeton University Press, 2019.
Rogers, Ed. "Democrats' Frightening Embrace of Socialism." *Washington Post*, May 7, 2018.
Rogers, Katie. "Protesters Dispersed With Tear Gas So Trump Could Pose at Church." *New York Times*. June 1, 2020.
Roll, Jarod. *Spirit of Rebellion: Labor and Religion in the New Cotton South*. Urbana: University of Illinois Press, 2010.
Roll, Jarod, and Erik S. Gellman, eds. *The Gospel of the Working Class: Labor's Southern Prophets in New Deal America*. Urbana: University of Illinois Press, 2011.
Roxburgh, Kenneth. "James Morison (1816–1893)." *Scottish Church History* 32, no. 1 (2002): 115–41.
Saldarini, Anthony J. "The Gospel of Matthew and Jewish-Christian Conflict." In *Social History of the Matthean Community*, edited by D. Balch, 38–61. Philadelphia: Fortress Press, 1991.
Salvatore, Nick. "Herbert Gutman's Narrative of the American Working Class: A Reevaluation." *International Journal of Politics, Culture, and Society* 12, no. 1 (1998): 43–80.
Salvatore, Nick. *Singing in a Strange Land: C. L. Franklin, the Black Church, and the Transformation of America*. New York: Little, Brown, and Company, 2005.

Scheffler, Eben. "Caring for the Needy in the Acts of the Apostles." *Neotestamentica* 50 (2016): 131–66.
Scott, Eugene. "Trump Says Bible is His Favorite Book, But Declines to Share Favorite Verse." CNN. August 27, 2015.
Shankar, Pradha R. "Socialist Labour Leader James Keir Hardie's (1856–1915) Contribution to India's Struggle for Freedom." *Proceedings of the Indian History Congress* 60 (1999): 675–83.
Shapiro, Hyman. *Keir Hardie and the Labour Party*. Then and There series. London: Longman, 1971.
Smith-Christopher, Daniel. *A Biblical Theology of Exile*. Overtures to Biblical Theology. Minneapolis: Fortress Press, 2002.
Smith-Christopher, Daniel. "Cross Cultural Exegesis." In *The Oxford Encyclopedia of Biblical Interpretation*, edited by Steven L. McKenzie, 138–50. Oxford and New York: Oxford University Press, 2013.
Smith-Christopher, Daniel. *Micah: A Commentary*. Old Testament Library. Louisville: Westminster/John Knox Press, 2015.
Smith-Christopher, Daniel. "Reading the Christian Old Testament in the Contemporary World." In *The Pentateuch: Fortress Bible Commentaries*, edited by Gale A. Yee, Hugh R. Page Jr., and Matthew J. M. Coomber, 43–66. Minneapolis: Fortress Press, 2014.
Smith-Christopher, Daniel. *The Religion of the Landless: The Social Context of the Babylonian Exile*. Eugene: Wipf & Stock, 2015.
Snowden, Philip. *An Autobiography*. London: Nicholson and Watson, 1934.
Snowden, Philip. "The Religion of the Labour Movement." In *Labour and Religion*, edited by Anon. Browning Hall: Labour Week, 1910.
Stevens, Carolyn. "The Objections of 'Queer Hardie', 'Lily Bell' and the Suffragettes' Friend to Queen Victoria's Jubilee, 1897." *Victorian Periodicals Review* 21, no. 3 (1988): 108–14.
Stewart, William. *J. Keir Hardie: A Biography*, London: Cassell and Company, 1921.
Still, Todd D. "Did Paul Loathe Manual Labor? Revisiting the Work of Ronald F. Hock on the Apostle's Tentmaking and Social Class." *Journal of Biblical Literature* 125, no. 4 (2006): 781–95.
Stromquist, Shelton. "Labor Historians and Traditions of Engaged Scholarship: Progressives, Insurgents, and the Making of a New Labor History." In *Civic Labors: Scholar Activism and Working-Class Studies*, edited by Dennis Deslippe, Eric Fure-Slocum, John McKerley, Kristen Anderson, Matthew Mettler, and John Williams-Searle, 11–34. Chicago: University of Illinois Press, 2016.
Suggs, Jon-Christian. "Marching! Marching! And the Idea of the Proletarian Novel." In *The Novel and the American Left: Critical Essays on Depression Era Fiction*, edited by Janet Galligani Casey, 151–71. Iowa City: University of Iowa Press, 2004.
Sugirtharajah, R. S. *Asian Biblical Hermeneutics and Postcolonialism: Contesting the Interpretations*. Biblical Seminar. Sheffield: Sheffield Academic Press, 1999.
Sugirtharajah, R. S. *Exploring Postcolonial Biblical Criticism: History, Method, Practice*. London: Wiley-Blackwell, 2011.
Sugirtharajah, R. S. *Jesus in Asia*. Cambridge: Harvard University Press, 2018.
Sugirtharajah, R. S. *Postcolonial Criticism and Biblical Interpretation*. Oxford: Oxford University Press, 2002.
Sugirtharajah, R. S. *Postcolonial Reconfigurations: An Alternative Way of Reading the Bible and Doing Theology*. Des Peres: Chalice Press, 2003.

Sugirtharajah, R. S. *The Bible and Asia: From the Pre-Christian Era to the Postcolonial Age.* Cambridge: Harvard University Press, 2013.

Sugirtharajah, R. S. *The Bible and Empire: Postcolonial Explorations.* Cambridge: Cambridge University Press, 2005.

Sugirtharajah, R. S. *The Bible and the Third World: Precolonial, Colonial and Postcolonial Encounters.* Cambridge: Cambridge University Press, 2001.

Sugirtharajah, R. S. *Vernacular Hermeneutics.* Sheffield: Sheffield Academic Press, 1999.

Sugirtharajah, R. S., ed. *Voices from the Margin: Interpreting the Bible in the Third World.* 25th Anniv. edn. Maryknoll: Orbis Books, 2016.

Theoharis, Liz. *We Cry Justice: Reading the Bible with the Poor People's Campaign.* Minneapolis: 1517 Media, Broadleaf Books, 2021.

Trevor, John. *My Quest for God.* London: Labour Prophet Office, 1897.

Trocmé, André. *Jesus and the Nonviolent Revolution.* Scottdale: Herald Press, 1973.

Turner, David. *Israel's Last Prophet: Jesus and the Jewish Leaders in Matthew 23.* Minneapolis: 1517 Media/Fortress Press, 2015.

Turner, Jacqueline. *The Labour Church: Religion and Politics in Britain, 1890–1914.* London and New York: I. B. Tauris, 2018.

Wald, Alan M. *American Night: The Literary Left in the Era of the Cold War.* Chapel Hill: The University of North Carolina Press, 2012.

Wald, Alan M. *Exiles from a Future Time: The Forging of the Mid-Twentieth-Century Literary Left.* Chapel Hill: The University of North Carolina Press, 2002.

Wald, Alan M. "Literary 'Leftism' Reconsidered" (Review of James Murphy, The Proletarian Moment, 1991). *Science and Society* 57 (1993): 214–22.

Wald, Alan M. *Trinity of Passion: The Literary Left and the Antifascist Crusade.* Chapel Hill: The University of North Carolina Press, 2007.

Wallis, Lena, ed. *Life and Letters of Caroline Martyn.* London: Labour Leader Publishing, 1898.

Ward, Harry F. "The Bible and the Proletarian Movement." *The Journal of Religion* 1 (1921): 271–81.

White, Bouck, ed. *Songs Of The Fellowship, For Use In Socialist Gatherings, Propaganda, Labor Mass Meetings, The Home, And Churches Of The Social Faith.* 1912.

White, Bouck. *The Call of the Carpenter.* New York: Doubleday, 1911.

Wilkison, Kyle G. *Yeomen, Sharecroppers, and Socialists: Plain Folk Protest in Texas, 1870–1914.* College Station: Texas A&M University Press, 2008.

Wilson, P. W. "The Brotherhood Movement." *The Contemporary Review* 102 (1912): 680–7.

Wimbush, Vincent. *The Bible and African Americans: A History in Six Readings.* Minneapolis: Fortress, 2023.

Winter, Bruce W. *Seek the Welfare of the City: Christians as Benefactors and Citizens.* First-Century Christians in the Graeco-Roman World. Grand Rapids: Eerdmans, 1994.

Witherington, Ben, III. *1 & 2 Thessalonians: A Socio-Rhetorical Commentary.* Grand Rapids: Eerdmans, 2006.

Wood, Ian. *John Wheatley.* Manchester: Manchester University Press, 1990.

Yancey, Peter. "Steinbeck's Relationship to Proletarian Literature." *The Steinbeck Review* 9 (2012): 38–52.

Yeo, Stephen. "A New Life: The Religion of Socialism in Britain, 1883–1896." *History Workshop* 4 (1977): 5–56.

Yoder, John Howard. *The Politics of Jesus.* Grand Rapids: Eerdmans, 1972.

INDEX

Adamson, William 66
Aichele, George 215
Aitken, James K. 11
Anabaptists 66–7, 171, 197, 199, 201
Ardrossan and Saltcoats Herald 35, 38, 68–9, 130–2
Ayrshire miners 37, 40

Backstrom, Philip 18, 20
Baker, Kelly 16
Baptist, Edward 31
Barrett, James 15–16
Barrow, Logie 76, 93
Bartchy, Scott 200
Beavis, Mary Ann 203–5, 209, 211
Benn, Caroline 27, 37, 39, 42, 45–6, 48, 50, 55–6, 73, 75–6, 80–3, 89, 142, 160
Bevir, Mark 93
Bissett, Jim 18
Blatchford, Robert (*The Clarion*) 48, 72
Booth, Gen William 31, 45
Boring, Eugene 204–6, 207
Boxall, Ian x, 2, 183, 184, 214, 215
Braude, Ann 75, 78–9
Brotherhood Movement 85–7
Brown, Jeannine 188–9
Brown, Peter 195
Bryan, Pauline 28
Burnett, John 30

Cadbury, George 52
Callahan, Richard J. 17
Callow, John 50, 56, 74, 169–72, 192
Cantwell, Christopher C. 17
Cardenal, Ernesto 10, 221
Carter, Heath W. 17
Case-Winters, Anna 190
Catterall, Peter 18, 91, 202, 219–20
Central Labour College (London) 102–4
Chalamet, Christophe 83–5, 92

Christianity and Labor Movements ("second wave" studies) 17–21
Clark, Emily Suzanne 75
Clines, J. M. A. 11
Cockburn, John 28
Cole, G. D. H. 20, 81
Conner, J. McArthur 28, 33, 85–6
Constantine 171
Coomber, Matthew 19
Countryman, L. Wm. 193–4
Coxey's Army 50
Craig, Rev. Dan 71
Craik, W. W. 102–3
Cunninghame-Graham, Robert Bontine 42–3, 45

Daggett, Melissa 75
Davenport, Allen (Chartist poet) 119
Davidson, John Morrison xi, 95, 111–26
Davis, David Brion 31
Debs, Eugene 16, 50
Dibelius, Martin 196
Dickens, Charles 31
Dochuk, Darren 17
Dombrowski, James 18
Dorien, Gary 18
Downs, Kristina 3
Drake, Janine Giordano 17

Edgerton, William 200
Engels, Friedrich 29, 31
Etkind, Alexander 200
Evans, Craig 188–9

Fahey, David 70–2
Fallot, Tommy 84
Fee, Gordon 205
Ferguson, Robert Hunt 18
Finger, Reta 195, 200–1, 209, 211
Fivecoate, Jesse A. 3
folkloristics 3

Fones-Wolf, Ken 17
France, R. T. 189–90, 217
Fraser, Hamish 48
Friesen, Steven 193
Furnish, Victor 205
Fyfe, Hamilton 27

Garland, David 217
Gellman, Erik 18
Geoghegan, Vincent 75
George, Henry 118
Gerrard, Jessica 96
Gillingham, Susan x, 3, 183
Glasier, J. Bruce 51, 111, 113–14
Gold, Michael x, 4–8, 221
Green, Gene 205
Gutman x, 4, 10–16, 221

Harrill, J. Albert 198
Harrington, Daniel 187
Hauerwas, Stanley 218
Hayes, Rutherford B. 112
Hendricks Jr., Obery 126
Highland Clearances 43–4, 92
Hird, Dennis xi, 95, 102–11
Hirschfield, Claire 22
Hobsbawn, Eric 10
Hobson, S. G. 77
Hock, Ronald 210
Holman, Bob 20, 27, 34, 51, 54, 72, 73, 80
Horsley, Richard 215–16
Hostetler, John 21
Hughes, Emrys 28, 34, 36–7, 42, 48, 55
Hughes, Frank Witt 205
Hunter, James 43
Hutterites 21
Hyndmann 72
Hyslop, Jonathan 22

"Independent Labour Party" (ILP) begins 47–8
Irish Home Rule 40, 77

Jewett, Paul 207
Johnson, Luke Timothy 196, 211
Johnson, (Rev. Dr.) Neil 93
Jones, Peter d'A. 20
Jones, Rev. Rowland 89

Kampen, John 214
Keddie, G. A. 193
Keener, Craig 190, 198–9
Kenworthy, John Coleman 29
Kim-Cragg, HyeRan 203–4, 206, 209, 211
Kingsley, Charles 20, 31
K'Meyer, Tracy 22
Knox, W. W. 183
Kropotkin, P. 29

Labour Church 92–5
"Labour Leader" (Newspaper)
    Hardie starts 42
    Hardie writes most of 48
    Steps aside as editor 53
"Labour Representation Committee" (LRP) 50
Levine, Amy-Jill 214
Li, Xian 199
Liberation Theology 10
Lille, France (1910) 59, 83–8
Long, Thomas 187–8
Lowe, David 27, 34, 36, 45, 97
Lyon, Eileen Groth 18, 31
Luz, Ulrich 188–9

MacColl, Allan 18
MacDonald, Ramsay 51
Maier, Christl 11
Malherbe, Bruce 210
Malina, Bruce 208
Maloney, Linda 203–4, 206, 209, 212
Mann, Tom 63
Martyn, Caroline xi, 95–102
Martyrs Mirror 66–7
Marx, Karl xiii, 29
Maurice, F. D. 20, 31
McGiff, Meredith 3
McGinn, Sheila 204–5, 209–11
McLean, Iain 27, 30, 32, 34–5, 37, 40, 44, 46, 49, 51, 53–4, 56, 62, 64, 77
McMillan, Margaret 100
Meggitt, Justin 201
Merthyr (South Wales) Hardie as MP 49–50, 52
Mesters, Carlos 10
Michel, Louise 29
Milton, John 65

Montero, Roman 201
Morgan, Kenneth 27, 32-4, 36, 38, 41, 43-4, 45, 48-55, 64, 73, 75-7, 81, 85, 149, 160
Morison, James (Rev.) and "Morisonians" 59, 63-8
Morris, William 113
Murdoch, John (*The Highlander*) 43-4
Mutch, Deborah 22, 72
Myles, Robert 193

"National Council of the Pleasant Sunday Afternoon" 83, 85
New Labor Studies 10-16
Newport, Kenneth 216-17
Nick, Henri 84
Nicols, John 208
Nolland, John 190, 213

Order of the Good Templars 68-70
Oren, John 18
Osborne, Grant 190
Overtoun, "Lord" (J. Campbell White) 51, 142-9, 185
Owen, Robert 20

Page, Hugh 19
Pankhurst, E. 29
Passy, Frederik 85
Peel, Mark 18
Pervo, Richard 196-8
Philips, Morgan (famous quote on "Methodism" and "Marx") 18
Pilch, John J. 208
Proletarian exegesis 10
Proletarian literature 4-10
Pullman Strike 50

Rauchenbusch, Walter 84
"Reception History" 1
Reid, Fred 27, 32-4, 36-8, 40-2, 44, 62, 68-9, 71, 77, 80
Renan, Ernst 114, 120, 169
Rice, Joshua 208
Roberts, Kyle 188
Roberts, Jonathan 2
Robertson, Michael 21
Robertson-Smith, William 114, 120
Roll, Jarod 18

Rowland, Christopher x, 2
Rowntree, Joseph (and Arthur Sherwell) 72
Roxburgh, Kenneth 64-5
Ruskin, John (Ruskin College) 102

Sanders, Bernie xiii
Saldarini, Anthony 213, 216
Salvation Army 45-6
Salvatore, Nick 11-16, 22
Scheffler, Eben 194
Second Socialist International (Paris, 1889) 44
Segovia, Fernando 185
Shankar, Prabha 22
Shapiro, Hyman 28, 34, 55-6
Sinclair, Upton 51
Small, William 29
Smith, Frank 29, 45-6
Smith-Christopher, Daniel 185, 191, 222
Snowden, Philip 51, 78-9, 173
South Africa (and Boer war) 52-4
Spiritualism 75-83
Stevens, Carolyn 22
Stewart, William 27, 34, 43, 49, 52, 54, 64, 77, 83
Still, Todd 210
Sugirtharajah, R. S. 9-10, 185

Taff-Vale decision 53
Temperance 68-74
Tennyson, Alfred Lord 61
Theoharis, Liz 204
Thompson, E. P. 10
Tillett, Ben 63
Trevor, John 29, 81, 93-5
Trocme, Andre xii, 84-5, 126
Trump, D. 28
Turner, David 218
Turner, Jacqueline 93

United States (Hardie visits) 50

Wallis, Lena 96-100
Ward, Rev. H. F. 4
Ward, William 85-7
West Ham (Hardie as MP) 46-7, 52
Wheatley, John 16
White, Bouck 126

Wilkison, Kyle G. 17
Wilson [Hardie], Lily 37
Wilson, P. W. 85, 87
Wilson-Reitz, Megan 204–5, 209–11
Wimbush, Vincent 24
Winter, Bruce 208, 211
Witherington, Ben 206, 208

Wood, Ian 16
Woodbey, George Washington 9, 19

Yee, Gale 19
Yeo, Stephen 63
Yiddishkeit 13
Yoder, John H. 126

SELECTED SCRIPTURE INDEX

Genesis
1:27	176
2:15	210
4:24	210

Exodus
20:9	210
22:25-27	105, 137, 169
31:1-5	117

Leviticus
19:18	173
22:32	189
25	117, 137, 169
25:35-37	105, 118, 137
25:39-43	118
25:50-52	118
26:18	215

Numbers
26:54	117

Deuteronomy
15	117
15:7-9	105, 117, 198
15:12-18	118
23:15-16	118
23:19	105, 118, 137, 169
24:7	118
27:17	117
28:36-37, 41, 49-50	119

1 Samuel
8	119
8:13-16	120
28	88

2 Kings
4:38-44	198

2 Chronicles
36:15-17	218

Ezra
9	137

Nehemiah
5:7, 10, 11-14	118
9	137

Proverbs
6:6-11	210
6:31	215
10:4-5	210
19:17	106
24:30-34	210
31:13-27	210

Job
20:7-19	120, 137

Isaiah
1:16-17	141
2:9	137
5:8	117, 137, 169
10:1-2	119
25:8	159
28:23-26	117
61:1-2	159
65:21-22	154

Jeremiah
3:16	158
5:15	137
7	137
24	137
34:12	189
44	88

Lamentations
4:13	156

Ezekiel
13:19	189
20:9, 14, 22, 27, 29	189

Selected Scripture Index

22:12-13, 31	118, 189	9:58	161
36:20	189	10	156, 161
39:7	189	11:10-13	123
		11:39-52	215
Daniel		11:45-54	106, 137
9	137	12:13-15	153
		12:16ff	108, 176
Matthew		12:28-32	155
3:2	190	12:32-33	109, 198
3:7	140	13:31-33	107
4:17	190	14:16-24	115, 121
5:21-26	175–6	16	176
5:38-41	122, 175, 218	16:13	176
6:5-6, 7-8	123, 160–1, 176	16:19ff	108, 161
6:10 (11-13)	141, 155, 166,	18:18	107
	186–91	22:42	190
6:33	166	25:25-27	109
8:20	161		
8:36	176	**John**	
10:8-11	206	4:19-24	124, 175
10:10-13	134	6	156
12:28	190	8	175
12:34	140	15:12	92
12:37	115		
12:50	175	**Acts**	
16:26	176	2	110, 116, 137, 153,
19:19	103, 109, 173		164, 176, 191–202
20	124, 153, 175	4	110, 116, 134, 137,
21:28ff	153		153, 164, 176,
22:17	108		191–202
22:39	103	5:1-12	192–202
22:36-40	121		
23	107, 140, 144–6,	**Romans**	
	176, 212–19	9:3	210
23:13-33	106, 140	11:1, 2	210
25:32-40	124		
26:42	189, 190	**I Corinthians**	
26:52	175	13	92
27:6	156		
		2 Corinthians	
Mark		11:22	210, 218
9:34	176		
10	153	**Galatians**	
		1:13-14	210
Luke			
2:41-52	175	**Philippians**	
3:7	140	3:4a-6	210
4:18-21	107, 115		
6:39	140	**2 Thessalonians**	
7:12	109	3:10	170, 202–12

James
2	38–9, 163
5	39, 161, 170

Revelation
3:14-15	89
8-9, 16	215

Sirach
7:15	210
38:24-34	210
51:30	210

2 Maccabees
6:12-17	218

www.ingramcontent.com/pod-product-compliance
Lightning Source LLC
Chambersburg PA
CBHW051520230426
43668CB00012B/1676